Organizing for Educational Justice

Organizing for Educational Justice

The Campaign for Public School Reform in the South Bronx

Michael B. Fabricant

University of Minnesota Press
Minneapolis
London

Published by the University of Minnesota Press
111 Third Avenue South, Suite 290
Minneapolis, MN 55401-2520
http://www.upress.umn.edu

Library of Congress Cataloging-in-Publication Data

Fabricant, Michael B.
    Organizing for educational justice : the campaign for public school reform in the South Bronx / Michael B. Fabricant.
        p. cm.
    Includes bibliographical references and index.
    ISBN 978-0-8166-6960-8 (hc : alk. paper)—ISBN 978-0-8166-6961-5 (pb : alk. paper)
    1. Public schools—New York (State)—New York. 2. School improvement programs—
New York (State)—New York. 3. Educational change—New York (State)—New York.
4. Community organization—New York (State)—New York. 5. Social movements—
New York (State)—New York. 6. South Bronx (New York, N.Y.)—Social conditions. I. Title.
    LA339.N5F34 2010
    371.2´0709747275—dc22
                                                        2010008810

Dedicated to the men and women of CC9,
who inspired this book,
and to Betsy Werner Fabricant,
who inspires me every day.

Contents

Acknowledgments

It is always a daunting task to thank all of the people who have contributed to the development of a book. First, I want to acknowledge the consistent support I received from the staff and parents of CC9 (Community Collaborative to Improve District 9 Schools). They welcomed me to their family and opened any door necessary to tell CC9's story. I hope I have in some small way repaid their trust with a book that faithfully captures their vision, risk taking, and practice work on behalf of neighborhood schools. Eric Zachary was especially important to the development of this writing project; he was always willing to sit for an interview and never censored the complexity and contradiction associated with reconstructing change work. Michelle Fine helped me to refine key elements of the manuscript; her insight enabled me to more fully understand the potential contributions of the emergent analysis while challenging me to address a number of unanswered questions. Steve Burghardt offered important comments that strengthened the conceptual and structural underpinnings of the manuscript.

I am especially grateful to Steve Kruger for providing initial entrée to the University of Minnesota Press. Richard Morrison helped to tighten the manuscript through his acute sense of narrative rhythm and structure; his comments were indispensable during the final stages of manuscript refinement. Emily Steinmetz made critical editorial contributions during a relatively early stage of development; her attention to the logic, detail, and frames of the analysis added both polish and weight to the project. Early contributions to the editing of the manuscript were also made by Michael Marcus. I am indebted to Sharon Tonge; her skill in preparing and formatting the final manuscript was consistently impressive. Amanda Dejesus Magalhes helped to organize early contact with publishing houses.

I could not have completed the book without the support of a cross section of colleagues who in large and small ways sustained my enthusiasm despite a series of difficult moments. This supportive network included Harriet Goodman, Andrea Savage, Jackie Mondros, Barbara Bowen, Niki

Fabricant, and Kelvin Wallace. Perhaps most important, Betsy Fabricant, as always, stayed the course: she allowed me to labor on weekends and late into the evening because she shares my passion for contributing, however modestly, toward the improvement of public education in the poorest neighborhoods. As in the past, I am deeply indebted and inspired by the basic truths she continues to teach me.

Abbreviations

ACORN	Association of Community Organizations for Reform Now
CAB	Citizens Advice Bureau
CBO	community-based organization
CCB	Community Collaborative to Improve Bronx Schools
CC9	Community Collaborative to Improve District 9 Schools
CDC	community development corporation
CEJ	Coalition for Education Justice
CFE	Campaign for Fiscal Equity
CIP	Community Involvement Project
DOE	Department of Education
EJC	Education Justice Collaborative
IAF	Industrial Areas Foundation
IESP	Institute for Education and Social Policy
KTP	Keep the Promises Coalition
MOM	Mothers on the Move
NSA	New Settlement Apartments
NYU	New York University
OCO	Oakland Community Organization
PAC	Parent Action Committee
UFT	United Federation of Teachers
UPOH	United Parents of Highbridge
WHEDCO	Women's Housing and Economic Development Corporation

Resetting the Agenda

During summer in the South Bronx much of the life of the community is lived in public. In Mount Eden on a late afternoon in August 2003, for example, the heat radiating throughout the neighborhood was driving people out of their apartments and onto the streets. To cool off, hydrants were opened, and kids sat under and ran through the intense water streams. Rhythms circulated up and down the street from car radios passing through and boom boxes fixed to the curb. Bright fabrics of every color were worn and used to cover makeshift card tables. Kids ran and played their games while adults sat and played theirs. The sweltering heat seemed to catalyze a swirling kaleidoscope of color, games, and music that cohered into a spontaneously combusted carnival.

The public festival on the street provided a backdrop to a meeting occurring at New Settlement Apartments (NSA), a nonprofit agency with deep roots and substantial legitimacy in the community. The meeting convened a group of parents representing various community agencies committed to improving the learning environment and achievement outcomes in neighborhood schools. The group called itself the Community Collaborative to Improve District 9 Schools (CC9). The informal conversation among seasoned leaders of the group focused exclusively on developing a campaign for the following year. As new parents entered the room, however, the conversation quickly shifted: leaders welcomed new parents, asked about the schools their children were attending, and guided them to the dinner. Stories of neighborhood events, mutual friends, and the failure of the schools were shared. Quickly, this informal conversation ended, and the meeting began. Parent leaders, not the professional organizers in the room, facilitated and led the conversation. Attention was paid to involving the neophyte and the reticent by both providing translation services to everyone in the room—about half of the parents did not speak English—and encouraging parents to speak up. Eliciting participation was not easy, but the safety of weighing in was palpable. When parents spoke, no matter their position, they were never rebuked. Disagreement was offered gently, and leaders consciously laced their comments with affirmation directed to others who had spoken earlier.

These group dynamics created a cascading formal discussion involving at one point or another all of the approximately thirty parents in the room, and a number of informal side conversations. Intensity and pain marked much of what parents shared with each other as they revealed the ways in which the local schools had failed their children. That part of the discussion segued into how the schools might be changed. Here, too, passion and energy were evident throughout the room. Parents talked about many needs, including safety, smaller classes, effective professional leadership, and investment in dilapidated buildings. A touchstone to which parents consistently returned, however, was the need to improve classroom instruction. At the conclusion of the meeting every parent in the room volunteered to work on committees, to begin to more sharply formulate the goals of the next campaign, and to get more parents involved in the organizing work.

What parents recognized throughout the meeting was the relationship between targeted investment in public education and increased achievement in the neighborhood schools serving very poor children of color. Their particular expertise is a product of witnessing daily the failures of local schools through the experience of their children, yet it is systematically ignored by policy makers. Their voice is notably absent in the discourse about reforming public schools, which is monopolized by academics, policy makers, and politicians with greater power and access to media. The parents of CC9 are engaged in building organizing campaigns that both correct for this imbalance in power and in turn create seats at the table for grassroots leadership in the negotiation of public school reform.

The crisis of public education has been systematically documented by both the media and the academy during the past half century. As the problem of failing schools and students has persisted, the strategies for addressing this breakdown have clustered around three approaches: market initiatives intended to stimulate competition, standards as a spur for accountability, and community organizing as a tool for creating the necessary parent power to leverage both a redistribution of resources and influence that tilts to poor communities of color. These approaches, however, have generated dramatically different levels of resources and legitimacy. Equally important, the political economic context that in large part accounts for this crisis is all but ignored.

The crisis of faith in public education, and the public sector more generally, is part of a more sweeping trend referred to as neoliberalism. As the anthropologist Micaela di Leonardo notes, in *New Landscapes of Inequality*, neoliberalism "is a widely used term in Europe and Latin America, but largely confined to academic circles in the United States" (94). Critically, neoliberal ideology has evolved into the dominant policy framework over an approximate thirty-five-year period. Neoliberal policy initiatives were ushered in with the contraction of the welfare state and the massive domestic budget cuts of the Carter and Reagan administrations. The ascendance of neoliberal policies was triggered, in part, by intensified global market competition, new forms of technology, the increased costs of natural resources such as oil, the costs of labor internationally, policies that overtly undermined labor unions, and the outsourcing of jobs. These processes of globalization left in their wake substantial dislocation and immiseration.

Neoliberalism has had a profound impact on the welfare state. The state's capacity to act autonomously and to have the resources to implement public projects has been dramatically squeezed by privatization, disinvestment, and managerial standardization. As market approaches take hold, numerous historically state-run functions have been outsourced to private and/or market-based institutions. Market alternatives to public institutions, such as prisons, hospitals, and schools, are characterized as more efficient than bloated, self-serving state bureaucracies. Accompanying the shift to privatization are new forms of standardized state practice intended to evaluate and measure public sector initiatives. New education policy has been enacted through federal legislation, most notably the No Child Left Behind Act, which mandates increased academic performance with little if any additional funding. The combination of privatization and standardization is expected to produce an increasingly efficient state apparatus. Linda McNeil suggests in *Contradictions of School Reform: Educational Costs of Standardized Testing* that these new efficiencies are elemental to neoliberalism's intention to shrink welfare state expenditure and more largely hollow out the functions of the public sector.

What often remains underexplored, however, are the subtle implications of reform proposals that rely on standardized testing and privatization as a substitute for the kinds of targeted economic investment necessary to alter the learning and instruction culture of public schools. Importantly, the larger context of public school failure is all but ignored. Critical but largely unanswered questions include the following: How have public investment policies had a differential impact on the success of inner-city students as compared to their suburban counterparts? In what ways do these reform agendas advance or impede development of students as critical thinkers and, over time, as informed citizens? Finally, a critical question with respect to any reform initiative is how do its architects imagine the role of the public sphere in a democratic society? These are especially important questions because the proposals being considered and implemented are intended to reform institutions that are considered essential to nurturing democratic values and extending economic opportunity. The strategy for fixing the public schools has, therefore, powerful political, social, and economic implications.

The proponents of neoliberal policies have also suggested that such initiative will lead to greater freedom for citizens and consumers. As resources are distributed directly to parents through vouchers, it is believed that parents will have greater opportunity to select schools that are a best fit for their child. Charter schools are also seen as offering greater choice or an alternative to public schools by providing enriched learning and more varied instructional opportunities for students. Choice is associated with the stimulant of competition in public education environments increasingly structured to mimic the dynamics of the marketplace. Choice is also cited when, for example, parents are offered the option of selecting a school for their child. Most generally, however, neoliberal policy is described as yielding a more democratic public sector.

Market Reform and Public Education Policy

Alexander Astin, in his article "Educational Choice," notes, "who would argue with the proposition that students and parents should have greater freedom of choice?" (259). Market reformers tend to emphasize exit, or the parents' choice to leave rather than remain in public schools, as the preferred option. Myron Lieberman, in *Privatization and Educational Choice,* indicates that the very assumption of exit from public schools as remediating the circumstance of public education has been called into question by the internationally renowned economist Albert Hirshman, who first developed this terminology in 1970. Lieberman cites Hirshman, who raised several reservations about the Nobel laureate economist Milton Friedman's strong support for the exit option in education. Hirshman notes:

> In the first place, Friedman considers withdrawal or exit as the "direct" way of expressing one's unfavorable view of an organization.

A person less well trained in economics might naively suggest that the direct way of expressing views is to express them! Secondly, the decision to voice one's views and efforts to make them prevail are contemptuously referred to by Friedman as a resort to cumbrous political channels. But what else is the political and indeed the democratic process than the digging, the use and hopefully the slow improvement of these very channels. (145)

The policies supported by market advocates include tuition tax credits, vouchers, and the development of private and nonprofit options, all of which emphasize exit from public schools. Tax credit proposals call for deductions for sending children to private schools. Alternatively, tuition vouchers are seen by many as the least intrusive way for government to support education reform. The underlying assumption, as Lieberman notes in *Privatization and Educational Choice,* is that the best way to strengthen parental choice of schools is to strengthen parents' ability to pay for education whether in public or private schools.

Vouchering is a hot-button issue in education reform circles. Voucher proposals are intended to intensify demand for more effective schools. Some plans give the child a voucher that is redeemable in any school, even one with a religious affiliation. In most plans, the voucher pays for only a part of the cost of the child's education. Such initiative has encountered strong resistance from labor unions, such as the American Federation of Teachers, and from a broad cross section of elected officials and policy makers.

In general, this resistance has successfully thwarted broad efforts to initiate vouchering programs. In the 1990s, however, a far-reaching vouchering program was implemented in Wisconsin. Margonis and Parker, in their article "Choice: The Route to Community," note that the "Wisconsin Supreme Court held that the Milwaukee Parental Choice Program violated neither the establishment of the religion clause of the First Amendment nor the Wisconsin constitution against using state funds for spending on private religious schools through vouchering" (204). In *Jackson v. Benson,* the court ruled that public dollars went directly to consumers rather than to the schools. The court rejected the argument that vouchers fostered the enmeshing of religious and state institutions. The U.S. Supreme Court refused to hear the case, thus allowing the decision to stand. This legal precedent is expected to have significant policy reverberations as more targeted vouchering programs are introduced in other states. Although the coalition of groups opposing vouchering has been relatively successful, it will remain a battle line in the continuing struggle to reshape public education.

At least one organizational alternative to public education envisioned by choice proponents is charter schools. Chris Lubienski indicates in "Redefining 'Public Education'" that

> their increased popularity can in part be traced to the belief that charter schools represent a middle way between traditional public education and choice proposals that rely on vouchers. The charter school movement is national in scope and between 1980 and 2005, the number of charter schools increased dramatically. (635)

Charter schools are commissioned and funded by the state but managed outside the public bureaucracy. In general, nonprofit agencies are the sponsoring group. They are subject to some, but not all, of the regulations that govern public education. Charter schools have the authority to rewrite historic understandings regarding salaries, benefits, credentialing requirements, and unionization of school professionals. Such practice latitude is consistent with the presumption that much of the failure of public education can be traced to both incompetent teachers and unions that foster and protect an unproductive workforce. Charter schools are seen by many proponents of privatization as an early stage of reform that will ultimately lead to vouchering. Lubienski cites DeWeese's assertion that "the significance of the charter school reform cannot be overemphasized in terms of helping to prepare the public for broader educational reform and the most far reaching reform envisioned by market advocates is vouchering" (638).

The choice for exit has had very concrete fiscal consequences for public schools. In a number of urban districts, the migration of students to charter schools has resulted in an evaporation of public resources for many public schools. In Houston, Texas, for example, the independent school district lost fifty million dollars in state aid to charter schools. John Bohte has examined the impact of charter schools and notes that in the late 1990s Kansas City, Missouri, diverted $41 million to charter schools, and Dayton, Ohio, lost 17 percent of its total school budget to charter schools. Researchers have reported modest performance gains in the public schools affected by these changes, and advocates of privatization argue that these improvements were stimulated by the intensified competition spurred by charter schools. Evidence suggests, however, that this change was largely a consequence of the movement of at-risk students to charter schools. This pattern enabled public schools to shed their lowest-scoring, lowest-achieving students. What remains indisputable is that public schools were left with fewer resources to provide an education to the remaining students. Such trends raise an important question: What happens to those left behind in districts that are already resource poor and facing a period of limited investment in public schools? Regardless of the form of privatization, public education is further impoverished as the dollars flow away from it.

Market arguments regarding school failure are not without merit. Clearly, public bureaucracies tend toward control, caution, and hierarchy, which can slow and undermine reform initiatives. As well, the resources that are allocated to public schools are often expended in inefficient and unproductive ways. As Jonathan Kozol remarks in *The Shame of the Nation,* poor children of color pay the dearest price for the failures of public schools. Critically, the response of public sector decision makers to present conditions in the schools is simply not commensurate with the depth of the crisis. Consequently, charter schools have had an increasingly receptive audience in very poor communities, reaching across the political spectrum.

Market arguments regarding declines in student achievement have captured much of the public's attention. In turn, they have drowned out many of the competing explanations for the declining condition of public schools. Matters of investment, teacher supports, and parent leadership are rarely included in market analyses. Instead, the complexity of both the aspiration and practice of public education is reduced to a simple dichotomy: bureaucracy versus free market. The discussion occurs at the policy level, and matters of educational practices are rarely, if ever, introduced.

Repeatedly, achievement on standardized tests is presented as synonymous for productivity and educational accomplishment. Conversely, little attention is paid to public education's role in developing critical thinkers capable of meaningfully participating in democratic decision making. It is within this context that the discussion of choice is silent on the participatory roles of parents and the community in holding public schools accountable for their performance. Consequently, the very relationship between the public schools and the ongoing invigoration of democratic institutions and dialogue is at risk in a more privatized system precisely because any accountability to the communities it serves is less clear. Critics suggest, therefore, that privatization promises to reinvent not only the culture of schooling but the very future of the larger democratic experiment. This is not to romanticize the history of public education as a democratizing force but rather to simply rearticulate a hope and possibility voiced much earlier by reformers such as John Dewey.

Standardized Testing Reform

Recent legislative initiatives to reform public education have also focused on holding public educators accountable through standardized testing. The intention, as McNeil suggests, is to use "a very narrow set of numerical indicators (student achievement on statewide tests) as the only language of currency within the state" (xxv). In *Contradictions of School Reform,* McNeil remarks that teachers' and principals' rewards and penalties are increasingly aligned with student scores. Critically, new forms of curricula have been proposed, developed, and structured to address specific demands of the testing. This accountability and testing reform movement is intended to regain public confidence in public education by demonstrating that student achievement can be increased without substantial new investments of public dollars or dramatic reorganization of the public bureaucracy.

As public education redefines its mission to prepare students to perform on standardized tests, Taylorist, or factorylike, principles are employed to reengineer the day-to-day work and working conditions of public school staff. Lizbeth Schorr suggests in *Within Our Reach* that increasingly in striving for efficiency by deploying "personnel to focus on sharply defined, single problems, bureaucracies fragment services into absurd slivers" (263). But at the center of such reform is a fundamental contradiction astutely observed by McNeil. She notes that "a school that is designed like a factory . . . is tightly organized, highly routinized, and geared for the production of uniform products; educating children is complex, inefficient, idiosyncratic, uncertain and open ended" (11). One critical objective of the public education system is to nurture students and prepare them with the knowledge and skills needed to function effectively and critically in the larger world. From a different perspective, the purpose of public education is to process large numbers of students through the standardized requirements of credentialing. Every bureaucratically organized school struggles with this inherent contradiction. However, when the pull toward uniformity effectively overwhelms other purposes, then the very project of public education may be undermined.

Reforms that tighten administrative controls through heightened accountability have less than optimistic views of teachers' skills and knowledge, which may independently contribute to improved learning. For teachers, this is especially disheartening as they face full accountability for improved scores with little, if any, opportunity to influence curricula or instruction. Clearly, the public education reform/policy environment systematically reinforces the message that no matter the contextual factors influencing learning outcomes, ultimately staff have failed if scores do not improve.

The promise of improved achievement at no additional cost often wins support among business interests resistant to paying for more expensive forms of public education, as well as among the middle class, which is shouldering a disproportionate share of the tax burden. The standardized testing initiative's features of fiscal constraint, individual responsibility, productivity, and distrust of the public sector make it an especially compelling fit with the conservative political mood of the 1980s and 1990s.

The reformers' ideological resistance to adding resources to the educational systems has been criticized on the basis of equity. As Kavitha Mediratta, Norm Fruchter, and A. C. Lewis of the Institute for Education and Social Policy indicate in their monograph *Organizing for School Reform*:

> The Chicago, Baltimore, Philadelphia and New York systems have all
> registered gains in test scores performance at the elementary level.
> But these gains still leave at least half . . . reading below grade level.
> Outcomes in middle and high schools are far worse: fewer than
> 60 percent of all entering ninth graders graduate from many of
> our large city school systems . . . it is also not clear that these
> improvements can be sustained over time. (3)

They conclude that standards, testing, and mandated reforms are insufficient to "improve the education provided to poor students of color in most urban districts" (3).

Noted education scholars Jeannie Oakes and Martin Lipton, in *Struggling for Educational Equity in Diverse Communities,* suggest that "the usual approaches to school reforms altering rules, structures, and practices are necessary but not sufficient to change profound inequality within and between schools" (15). These economic and political differences between communities will influence the outcomes of any centralized reform initiative. Too often, education efforts offer a bipolar discourse of either ideological distrust of all things public or an implacable faith in all things that are privatized or standardized. Policy makers who adhere to the latter of these perspectives ultimately advance an agenda that abandons public education while substituting privatization. This willful ignorance of the relationship, for example, between targeted investments in teaching or classroom instruction and student performance results, as Seymour Sarason, an influential organizational analyst, notes, in the predictable failure of education reform. Consistent with Sarason's point, Paul Hill, Christine Campbell, and James Harvey note in *It Takes a City* that none of these initiatives has narrowed the performance gap between poor inner-city students of color and other American children.

Where, then, does this leave us regarding the seemingly Herculean task of changing public schools so that they effectively serve the poorest children? What resources and ideas are most likely to advance such a change trajectory? Recent failed school reform initiatives share a common conceit that public education can be improved without the active involvement of community members setting a direction for reform.

Organizing Community for Educational Justice: Redefining the Agenda and Locus for Change

In the past ten years, poor parents increasingly dissatisfied with the performance of public schools in their communities have begun to develop organizing campaigns to create pressure for needed change. The emergence of community organizing as a strategy for changing schools and improving learning culture is only fifteen years old. Yet research by the Institute for Education and Social Policy (IESP) in New York City indicates that the work has proliferated across the country to sixty-six groups involved in issues ranging from school safety to quality of classroom instruction. These groups are located in a number of cities including, but not limited to, Los Angeles, San Antonio, Chicago, Philadelphia, and New York City. Mediratta, Fruchter, and Lewis note that "when combined with groups identified through other studies at least 200 community groups are currently engaged across the country in specific organizing campaigns for better local public schools" (3).

A premise of these campaigns is that public officials must be held accountable by the communities they serve if schools are to be improved. The organizing is intended to both publicize the poor performance of local schools while fighting to make certain the public investment necessary to change those conditions is made. Schools in these communities share common problems of crumbling facilities, overcrowded classrooms, shortages of qualified teachers, high turnover of principals, and very low achievement levels. Organizing has taken place where these conditions are most intolerable. To enforce such perspective, parent power sufficient to challenge policy decision making must be developed. In general, parent groups are too weak to unilaterally build a campaign around complex school-based issues. Organizers and advocates for parent involvement have indicated that the most effective groups, such as the Parent Action Committee (PAC) of the Mount Eden section of the Bronx, have built a base outside the school through relationships with community-based organizations. Eric Zachary, an organizer at the Institute for Education and Social Policy, and Shola Olatoye suggest, in *Community Organizing for School Improvement in the South Bronx,* that a proposition being advanced by parent groups is that building "parent power in low income communities can be a viable alternative to free market solutions (like vouchers, tax credits, charter schools) for holding public schools accountable."

Importantly, some part of the call of parent groups is for a more just distribution of resources to low-income schools. As Jonathan Kozol noted in *Shame of the Nation,* it is clear that the "resources devoted to public schooling have never been distributed equitably; instead the resource distribution has always been highly correlated with the class and racial composition of local communities." These discrepant funding patterns largely explain the lack of adequate educational preparation of low-income students of color. Critically, money matters for poor and minority students. But money alone will not solve the problem of low student achievement. Zachary and Olatoye note that Connell indicates in *The Midnight Hour* that both money and targeted investment are essential to improving the quality of education, "and neither will happen without the other" (2). Conservatives have consistently failed to acknowledge the importance of increased strategic investments in public education.

Zachary and Olatoye have indicated that the challenge for progressive activists and scholars in and outside the academy is to present a "compelling paradigm of how to transform schools so that all children receive a high quality education" (2). This must be done without defending the generally poor performance and practices of inner-city low-income schools. Such a progressive paradigm must trace the failure of public schools and offer as a potential corrective the political will to make certain that investments are made and programming implemented that have the potential to transform learning and achievement. A number of local communities have determined that the struggle to change conditions in local public schools that produce and reproduce failure will not come from policy makers but rather from the neighborhoods in which the schools are located. Parent education organizing represents to date the most powerful assertion of a communal will to transform the learning and achievement cultures of local public schools. That assertion when combined with strategic organizing is a ray of hope for altering the policy discourse regarding public schools.

As noted, the discourse on education reform has been monopolized by politically conservative policy makers and bureaucratic technicians emphasizing privatization and high-stakes testing. Missing from this discourse are the politics and expertise of parents who live daily with the failures of public education. Parents have the least complicated motives for improving public education: the success of their children. In the absence of parent-led initiatives to reform public education, the prospects for fundamental improvement are likely dim. Present policy direction promises to transform public education into ever-more-degraded testing centers, offering students an increasingly static and dead-end education.

The broad context for this Bronx organizing initiative is the largest school system in the nation. As the IESP has suggested, it serves largely poor (75 percent), black (72 percent), and Latino (13 percent) students with limited English proficiency. It is a school system where half of high school students fail to graduate. Perhaps most important, the New York City public school system has been undergoing a significant restructuring of financing, school units, and educational standards as well as policies under Mayor Michael Bloomberg.

The Purpose and Structure of the Book

The primary purpose of this book is to describe and learn from a unique, parent-led organizing campaign in New York City. The Community Collaborative to Improve District 9 schools (CC9), a parent-led consortium of six neighborhood-based agencies in the South Mid-Bronx, is unique for two reasons. First, having started as a small group of parents who discovered that their children's elementary school reading achievement was among the lowest in the city, the collaborative grew until it attained the power to bring the reforms it demanded to scale: in 2005, New York City applied the reforms CC9 had sought to one hundred low-performing elementary schools. The CC9 campaign for lead teachers, as Anne Bastian notes in *Making a Difference,* is the most significant policy reform achieved by a parent-led collaborative in New York City in several generations. The effort illustrates how a community initiative shifted relationships of power between three major stakeholders: low-income parents, the United Federation of Teachers (UFT), and the Department of Education (DOE). Recent data developed by the Academy for Educational Development in fall 2006 suggest the reforms have contributed to improvements in student reading and test scores. CC9's success demonstrates that parent-led initiatives are perhaps the best hope for promoting the increased investment and targeted reform necessary to improve student achievement.

Second, the story in this book is unique because CC9 combines many of the processes of social change often depicted in texts but rarely implemented in practice. CC9's groundbreaking, successful parent-led effort built a collaboration among a university, labor union, and community that not only agitated publicly for change but worked cooperatively with educators to put their reforms into practice. At both levels what CC9 achieved must be situated within the framework of disinvestment and disenfranchisement brought about by neoliberal policies. What CC9 contested was nothing less than the hegemony of neoliberal policy and practice. That said, a central question of the inquiry is how CC9 built the power necessary to enforce its agenda and will on New York City education policy makers. Of equal importance is how this model can be applied to other communities across the country.

The CC9 narrative is also situated within a broader exploration of parent participation as a historic impetus for reform. This discussion will describe the shifting political economy of education while integrating the concepts of social and political capital. The conflict between poor parents of color and the teachers' union, the UFT, in Ocean Hill–Brownsville during the late 1960s and early 1970s over decentralized control of neighborhood schools illuminates how the nexus of organizing, parent power, and public education reform can produce deep distrust and division between stakeholder groups. The precedent-setting work of CC9, however, lies in its strategic shift from governance/decentralization to learning and instruction issues and in the tactical utilization of both conflict and collaboration in framing parent-led organizing campaigns. In the case of Ocean Hill–Brownsville, parent organizing led to a decade-long rift between grassroots groups and the UFT, which in turn diminished their power to effectively advance a reform agenda for public schools. Within this context of deep distrust, it is remarkable that CC9 managed to successfully build a labor community coalition to leverage a targeted reinvestment of public dollars in public schools.

Study Methods

The inquiry was underpinned by qualitative data collected between 2003 and 2005. During that period, seventy-nine interviews were conducted with forty respondents. The interviews included a cross section of parent leaders, organizers, staff of the IESP, agency administrators affiliated with CC9, public education officials, and UFT officers. Multiple interviews were conducted with key informants who had important decision-making roles and a long history with CC9. Multiple interviews demanded that guides be developed to probe specific themes, examples, or insights that emerged in an initial data collection encounter. Follow-up interviews tracked key decision-making processes with critical leaders. Initial interviews were tailored to the specific institutional and individual experience of informants. The questions that were posed to UFT officials, parents, or community-based organization (CBO) administrators were quite different. Additional qualitative data were obtained through observation. During the course of the study, ninety-eight events associated with CC9 were observed and recorded. These events ranged from parent decision-making meetings to rallies and informal conversations between the UFT and CC9 leadership. I was granted total access to CC9 meetings and events, including discussions that were critical to shaping the strategic direction of CC9. Finally, relevant organizational memos, newsletters, and newspaper articles were collected during the course of the investigation and used in data analysis.

Data analysis of approximately three thousand pages of interviews and observations was initiated in fall 2005. A full year was devoted to data analysis and coding. The first stage of analysis resulted in descriptive codes, which over time were assembled and reassembled into more complex constructions that were more conceptual and analytic. Most important, the categories that were constructed cohered into a narrative structure. Once the categories and narrative structures were created, the writing began in fall 2006. A first draft manuscript was developed over two years, between 2006 and 2008. The next year was spent soliciting editorial feedback from colleagues and rewriting sections of the manuscript.

The leadership of CC9 systematically directed me to data sources that helped to illuminate aspects of the inquiry. For example, Eric Zachary referred me to Michelle Cahill, an aide to Chancellor Klein, to gain sharper understanding of the DOE's perceptions of CC9. As well, parents guided me to other parents whom they perceived as having rich, detailed understandings of the CC9 lead teacher campaign. This snowball sampling helped me to fill in missing parts of the emergent analysis and enrich large parts of the narrative. Finally, I was granted carte-blanche access to every CC9 meeting no matter how sensitive the discussion. Importantly, the transition of CC9 into its later boroughwide and citywide work organizing campaigns was also documented through subsequent interviewing in 2007–9. That part of the school reform experience is discussed in the book's epilogue.

The Book's Structure

Increasingly, urban parents are searching for ways to hold public schools accountable for their failures. Chapter 1 describes how parents and community groups are building organizing initiatives that empower parents and advance specific community proposals for change. It identifies instances of especially notable parent-led organizing initiatives beginning in the late 1960s. These efforts include, but are not limited to, Ocean Hill–Brownsville, Logan Square in Chicago, New Settlement Apartments in New York City, the Industrial Areas Foundation's work in Texas, and local organizing in Philadelphia.

This chapter also describes the record, change theory, or logic of campaigns, as well as salient strategic features. Importantly, the limitations and dilemmas of these local campaigns are considered, as are recent attempts to spur education reform in New York City and more specifically in the Bronx. In this way, the groundbreaking organizing work of CC9 is situated within both the larger struggle for parent-led reform on the national level and local campaigns organized to improve the dire condition of public education in the South Bronx.

Chapters 2 and 3 explore the context and process associated with forming CC9. By the late 1990s, parent-led organizing campaigns for education reform in New York City were stalled by the ubiquity of neoliberal policy making. A group of Bronx CBOs and New York University's IESP began to rethink strategies for change. These strategic conversations promoted a deepened understanding that the South Bronx neighborhoods could not be revitalized without a more effective public education system. Brick and mortar projects would no longer suffice. As well, leaders concurred that individual agencies could not challenge education policies that were systematically undermining every public school in the community. This gradual shift in perspective led to the founding of a collaborative (CC9) of six Bronx-based community agencies committed to improving public education through parent-led organizing.

Describing CC9's early efforts to develop a proactive agenda to change the learning and instruction conditions in public schools, these chapters illustrate how relationships with critical public education stakeholders created an internal organizational structure that emphasized democratic decision making as well as parent leadership. These features of CC9's practice were foundational to its building the necessary political and social capital to effectively implement future campaigns. As well, they contributed to the development of an alternate local public space capable of considering, critiquing, and contesting education policy.

The fourth chapter explores CC9's effort to build both internal capacity and external partnerships. Practices were introduced to expand parent involvement and develop leadership capacity. As well, CC9 convened strategic meetings to build and consolidate relationships with other community groups, politicians, the teachers' union, and key professionals in the public education establishment. What set CC9 apart from its predecessors was a recognition that change could not be won unilaterally or simply through community resistance. Effective campaigns for changing the public schools would require the involvement of powerful partners; otherwise, they were fated to fail. But such partnership also posed dilemmas and challenges. This part of CC9's practice was a pragmatic accommodation to the dynamics of social change and recognized that community groups must search for partners beyond the locality in order to leverage enough power to alter public schools embedded in a large system. Critically, CC9 recognized that parents, although necessary to the success of their campaigns, simply were not sufficient. CC9's outreach to other stakeholders contributed to the growing power and social capital of CC9.

The fifth chapter focuses on practices that contributed to the accumulation of CC9's social capital. Of particular interest is how specific practices contributed to the development of expansive relationships between parents and CC9. This is especially important for two reasons. First, what these practices offer is a way of thinking about how solidarity can be achieved through building activist communities. Second, they offer an important example of how alternative public space can create forms of democratic decision making, capacity development, and policy agendas that promote a more enfranchised and collectively empowered citizenry. Such experiences offer an important counterpoint to the withered relationship between citizens, particularly the poorest and most newly arrived, and the public sector.

Citizen empowerment was accomplished, in part, through the use of dialogue. CC9 has taken the abstract idea of democratic dialogue and translated it into a social reality, fusing individual relationships, solidarity, and collective action. Additionally, CC9's efforts to rethink expertise, private/public boundaries, leadership, and the conditions of respect are examined as conscious practice choices that promoted affiliation or membership. This part of the analysis offers a preliminary practice framework for creating social capital derived from the CC9 experience. These lessons can assist other community groups as they struggle to improve public education and contest neoliberal models of citizenship.

Chapter 6 describes how CC9 organized its political and social capital to leverage reform and explores the strategies and tactics employed during the campaign to target adversaries and maximize CC9 power. Additionally, it discusses the reasons for selecting the lead teacher campaign as the lever to improve learning and instruction. Finally, CC9's complex and pioneering role is examined as it transitioned from an external change agent to an internal partner.

In chapter 7 the organizing approaches employed by CC9 in developing its groundbreaking lead teacher campaign are more deeply explored, as are the organizing choices and practices that surfaced in the previous chapter. The distinctive contributions of CC9 to maximizing parent power are highlighted through recognition of the dynamic interplay of internal community building, external partnerships, and organizing campaigns.

The final chapter considers some of the policy, theory, and practice themes inspired by the work of CC9. It focuses on the lessons learned "scaling up" from local to districtwide campaigns. As well, it identifies a practice framework that emerges from CC9's campaigns. Finally, it explores the more general prospect of parent-led reform, offering an alternative to the failed policies of individual blame, privatization, and bureaucratic standardization. This last point is particularly important in a neoliberal context in which poor people are assumed to have little agency and in which alternate forms of discourse are disappearing. Four primary themes help to frame and deepen the discussion: (1) organizing lessons learned from CC9 in building parent power; (2) the challenge of building effective grassroots campaigns for education reform in a conservative/neoliberal era; (3) CC9 as a prism for rethinking a theory and practice of solidarity; and (4) the fragile dual project of public education and democracy.

This book will help to correct for the dearth of critical case studies on organizing and school reform. The intellectual labor of developing concepts, frameworks, and case studies to evolve a literature on the practice of education organizing remains in its infancy. What distinguishes this book is its focus on how a collaborative organizing initiative built the parent power necessary to produce landmark education reform in New York City. The analysis is constructed to address practice questions about how relationships of solidarity, the incremental work of forging an alliance between labor and community, erecting a platform for change on democratic dialogue, and the development of indigenous leadership contribute to effective organizing as well as strategic decision making. (For the purposes of this study, *indigenous* will refer to grassroots efforts from individuals within the community who may or may not have formal training as community organizers.) Each of these themes is addressed within the context of a community collaborative of parents and agencies contesting the degradation, privatization, and neoliberalization of public education.

CC9's efforts to change the discourse and performance of education in a section of the South Bronx offer a narrative of resistance to both local policy and international forces. It is a narrative that not only has the audacity to imagine that collective parent power can change the conditions within schools in one of the poorest communities in New York City, but also offers us a lesson in how such hope can be channeled into successful organizing campaigns elsewhere.

I

Community Power and Education Reform

1

Democracy, Community, and the Crisis of Public Education

The economic changes of the late twentieth and early twenty-first centuries have had devastating effects on the most vulnerable communities. As manufacturing jobs have been exported to other parts of the world and replaced with lower-paying, nonunionized service sector work in industries such as health care, fast food, and retail, the impact on urban communities has been substantial. The capacity of many poor and working-class families to make ends meet is increasingly tenuous. William Julius Wilson indicates in *The Truly Disadvantaged* that these economic trends have also contributed to the destabilization of churches, local voluntary associations, and other intermediary institutions that have historically helped to organize and channel local political power. In turn, the influence of these communities on the public policies of the larger city has diminished. This dynamic has had an especially profound impact on the fiscal base and performance of public schools in poor neighborhoods.

Clearly, other factors, such as teacher capacity, school leadership, and learning culture, have also affected the performance of public schools in very poor communities. That said, what remains indisputable is that at the convergence of political economic forces, differential investment in public schooling and student achievement is an especially critical dynamic affecting every other choice made by education professionals. Yet this part of the story of public education failure receives scant attention from policy makers favoring market incentives or testing initiatives to arrest and reverse the tide of public education failure. More to the point, this reality is systematically ignored.

Poverty and Public Education

The living conditions of poor students greatly affect their performance. Inadequate health care, housing, nutrition, and safety often impede learning. Poor children living in shelters or substandard housing face many challenges completing school assignments outside the classroom. Insufficient nutrition and health care undermine students' capacities to concentrate on schoolwork during the day. Finally, lack of safety is characteristic of the environment inside and outside of the schools and is distracting to students who want to learn. Here, too, the argument can be made that these conditions do not exist apart from the history and forces of a larger political economy but rather are its consequences.

The turbulence within public education is not entirely attributable to larger political and economic forces. The internal organization and culture of public schools are also contested by policy makers. Edgar Schein, an innovative organizational theorist, argues in "Culture," for example, that what is different today is that organizations, particularly public organizations, are more in trouble and that the environment is changing faster. Leaders in the private and public sector are wrestling with difficult economic problems. He notes that the electorate has become increasingly cynical about the social value of money spent on public organizations, and he refers to one school of thought on how to address these organizational stresses as "engineering." Engineers, like conservative policy makers shaping public education, he states, "view the need for complex human teams, the need to build relationships and trust, and the need to elicit the commitment of employees as unfortunate derivatives of human nature to be circumvented, if possible, because they are so hard to manage and control."

Organizational culture plays a pivotal role in enabling or disabling effective adaptation to environmental turbulence such as that experienced in the very poorest urban neighborhoods. Critically, an organization's culture and its consequent practices have political as well as social implications. For example, a school system that determines that student achievement is essentially a technical matter is likely to favor increased managerial control, simple outcome measures, and an increasingly scripted role for teachers. What is left out of such an equation? To begin with, parents and the communities served by public schools are largely ignored. A question rarely asked is, How can parents from the poorest communities contribute to repairing their schools? Given their messiness and complexity, undertaking more democratic approaches to transforming public education is not discussed as a serious policy option.

Equally important, legislation such as No Child Left Behind creates a plethora of new demands for improved student achievement with little attention paid to the persistent scarcity of resources in the poorest communities. Power and politics influence the flow of public dollars. Education reform that is not accompanied by new public dollars can only mean that there is little political will among decision makers to improve schools. To address these shortfalls, stakeholders will have to realign, increase their power, and organize campaigns for educational justice. Much of the push will have to come from those communities most affected by the disinvestment in public education. To win any substantial change, alliances will also need to be created with other stakeholders such as teachers' unions. To be effective, however, this reform movement must build its campaigns for educational justice and improved school performance on a foundation of independent parent power.

Democratic Experience, Citizenship, and Effective Schools

Salient to this discussion is John Dewey's body of work, which pointed to parent or community involvement as essential to meaningful school reform. Dewey believed that citizens' capacity to effectively observe, report, and organize to improve public education was an underpinning of effective schools. Critically, parents would offer a powerful and important counterweight to expert perspectives on the needs of public schools. Dewey was clear on the limits of professional expertise. Jeannie Oakes, John Rogers, and Martin Lipton, in *Learning Power,* cite Dewey for pointing out that a "class of experts is removed from common interests, and consequently, it becomes a class with private interests and private knowledge which in social matters is not knowledge at all." Oakes, Rogers, and Lipton go on to note that for Dewey, "aristocracy was perceived as eliminating the social intercourse so crucial to the problem solving process itself" (37). Therefore, Dewey concluded, "the man who wears the shoe, knows best where it pinches" (37). For these reasons Dewey argued that school officials or experts were responsible for involving parents in a dialogue regarding public education. Only through such dialogue could education experts identify critical problems and begin to jointly formulate effective resolution. Critical to authentic dialogue, however, is a mutual respect more easily described than practiced.

Michael Williams in his book *Neighborhood Organizing for Urban School Reform* has described practices within public schools as a balance, where parents "stick to providing nonexpert tasks, and staff the expert functions." In keeping with this presumption is Pierre Bourdieu's assertion that often between dominant and dominated groups an overt opposition exists between the right opinion and left, or wrong, opinion, which limits possible discourse. The universe of discourse, Bourdieu states in *Structures, Habitus, Power*, "is a range of ideas expressed or understood as containing the whole matter under discussion. Such discourse is essential to an enfranchised citizenship drawing on its own experience in order to reimagine public education" (120). However, on matters of policy and practice regarding public institutions, the role of parents is restricted. Successful linkage with parents, school professionals often note, is contingent on parent recognition that they are essential to the student's out-of-classroom preparation and development. Conversely, decision making on the structuring of the classroom environment is restricted to professional teachers, administrators, and planners.

A countertrend regarding the importance of parent involvement to school performance has emerged within professional education circles. For example, recent research by the IESP maintains that parent-school interconnectedness is associated with higher levels of achievement. James Comer's research during his tenure at the Harvard School of Education, however, indicates that without a significant change in the mechanisms of democratic governance and discourse, it will be difficult to engage parents in the work of changing public schools. These findings underscore the importance of designing a governance structure that offers parents authentic opportunities to use what they know to influence public education.

These research findings have helped to inform and shape professionally initiated experiments intended to promote parent inclusion. These experiments challenge historic understandings of the sharp boundary between schools and communities. In *The Sharp Edge of Educational Change*, edited by Nina Bascia and Andy Hargreaves, the authors argue that the school is not an isolated society, but rather has its own culture that is formed in contact with the wider society, in the particular local context. These influences are critical in shaping the school. It was on this basis that education reformers such as Comer developed school-based experiments that emphasized the importance of parental influence on student learning. The initiative was intended to systematically include parents in much of the day-to-day work of public schools. More specifically, the objectives of Comer's project in New Haven were to involve all adults in the school program so that they would come to know one another as persons rather than as stereotypes, to help teachers and parents through workshops and other means to increase their skills in dealing with the children, and to aid the education staff in improving the curriculum. Critically, both dialogue and utilization of parent expertise were elemental to this approach. Equally important, as Williams notes in *Neighborhood Organizing for Urban School Reform,* Comer intervened to bridge the divide between professional education staff and adjacent communities by "emphasizing cooperative forms of participation within the schools."

The effort to build a school community that draws upon the expertise and participation of members of the neighborhood was also a part of Deborah Meier's work as principal of an East Harlem elementary school. She notes, in *The Power of Their Ideas,* that "we also saw schools as examples of the possibilities of democratic community.... For us democracy implied that that people should have voice not only in their individual work but in the work of others.... we knew that it would require authentic forms of collaboration between the school and the family." However, Meier concludes that "we eschewed formal teacher/parent co-governance."

In the development of a school community, both Comer and Meier are silent on the necessity of independent parent power. More specifically, they did not consider how independent power derived from parents working together outside the school system was fundamentally different from an enlarged parent influence entirely dependent on professional belief in its potential to shape democratic community within public schools. Their notion of a democratic community is contingent on the commitment of professional leadership to parent participation. Although the aspiration is laudable, it is also fraught with dilemma. As Annette Lareau suggests in her book *Home Advantage,* teachers may want parent involvement, but their practices often "challenge the dominant view that teachers want a partnership with parents." She further remarks that the professional socialization and training of most teachers and principals is to devalue the expertise of parents. An initial question that must be asked is, What forces are aligned to enforce such a vision and translate it into institutional practice over time? Can a third party, such as Comer or principals like Meier, be expected to successfully implement projects promoting democratic decision making within public schools that include parents as full partners? Perhaps, but the forces aligned against such reform may quickly overwhelm even the most talented academic or professional leader. Such reform would be isolated and sustained on the basis of individual professional capacity and always vulnerable to turnover and burnout. At worst, such an isolated initiative, no matter how well intentioned, might be washed away by powerful forces outside the schools that enforce bureaucratic norms and allocate increasingly scarce resources.

What is missing from the analysis of professionally led reform is the relationship between power and change in public education. In Meier's democratic experiment, parents' independent power remains modest at best. Their roles are proscribed by professionals and fit within a structure developed by "experts." Alternatively, as Williams notes in *Neighborhood Organizing or Urban School Reform,* "Comer's analysis fails to come to grips with how people create the circumstance that enables them to share power. In his project, poor people had the school improved for them once again by professionals" (67). Seymour Sarason adds in *The Predictable Failure of Educational Reform* that "any effort to reform (literally give new form to) our schools has to deal with the nature and allocation of power" (73). In the absence of parents having an independent base of power outside of the school system, what they say is more easily ignored by public school staff and undermined by the commands of the larger bureaucracy. Critically, community participation in public education decision making is more imagined than real unless parents have first created an independent change agenda largely drawn from their experience with school failure. The process of community members building such a platform for change is essential to the development of an independent parent voice and power that stands outside the education bureaucracy and thus better positions community members to make a uniquely grounded contribution to the present policy discourse focused on restructuring public schools.

The Political Economy of Public Education

The recent trends in public education are reasonably clear. There has been an intensification of various forms of privatization and increased test taking to measure improvements in achievement. These policies have generally failed to reverse low reading and math scores as well as drop-out rates in inner-city schools. There is a paradox at the center of recent public education policy: persistent failure but continued adherence to privatized and standardized test taking approaches that yield little benefit. This contradiction certainly begs for an explanation. Some part of the explanation can be traced to the political economy and the move toward privatization of public education.

Critically, policies of privatization create an economic dynamic that intensifies the breakdowns of the public sector. As more resources are directed away from public institutions, their capacity to address persistent difficulties, particularly in public schools, is diminished. This environment maroons poor students in many of the poorest communities in schools that are decreasingly capable of meeting even their most basic learning needs.

In *Social Class, Poverty, and Education,* edited by Bruce Biddle, a number of authors argue that several well-designed studies have shown a relationship between funding levels and achievement. Clearly, resources alone will not reverse the failures of public education. However, without additional resources it is reasonably clear that there is little hope of arresting and reversing present trends regarding achievement in the poorest urban neighborhoods. Current policies that funnel resources away from public schools assure that teachers remain undersupported, class sizes continue to grow, salaries remain insufficiently competitive to attract the best teachers, and the physical infrastructure of public schools decays. Serious public reforms require increased resources.

If this cycle of reform and failure is to be broken, basic presumptions regarding education policy will have to be challenged. The present political economy of public education, which demands that public schools in the poorest neighborhoods increase levels of achievement with diminished or static funding, is untenable. The pressure for a substantial redistribution of resources, however, will not come from either policy makers or the public bureaucracy. Rather, it will have to come from outside the system and from those who are ideologically and experientially predisposed to a reinvestment in public institutions. Equally important, the timing and scope of the reforms must reflect the urgency of the present crisis. That urgency is most deeply experienced by poor parents and students presently caught in the downward spiral of underachievement and dead-end jobs.

The power necessary to enforce a community agenda for change is not easily acquired. It demands that parents create the necessary collective force to both gain a seat at the table with policy makers and advance an independent reform agenda. Such power is built through the steady accumulation of social and political capital that over time "scales up the influence" of parents.

Parent Power and the Accumulation of Social Capital

The concept of social capital has a particular history within the field of education scholarship and policy making. James Coleman, the noted Harvard sociologist, introduced this concept to education decision makers in a very particular way. Coleman understands social capital as both the latent and active resources inherent in the structure of relationships. He noted in "Social

Capital in the Creation of Human Capital" that the reproduction of specific norms and social networks is essential to improving a school's performance. In accumulating social capital, then, a parent seeks to build his or her individual child's predisposition and capacity for education. Such definition and practices have less to do with building a collective parent power than with creating a familial or school dynamic of norm transmission and, in turn, educational achievement. Although Coleman's analysis is valuable, he misses what Bourdieu in his original conception of social capital understood: unequal relationships of power affect parents' capacity to influence their child's education. Consequently, the accumulation of social capital is not simply about the transmission of norms but also about the acquisition of an independent power that rests on a web of relationships. Bourdieu's definition allows for an analysis in which race and class, as structural factors, affect parent involvement. It also sheds light on the ways in which the accumulation of social capital can change the balance of power and, in this case, support parent-led social change movements that directly address structural inequalities.

In keeping with Coleman's argument, Mark Warren notes that social capital refers to the set of resources that build relationships of trust and cooperation between and among people. He departs from Coleman, however, when he indicates in his book *Dry Bones Rattling* that "theoretical work on social capital highlighted the benefits of trust, cooperation and collaboration, but only sometimes has it directly confronted issues of power" (4).

Yet the lack of power that lies at the core of poverty and racism plays a key role in community decline and school failure. Warren remarks that urban schools will continue to fail their students "when communities lack the power to demand accountability, when they are captured populations." How, then, can social capital accumulation become a basis for increasing the power of parents? The sociologists Alejandro Portes and Patricia Landolt suggest that as social capital is transformed into bonds of social solidarity within a community, it can become an important factor in the success of economic and political initiatives. They caution, however, that such bonds are difficult to establish. They are particularly critical of social engineering initiatives that seek to build solidarity networks when few or none exist. Instead, they note in their article "Social Capital" that "it is advisable to build on whatever exists, that is to reinforce existing social ties and work alongside the definitions of the situation of community members rather than seeking to impose them from the outside." Social capital that coheres into bonds of solidarity helps to build activist communities. This dynamic is underpinned by democratic processes that honor the expertise and history of citizens.

What remains unclear, however, is how to accumulate the trust necessary to promote relationships of social network and solidarity. Solidarity is most vividly expressed when poor communities are fighting battles essential to their immediate survival and the larger society's sustainability. Certainly education is one of those frontline battles that poor communities are presently fighting. Still the question remains, how can fractured and dispirited poor communities in the United States build the social network and solidarity necessary to wage such campaigns?

Portes, in his article "Social Capital," suggests that relational social capital between members of a group is formed to some extent through (1) early introjection of shared values, particularly justice, into conversation; (2) norms of reciprocity in exchanges between participants; (3) an embeddedness or bounded solidarity that is often reactive to conditions that are exploitive and or oppressive; and (4) enforceable trust that distributes highly particular rewards and sanction to group members.

These dimensions offer a way of framing dynamic exchanges that, over time, promote the accumulation of relational social capital and eventually solidarity. The interplay between shared values, oppression, and reciprocal exchange helps to explain how relational bonds of solidarity are built. Ultimately, however, such collective identity is animated through the shared agency of political struggle.

This transformation of social capital into forms of solidarity and political power does not happen accidentally. Rather, it is tied to the conscious use of specific practices, some of which will be more fully discussed and elaborated in subsequent chapters. One such practice is to create opportunities for participants to engage each other in dialogue to generate hopeful alternatives to their present situations. Such dialogue, as Oakes and Lipton note in "Struggling for Educational Equity in Diverse Communities," not only reframes problems but also fosters a sense of collective identity. Activist communities can emerge from such dialogue if particular objectives are targeted and organizing is initiated to change conditions. Conscious attention to building collaborative relationships with key stakeholders in public education is another practice that leverages social and political capital (building bridges to other institutions and groups).

With practice, the social capital of parents can mutate into various kinds of political capital. Alliances with key decision makers, access to the media, the legitimacy of a collective parent voice, and pressure tactics are key elements of a potential political capital spawned by the cohesion and solidarity of parents. As Portes and Landolt indicate, it is difficult to create, sustain, and continue to build such social capital or solidarity. It is with this in mind that we now turn our attention to examples of parent-led initiatives intended to improve public education.

Organizing Community Power to Reform Public Education

Community organizing as a strategy for both local and broad-based reforms has both a deep history and mixed record. Recently, community organizing has been employed as a primary change strategy in campaigns as disparate as environmental protection, immigrant rights, neighborhood enfranchisement in political decision making, resistance to community development projects, and police brutality. It has been suggested by Michael Apple in *The State and the Politics of Knowledge* that much community organizing emphasizes alignments along economically defined classes struggling to defend their interests, end exploitation, and win redistribution. The political imagination of these class-based struggles was largely restricted to matters of justice and unequal distribution of resources. A number of academics have argued that this socialist framework is no longer operable. As noted in Apple's volume, the political scientist Charles Tilly indicated four decades ago that community organizing's historic role as a stimulant for reform was being supplanted by nationwide, centralized groups, such as political parties, trade unions, and government. Also in Apple's volume Nancy Fraser argues that new communities are emerging that are not identified with neighborhoods or matters of economic redistribution. Rather, Fraser notes, they "are culturally defined groups or communities of value . . . struggling to defend their identities, end cultural domination, and win recognition" (224).

Importantly, as Fraser indicates, the postmodern era is marked by an identity politics that has forged solidarity among some groups but has simultaneously contributed to a fracturing of broader-based social movements along racial, ethnic, and gender fault lines. The arc of neighborhood community organizing is also significantly affected by factors cited by William Julius Wilson in *The Truly Disadvantaged,* including depletion of social capital in poor communities, the multiple pulls on leadership, intensifying problems, racial and ethnic divisions, and the scarcity of economic resources necessary to sustain change campaigns.

Fraser's and Tilly's arguments, however, must be counterposed with the growing inequality between the richest and poorest segments of the country. A number of scholars have written extensively on the heightened inequalities and disappearing middle classes created by post-Fordist deregulation and the shift to regressive taxation in the late twentieth century. In 2004, the U.S. Gini index reached its highest, most unequal level since the early 1940s. Equally important, the capacity of identity politics, unions, and political parties to effectively respond to policies that have intensified these trends has diminished. Perhaps most notably, labor power has declined dramatically as the proportion of unionized workers has plummeted during the past thirty years.

These trends raise a number of compelling questions regarding the development of new social movements. Given intensifying economic and social divisions, is there an alternative to building change movements geographically and from the ground up? Additionally, can a progressive agenda for school reform ignore inequitable resource distribution and the intensifying deprivation of the poorest inner-city communities? Has any social change project of substantial ambition been spared the struggles of racial/ethnic division, leadership development, or building social networks? Finally, can the public education system be transformed to meet the needs of the poorest students and communities without building parent capacity and power to advance a change agenda? Recent history suggests that the answer to each of these questions is no.

Presently, few movements exist that are sufficiently powerful or attentive to matters of public education to offer much hope that they can alter present neoliberal trends. Critically, national or even regional social movements do not represent a significant countervailing force to the unrelenting march toward privatization. Where does this leave citizens interested in advancing a more progressive agenda for public education reform? Certainly, no short cuts or easy answers are available to activists. Power will have to be built from the bottom up one neighborhood at a time and "scaled up" over time in order to create the political energy necessary to leverage new forms of targeted investment in public education. Much of that will have to come from parents, the single group of stakeholders in public education whose allegiance is most focused on the needs of students and grounded in the historic injuries of class and race injustice that are systematically expressed through the breakdowns of local schools.

A starting point for creating the necessary parent agenda and power to change public education is the formation of strategic approaches to local organizing. These strategic approaches must consider (1) how alliances can be built with other stakeholder groups such as teachers, (2) the development of change agendas that have a long-term trajectory but begin with achievable goals, (3) the complex transition from protest to advocating for specific proposals, (4) building solidarity with often culturally disparate groups, (5) the necessity of drawing community-based organizations (CBOs) into this struggle, and (6) the development of practices most likely to promote parent leadership. Clearly this is, as Portes and Landolt indicate, a complex and difficult undertaking. Local struggles are a key to the development of a progressive agenda that will ultimately translate into policy changes. The hope is that over time these very local or community-based initiatives will cohere into a broader parent-led movement for education reform. But the work of building the local and regional agency for effective campaigns will be painstaking and gradual.

Recent history through 2005 suggests that parent-led campaigns for education reform have not led to the creation of strategic alliances or sustained change. Instead, the organizing work has resulted in forms of confrontation that often marginalize parent voices in the struggle for resource redistribution and improved public schools. Perhaps the most vivid example of the polarization frequently associated with parent-led campaigns for education reform is the Ocean Hill–Brownsville struggle for community-based control of the schools.

Ocean Hill–Brownsville and the Politics of Polarization and Confrontation

In the early to mid-1960s a coalition of government, business elites, educators, and activists emerged in New York City. This coalition rallied around the idea of what Jerald Podair describes as "community control of education in black neighborhoods." In his volume *The Strike That Changed New York*, Podair notes that the teachers union, the UFT, refused to join this coalition. The Ocean Hill–Brownsville community was in the vanguard of pushing for community control of public schools. Parents and activists, increasingly exasperated with the failures of the local public schools and their lack of voice in the decision-making process, chose to boycott the local school board and form their own governance structure. The UFT chose not to support community leaders' positions regarding local governance at a very early stage of the conflict. Podair suggests that union leaders favored an alliance . . . for two interrelated reasons. First they wished to curry favor with black parents by joining with their demand that 110 Livingston Street pay more attention to the Ocean Hill–Brownsville community. And second, to the UFT, attention meant services—more teachers, more specialists, more equipment—in a word, more.

He adds that

in 1967, most UFT teachers felt that residents of neighborhoods such as Ocean Hill–Brownsville shared their belief that more services and facilities would cure what ailed the New York City public schools. But even as they marched with the UFT . . . parents were showing signs that their understanding of school reform was very different from that of the union. (6)

Fractures between parents and teachers deepened over time, and the continued failure of local public schools, in spite of collaborative efforts, created a deep gulf between parents and the school system. In a language that could be used today to depict the failures of large urban public school systems, Alfred Hess, in his article "Understanding Achievement (and Other) Changes under Chicago School Reform," cites David Rogers's description of the specific failure of New York City public education during the 1960s and 1970s:

In New York City public schools, one out of three pupils is a year or more retarded in arithmetic. . . . the gap between . . . achievement and national standards widens as pupils remain in school. In the past ten years reading scores have gone down, drop out rates have gone up. . . . Many employers are angry at the school system's failure to produce an employable black and Puerto Rican population. (218)

The reality of such failure in the midst of a still vibrant civil rights movement produced both profound distrust between parents and the boards of education, and a belief that only a dramatic redistribution of power could fix the school system. This prompted parents to demand not only a voice but the power to influence the policy and practices of board decision making.

The parents' call for sharing power resulted in community control experiments organized by the City of New York in three demonstration districts each with several schools. One of those districts was Ocean Hill–Brownsville. School professionals, however, did not trust the parents as they pushed for community control of local schools. Teachers, and more specifically the teachers union, had greater faith in and allegiance to the centralized board of education. For the mostly white teachers in Ocean Hill–Brownsville, the public school system had been a primary vehicle for both upward mobility and professional status. The stability of these gains was seen as highly inter-related with the maintenance of a powerful central public education author-ity. The UFT, at that time a relatively young union, recognized that its power and capacity to advance the contractual interests of teachers was maximized by negotiating with a single, centralized authority. The more such authority was diluted through decentralization, the greater the likelihood that victories won in the past might be overturned by local boards and that variability in contracts across districts would create greater internal tension and rift for the UFT central leadership.

Over time, Ocean Hill–Brownsville became a battleground between the teachers' union and parents. At the center of this battle was the contested terrain of whose voice should have the greatest authority in education deci-sion making. In the 1960s, the failure of the New York City public education system to increase academic achievement in the poorest black and Puerto Rican neighborhoods was eclipsed by a narrative of intensifying conflict between community and union leaders. Transfer and hiring policies provided a catalytic spark for the collision between parents and the union. The UFT claimed that parent decision making had abrogated the due process rights of teachers, and called a strike. Podair notes in *The Strike That Changed New York* that parents charged that every attempt was made by the UFT to elimi-nate community control and that racism was rampant. An underlying con-cern of the UFT was that merit systems of hiring and promotion would soon be displaced by an idiosyncratic system of parent preference.

Podair suggests a particular concern was Rhody McCoy, a district educa-tion official, stating that "an eventual goal was an all-black teaching staff in Ocean Hill–Brownsville." Albert Shanker, the president of the UFT, under-stood that "merit" hiring was a visceral, emotional issue for his rank-and-file members. Community leaders, however, were equally adamant regarding the historic failure of "merit" hiring to improve educational outcomes for their children. They concluded that such failure demanded an infusion of new teachers more committed to the education of black youth. A guid-ing assumption was that black teachers best understood the urgency of the crisis, could identify with the struggles of students, and would commit the personal resources necessary to change the learning conditions within the schools.

The parents, however, underestimated the power of the UFT to short-circuit the decentralization movement. The UFT organized a series of strikes that first targeted the district and later the entire system, bringing a quick halt to community control by 1970. Subsequent forms of local control were substantially diluted. As Michael Williams notes,

> The residue of this struggle between parents and system, however, was the decentralization of the nation's largest system into 32 districts, each with the population of a medium sized city. The power of the Community School Boards (CSB) that governed them was far more circumscribed than under the original community control experiment. The CSB could hire the district superintendent and later could fire principals as well, but they could only function in an advisory capacity on budget and curricula matters. (99)

Ocean Hill–Brownsville continues to be a powerful reference point in New York City for the distrust that separates overwhelmed, undersupported school staff and parents who are increasingly frustrated with the failures of public education. The conundrum faced by both parents and teacher unions, however, is that alone they simply have not been able to muster the power to revitalize public education. At the same time, the prospects for alliance are undercut by a tactical, cultural, and aspirational divide. Importantly, the confrontational tactics employed in Ocean Hill–Brownsville did not contribute to improving the state of public education in poor communities of color.

As teachers, parents, and students are increasingly caught in the web of conservative policies, intensifying resource scarcity, and the decline of public education, can they find the common ground necessary to forge an alliance? Ocean Hill–Brownsville illustrates how difficult it is to build such an alliance. However, other examples of parent-led initiatives offer greater encouragement. Critically, the political environment, increasingly hostile to unions and the public sector, may paradoxically open spaces for new forms of alliance between labor and community groups. It is clear that in the absence of such alliance, the prospect of building the necessary power to counter conservative policies or promote an alternative, parent-led progressive agenda for public school reform is seriously limited.

The Chicago Experience with Decentralization

During the 1980s, there was an intensifying call in Chicago for a radical re-organization of the public school system. The push began with grassroots organizations dissatisfied with the record of achievement of public schools. The political scientist Marilyn Gittell noted in "School Reform in New York and Chicago" that in Ocean Hill–Brownsville the initial push was to increase parent voice and authority in public education decision making. Similar to New York City, the reform momentum in Chicago focused entirely on matters of governance. Unlike the New York City campaign for decentralization, however, the Chicago coalition was not simply composed of grassroots groups. As momentum for change built throughout the 1980s, a number of business, education, political, foundation, and media interests joined the campaign for change.

In *Charting Chicago School Reform*, Bryk and colleagues suggest that rather than directly challenging the basic political structure of large-scale democratic control, arguments were made for systemic change within existing structures. This difference sharply distinguishes the potential reform trajectory for public education in Chicago from New York City. The reform agenda of this "large tent" coalition of many otherwise disparate groups often used the language of systemic dysfunction created by current governance structures. A greater role for parents was cited by advocates of the right and left as an essential ingredient for improving the public schools.

The grassroots groundswell for change in Chicago was a first step. Over time, community organizations had an essential role in building a broader, citywide coalition. Gittell has noted that the Chicago school reform is a story of the leadership role of community organizations in initiating and sustaining coalition politics and in engaging traditional civic groups, political officials, and business establishments as activist partners in the reform agenda. Critically, the decisive role played by these grassroots community organizations contests conventional social science wisdom that such agencies only deter elite actions but are unable to bring about structural change.

Community leaders and agencies in Chicago recognized that changing public school governance and learning culture would be a slow and arduous process, only achievable over the long haul and with other stakeholders. Additionally, early public confrontations with other interest groups were more likely to slow rather than accelerate reform momentum. Gittell suggests that no single elite necessarily controls education policy; however, school professionals and bureaucrats are in the best position to dominate the arena. Consequently, the campaign required pragmatic, strategic thinking about how to build collaborative momentum for a reform agenda. This broad coalition and agenda were shaped throughout the 1980s.

By 1988, the mayor of Chicago and the state legislature responded to and approved the Chicago coalition's sweeping plan to reorganize and decentralize the Chicago school system. Much of the decision making was relocated from the central bureaucracy to Local School Councils (LSCs). These LSCs, composed of teachers and parents, were given a degree of decision-making authority over personnel, budgeting, and curricula.

Critically, this initiative engendered little opposition. The reasons for the ease of implementation of this sweeping plan are complex. Certainly, the mayor's commitment to both community participation and school reform was critical. His support helped to shape a political culture in Chicago that was amenable to both a broad, representative coalition for school reform and a plan for fuller participation of parents and teachers in local school decision making. The business community in Chicago also had a history of working with diverse city groups on specific reform agendas. It might be argued, therefore, that the Chicago experiment with decentralization was idiosyncratic and rested on the historic commitments of important stakeholders to a practice of broad inclusion. What is left out of this equation, however, are the particular strategic choices that grassroots groups made to build a broad coalition around a common agenda.

This change process was initiated from the ground up and outside the system. Yet community groups understood that the power necessary to produce fundamental change could not be generated entirely from the outside. They needed to recruit other critical actors with relationships to the system. Parent-led initiatives and practices of building power through broad coalitions remain the primary lesson of the Chicago experiment in decentralization. As Michael Williams has suggested in reference to the more confrontational, isolated, parent-led initiative of Ocean Hill–Brownsville, "the bottom up, outside the system strategy of community control . . . was an effort doomed to failure in the heavily unequal struggle for resources with the giant public school systems" (96). Alternatively, he noted that "astute and adroit political maneuvering . . . coupled with a climate amenable to change and a militant organizational base will go far toward ensuring success."

Parent/community leadership capacity, an essential ingredient in joining the improvement of public education to policies of decentralization, was a daunting challenge in Chicago. Importantly, there was insufficient expertise among community groups and parents to support basic educational development work in the 550 public schools throughout Chicago. Equally important the Chicago public school system did not have the resources or will to develop parent leadership capacity. How, then, can reform momentum be sustained in an environment that, on the one hand, has embraced new decentralized forms of decision making but, on the other hand, does not have the community resources or leadership capacity necessary to meet the pressing needs of many inner-city schools?

This is a conundrum that extends beyond Chicago. Poor parents invest a great deal of time and energy in daily survival. Participation in public education is perceived by many as an unaffordable luxury. In general, this point is ignored in the literature, even by the most progressive academics associated with the new poverty literature. Often, it is presumed that if opportunities for participation are made available, the parents will show up. This is a misreading of parent circumstance and disposition. Consequently, a first order of business for organizers is to struggle to engage parents in a process that promotes sustained participation. A second and equally compelling need is for practices that promote leadership development that maximize parent voice, expertise, and contribution. These matters are intimately associated with moving from a public fight for decentralization to the effective exercise of parent voice in local public education decision making.

The Chicago experience also offers critical instruction on a number of strategic issues that must be considered in the complex work of building parent agenda, power, and leadership. Building coalitions with other stakeholders must be undertaken early. Campaigns need to focus on building a proactive agenda for improving schools that extends beyond new forms of governance. In Chicago, this more specific platform for change did not exist. The general features of such a reform proposal are relatively straightforward. Some part of this platform must address the need for additional resources. Critically, a call for heightened investment in public education must also be accompanied by a plan for how those dollars will be utilized.

The Chicago experience with decentralization implicitly and explicitly raises these important questions. These matters are elemental to the development of parent-led campaigns that seek to change power relationships as well as the ongoing learning conditions within the poorest urban districts. We will return to these themes in subsequent chapters.

Parent Organizing as the Strategic Lever for Reforming Public Schools

Although parents remain committed to amplifying their voices in the decision-making process of public education, governance and participation are increasingly seen as a means for improving schools, not an end. This shift has significant implications. To begin with, parent-led campaigns are more frequently developing platforms or proposals that challenge the present learning conditions and dynamics within public school classrooms. The proposed initiatives challenge business as usual by advocating specific reforms and explaining the logic or theory of change that will lead to improved achievement. This kind of proactive reform agenda, although ever more prominent in local campaigns, is not always featured in parent-led struggles for school reform.

The impetus for school reform is increasingly coming from specific community organizations. Generally, its point of origin is not a cohort of parents, as in Ocean Hill–Brownsville, or a broad coalition for change, as in Chicago. Rather, the campaigns more frequently percolate up from specific community agencies. Over time, these agencies may enlist other groups in broadened community or districtwide campaigns for school reform. Kavitha Mediratta, a researcher for the IESP, developed a study of eight parent-led campaigns for school reform, where the locus for change was in specific schools and community districts. About 75 percent of these organizing agencies were also part of a statewide coalition for improved public schools. Jean Anyon, in her book *Radical Possibilities,* notes that this trend is supported by the Collaborative Communication Group's study, which explains that "80% of the 66 parent organizations . . . are working not only in local neighborhoods but in regional and state coalitions" (157).

Mediratta begins with the proposition that organizing helps to create the pressure and relationships necessary to improve the learning culture of targeted schools and districts. Part of what remains unanswered is how community groups go about building the social and political capital necessary to change public schools. What is their practice? How might their strategic focus be characterized? As noted earlier, there is no single organizing approach or template that can by culled from the variety of agencies engaged in school reform campaigns. Certainly, the context of the neighborhood, the mission of the agency, the commitment of parents, decision makers' receptivity to the parents' change agenda, class, and race all greatly affect the development of specific campaigns. Although these differences matter, it is clear that recent shared experiences of state, district, and local parent-led campaigns are also instructive.

From the Industrial Areas Foundation's (IAF) work in Texas to campaigns developed by Mothers on the Move in the South Bronx to ACORN in Chicago, it is clear that organizers are explicitly working to develop parent leadership. In turn, leadership capacity is a linchpin in creating democratic, parent-led organizations. Parent leadership development, however, is a complex and difficult field of practice mined with a range of obstacles. As Lareau and others have documented, there is a relatively low level of involvement of working-class and lower-class parents in the work of strengthening schools. The explanations for this disengagement vary, but Bourdieu's suggestion that differences in class culture impede or facilitate both the child's adjustment to schools and the parent's negotiation of the process of schooling is especially salient. As Gilderbloom and Mullins note in their book *Promise and Betrayal*, the standards of schools are not neutral, and any call for parent involvement is influenced by the predispositions of intellectual and other elites. Consequently, for parents, the pull to challenge failing schools is likely to be washed away by the reluctance to engage a system that they experience as both threatening and hostile. For poor parents, the public schools are an especially uncomfortable territory that repels.

Engaging and Empowering: The Unique Needs of Parents in Poor Communities

For organizers, a central question appears and reappears: How do we engage and sustain parent involvement in campaigns when, historically, community members have been estranged from public institutions? This question has led many organizers and community agencies to conclude that campaigns to change public schools must create a decision-making process/environment that respectfully welcomes and elicits parent input. Critically, community or parent expertise must be incorporated into the development of campaigns. Finally, parents' capacity must be enlarged so that they can begin to develop the skills and knowledge to confidently lead meetings, think strategically, organize events, and discuss complex education reform proposals with professionals.

The work of establishing a parent commitment to improving public schools is largely a project of developing individual ownership of a collective change agenda. The strategic intention to build a parent-activist community to change neighborhood schools is bundled with the need to develop practices that create a strong network of relationships between parents around a common project. It is largely through the collective formation of a change agenda, leadership development, and organizing campaigns that specific practices are incubated and tested. The overarching intention at every stage of the work is to enable community agencies to leverage key decision makers to improve public schools.

Across the country, parent-led organizing has focused on a range of specific school improvement goals. For example, in Chicago, ACORN focused on matters of teacher quality and retention. The Texas IAF platform sought to change school curricula statewide through portfolio assessment, interdisciplinary education, and child-centered pedagogies. In New York City, ACORN organized a campaign opposing the privatization of parts of the school system. In California, the Oakland Community Organization (OCO), a federation of faith-based organizations, emphasized school construction, smaller class sizes, and after-school programming. Also in California, the Education Justice Collaborative (EJC) developed a statewide campaign to support litigation that challenged the state's denial of tens of thousands of minority children an adequate education because of an inadequacy of basic resources. The resulting legal case, *Williams v. California,* raised the issue of resource inadequacy for children of color across a range of education issues, from physical plant to teacher retention, from recruitment to class size. It was a keystone that enabled EJC to pull seemingly disconnected local campaigns into a larger and more coherent statewide movement for education change.

Parent-led campaigns, although differing in strategy, tactics, and agenda, almost always cohere around one common issue: the inadequate funding of public education in the poorest neighborhoods. As a result, the call for increased funding was joined to numerous reform proposals. Despite their disparate goals, each of these parent-led initiatives shared an understanding that meaningful reform required a redistribution of public dollars to low-income school districts. This is not a small point. Eric Zachary and Shola Olatoye, in *Community Organizing for School Reform in the South Bronx,* indicate that unlike proposals for privatization, community campaigns for the improvement of public schools tend to assert "that money matters for students from less advantaged backgrounds and minority students" (2).

Accountability for the performance of public schools is another theme that unifies the work of many community campaigns. Eva Gold and colleagues, in their article "Bringing Community Organizing into the School Reform Picture," suggest that public accountability is the hinge that connects community capacity with school improvement. They indicate that the broadening of accountability was the mechanism for creating the political will necessary to improve schools in low-income neighborhoods. In other words, an emphasis on accountability put public officials on notice that they must answer to the community for the failed record of public schools. This was a critical shift, effectively designating community groups and/or parents as overseers of neighborhood schools. In this way, parents and organizers could hold politicians to their promises despite competing pressure from other constituencies.

Zachary and Olatoye note that "the development of political will necessary to transform urban schools involves multiple constituencies and strategies and may vary by city" (2). Despite these differences, various community groups have argued that any reversal in the trends of public education failure demands that parents both assert their right to hold public officials accountable and have the power to effectively advocate a community perspective. Organizing was the basis for asserting parents' collective will and vision for public school improvement.

Framing Strategies, Tactics, and Issues

The strategic and tactical choices of parent-led campaigns fit no single profile. For example, a community group in the South Bronx, Mothers on the Move (MOM), in the mid-1990s developed a confrontational and highly charged campaign to replace a district superintendent who was widely considered incompetent. Public events were packed with speakers denouncing the superintendent. The media were contacted and carried this message to a larger public. Other campaigns have employed essentially collaborative strategies and tactics to advance their change agendas. The curricula reform campaigns of the IAF in Texas, for example, largely promoted collaborative alliances between parents and key decision makers in state and local government.

Another choice facing parent organizers was whether to build a membership base or work to develop institutional relationships in expanding community power. Mediratta notes that a number of campaigns have been organized around membership or one-on-one relationship building and outreach to community members, while others have emphasized building connections between institutions to leverage change. Examples of parent membership organizing are exemplified through the work of community-based organizations such as MOM and the New Settlement Apartments (NSA) in the South Bronx. Alternatively, organizing efforts in California and Chicago have focused more of their attention on building institutional relationships. It should be noted, however, that these approaches are not mutually exclusive and that a number of organizing campaigns have begun to integrate them.

Finally, parents and organizers have selected different issues to galvanize communities. In local campaigns, issue selection was largely determined by both the circumstances of the public schools and experiences of parents. This second point is especially important: parents largely determined the purpose or agenda of campaigns. Organizers understood that parent voice in such decision making was foundational to building an ever larger circle of participation, thus building the power necessary to produce change. Finally, broader organizing campaigns, such as the EJC's, focused on educating the public about the critical issues facing schools and promoting a change agenda commensurate with the crisis of public education in poor communities.

Many of these organizing campaigns produced palpable change. For example, Oakes, Rogers, and Lipton note that in Oakland, OCO convinced the district to adopt a small-schools policy for capital construction projects. Gold and colleagues suggest that the Alliance Organizing Project in Philadelphia increased school safety by gaining more crossing guards, better lighting, and improved traffic patterns. MOM succeeded in having the district superintendent removed. In Chicago, the Logan Square Neighborhood Association campaigned to reduce overcrowding and won five new annexes at elementary schools and two new middle schools. But as Zachary and Olatoye of the IESP suggest, the ultimate test of any public education change strategy is the improved performance of students. Although organizing initiatives have had success in changing conditions in targeted schools, their records in improving school performance are less certain. In Texas, for example, recent data suggest that school performance has not improved in the aftermath of the reform that was organized, at least in part, by the IAF. Alternatively, the 2008 report *Organized Communities, Stronger Schools,* by Kavitha Mediratta, Seema Shah, and Sean McAllister, makes a strong empirical case for the relationship between organizing campaigns and increased student achievement. For community organizing to gain legitimacy as an indispensable strategy for improving public education, it must establish that empowered communities are associated with improved student achievement.

Part of the challenge for organizers, then, is to develop a dual theory of change. To begin with, a theory of organizing must be developed that explains how the parent power necessary to transform or reform public education can be built. This task, of course, is daunting but it is simply not enough to discuss the ways in which parent power can be built. That discussion must be accompanied by a theory for changing public schools. It is necessary but not sufficient to demand more money or the expulsion of incompetent staff. The distinct proactive contribution of a parent agenda to changing the learning environment of public education must also be addressed. This is a tall order, but it is the challenge that community groups must meet in order to succeed.

Organizing Theory and Trajectories for Building Parent Power

Saul Alinsky is considered by many to be both a central innovator and founder of community organizing in the United States. Alinsky subscribed to an approach that first identified problems in poor communities and later created the power necessary to address the material conditions of poverty. The fundamental belief of Alinsky and his successors is that only by building and exercising collective power can poor people wrest concessions from those who skillfully use wealth and political position to maintain social and economic advantage. He sees direct action and mass mobilization as the most effective exercises of a community's collective power. Presently, the Midwest Academy and IAF advance Alinsky's organizing frame when they emphasize direct action organizing based on the power of people to take collective action on their own behalf.

Alinsky attempted to expand the collective power of poor communities by organizing around shared material conditions. Another organizing frame was developed by the Highlander school and introduced during the civil rights movement by Ella Baker, one of the founders of the Student Nonviolent Coordinating Committee (SNCC) among others. Highlander's statement of purpose, as described by Charles Payne in *I've Got the Light of Freedom*, was "broadening the scope of democracy to include everyone and deepening the concept to include every relationship" (68). The Highlander approach eschewed the dominant assumption that poor people would be led by their social betters. It also emphasized a nonbureaucratic style of work and local problem selection that was sensitive to the social structure and culture of specific communities. Payne remarks:

> Above all else, perhaps, they stressed a developmental style of politics
> in which the important thing was the development of efficacy in

those most affected by the problem. Over the long term, whether a
community achieved this or that tactical objective was likely to
matter less than whether the people in it came to see themselves
as having the right and the capacity to have some say-so in their
own lives. . . . this required participatory political and educational
activities in which people themselves had a say in defining the
problems. (68)

Baker insisted that leadership should be decentralized and come from community members, not from professional organizers. As Oakes, Rogers, and
Lipton note, "in contrast to Alinsky and the labor movement tradition where
professional organizers were outside agitators, Ella Baker's organizers worked
from inside the community and adapted organizing to a community's ways
of life" (105). The emphasis was on building relationships between community members, which over time was expected to cohere into a sense of
solidarity and, perhaps most important, shared identity.

Agitation, Political Capital Formation, and Confronting Established Power

These distinctive organizing frames are, of course, not mutually exclusive.
Organizers can employ approaches that build political power (political capital) and social networks (social capital) depending on the moment in a
campaign. This mixing of approach has, for example, characterized much of
the work of the IAF in Texas. The more fundamental question, however, is:
How do these frames inform thinking about change theory and practice? For
Alinsky, power enabled a flexing of political muscle, creating a shared identification around a public community struggle, promoting a visible urgency
around a problem, and building victories that were expected to contribute to
an enlarged base. During these early campaigns, relationships were neither
considered nor understood as germane to the task and tactics of building
power. It is important to note that this has changed; the more recent organizing work of the IAF increasingly focuses on attending to the development
of social networks. A presumption that guided Alinsky's work and those who
followed him was that poor people could build the power to change the conditions of their communities by shifting strategic alliances and developing
independent collective mobilizations. The emphasis was on an accumulation
of political capital through tactics that confronted the state and over time
mobilized larger and larger cadres of community members.

The theory of change undergirding Alinsky's work was that poor communities were in a constant state of near readiness to take action to advance their self-interest. What needed to be introduced, however, was agitation from outside the community. The organizer could play this role by offering an expert leadership capable of shaping a campaign and sustaining its momentum.

Although Alinsky's approach to organizing was quite effective in stimulating immediate actions, he was less successful in tending to leadership and community capacity development over the longer term. Consequently, local organizations and change agendas built within his framework tended to fade over time. Clearly, any explanation of the relatively limited life span of these change organizations would be quite complex. This complexity should not obscure, however, the relationship between such an outcome and the lack of attention to developing sustainable leadership and community capacity.

Critically the present political climate is markedly different than it was in the 1960s. Moral claims on the state registered by organizers like Alinsky have diminished. Public officials are more impervious to such demands because the power of progressive social movements has waned significantly. As well, Charles Murray, the author of the extremely influential work *Losing Ground,* and other neoconservatives captured the "high ground" in this discourse by suggesting that state intervention is counterproductive because it hurts the poor. Equally important, the recent demobilization, isolation, and political disenfranchisement of poor communities make it increasingly difficult to build grassroots power that is independently capable of altering state or public decision making. Consequently, a singular reliance on poor communities or supportive social movements to build the base of power necessary to change public institutions is likely misguided. This changed historic circumstance, in combination with the limitations of Alinsky's model in developing leaders and sustaining campaigns, requires that his organizing approach be reconfigured to meet the demands of the present struggle to reform public education.

Social Capital Formation, Solidarity, and the Development of a Collective Political Will

The Highlander school and Myles Horton, its founder, developed an alternate approach to community organizing. Horton's model focuses on building a collective and indigenous capacity to wage struggles to strengthen communities. Horton argues that this is achievable through building leadership capacity, creating democratic decision-making structures that privilege the expertise of community members, and developing more durable and dense social networks of community members to wage successful organizing campaigns. The search to find a best fit between change strategy, tactics, and the circumstances of a community is also weighed in deliberative decision making. However, such decision making does not proceed until more egalitarian relationships between community members and organizers are developed.

The organizing practice occurs, then, on two levels. Early attention is paid to creating expansive and deep relationships through various forms of dialogue and democratic decision making. Highlander practitioners did not see community members as simply an inert power to be mobilized and channeled by organizers. Rather, ordinary people were considered by practitioners like Septima Clark and Ella Baker as anything but ordinary because their contributions were essential to the short- and long-term success of social change work. Their potential contributions went far beyond showing up at a rally or putting a body on the line. Members of a community were seen as the primary source of ideas, energy, legitimacy, leadership, and networks capable of lifting both a campaign and community simultaneously. Payne, in describing the work of Ella Baker, notes, "they had a faith that ordinary people who learn to believe in themselves are capable of extraordinary acts, or better, of acts that seem extraordinary to us precisely because we have such an impoverished sense of the capabilities of ordinary people" (5). Importantly, practices that deepen and extend social capital are not separated from a campaign, but rather they are infused into its organizing culture and decision making.

Nonetheless, the mere existence of social capital does not guarantee its activation. Critical to this discussion, Portes and Landolt, in their article "Social Capital," suggest that the community development approaches most likely to activate social ties are consonant with the practice formulation of Highlanders. They indicate that there is no generalized formula for putting social ties to use in development. Instead, they assert that effective projects must be achieved one at a time by combining existing grassroots work with careful provision of resources and external support. The latter cannot be simply a top-down provision of support in the form of developmental formulas, but must be a part of the local environment, incorporating its understanding of the situation and its priorities.

The Highlanders' organizing framework, which influenced the course of the civil rights movement in the South thirty-five years ago, continues to have strong reverberations today in parent-led campaigns for school reform. A presumption that runs through the school reform work of IAF in Texas, Logan Square Neighborhood Association in Chicago, MOM in the Bronx, the EJC in California, and the Alliance Organizing Project in Philadelphia is that constituent engagement through consistent leadership development builds greater organizational power. Their shared intention is to enable parents to develop the skills and knowledge to act in their self-interest and, over time, to lead organizing campaigns. Gold and colleagues note in "Bringing Community Organizing into the School Reform Picture" that "too often these practices depart from parent involvement strategies and rather serve as a form of public relations to create greater institutional legitimacy for current educational practices."

Additionally, this body of organizing work has developed approaches toward internal governance and accountability that emphasize parent voice and leadership in decision making. The objective is to build parent power through authentic forms of participation and, ultimately, to hold school systems accountable for the performance of students. Warren indicates that this work increasingly emphasizes the importance of collaboration. The demands of collaboration, however, are especially complex. Such an approach requires working inside and outside of the government to advance a reform agenda. Unfortunately, examples of parent-led campaigns and more generally community organizing initiatives that have developed power both inside the public sector and outside by mobilizing a neighborhood's citizens are rare. Warren notes in *Dry Bones Rattling*, for example, that historically community organizing groups have followed a strategy that can best be understood as reflecting unilateral power. They organized the social capital of their community to leverage power

> into the political arena to force institutions to provide services or provide funds. . . . Some community organizations have used this strategy in the education arena. However necessary this outside strategy may be at times it is insufficient for improving urban schools. . . . Combative strategies can exacerbate a situation in which school principals and teachers are already wary of outside community groups. (4)

Clearly, organizing work is rarely, if ever, strategically or tactically pure. Consequently, the distinctive organizing approaches developed by Highlanders and Alinsky have been part of the strategic and tactical mix of many parent-led organizing projects.

Developing the Power to Hold School Systems Accountable

As suggested earlier, the relationship between parent power and school accountability is a recurrent theme. Pedro Noguera, an education scholar, has remarked that urban schools will continue to fail their students when communities lack the power to demand accountability. The question of how to build parent power is not easily answered. Some part of building an independent base of parent power can be traced to the breadth and depth of community involvement in a change campaign. However, this source of power is likely not sufficient to unilaterally leverage reform. As was noted earlier, public officials have the capacity to veto the change agendas of even the most powerful parent groups. It is on this basis that Warren suggests that parent collaboration with school officials and other public education stakeholders is a critical element of both building parent power and changing the system. He emphasizes the need to build an independent base of parent power outside the system while simultaneously building relationships within the system to forge collaboration or reform alliances.

The collaborative approach to organizing suggested by Warren is not without its problems, however. How can such collaborative relationships be fostered when public officials discount the expertise and policy priorities of parents? Is such collaboration possible in the aftermath of broken promises and rampant cynicism about the trustworthiness or commitment of school officials? Can parents sustain and expand legitimacy in their communities without confronting public officials about the failure of the schools? How can local community groups gain access to public education decision makers to build both productive conversations and collaborative projects? Finally, are confrontational tactics not part of the arsenal available to do this critical work? If confrontation is effectively eliminated as a strategy or tactic, will it not undermine the formation of oppositional collective identities?

Institutional Alliance and Parent Power

The work of education organizing has increasingly relied on mediating community institutions to build a base of power. As Williams notes, a mediating institution is "a group structure that stands between the private life of the individual and the giant mega structures of modern society, such as government, corporations and other bureaucracies" (111). It is precisely these mediating institutions that Mediratta refers to when describing the role of direct membership and institutional membership organizations in supporting parent-led education reform campaigns. These structures include churches, community-based nonprofits, and regional as well as state federations of local groups working to improve public education. They have offered parents and staff new forms of public space necessary to organize successful campaigns.

In the past, community campaigns often relied on a single agency to influence local and centralized decision makers. The disjuncture between the power of the single agency and the larger system, however, undermined parents' efforts to improve school performance were often stymied by the disconnect between the power of a centralized public education system and the limited reach and influence of a single community agency. This experience led to the formation of broad-based collaboratives comprised of agencies and churches. These collaboratives increasingly spearheaded education reform campaigns in cities such as Chicago, Philadelphia, Oakland, and Austin. Critically, they were more effective than single-agency campaigns in reaching decision makers and influencing policy. Questions remain about the enduring impact of these campaigns, the degree to which policy change has led to improved school performance, and the continuing struggle to maintain individual agency commitments to collaborative work. The formation of collaboratives, however, does represent an important shift in redressing the power imbalance between parents and school officials.

A Parent Platform for Change

Recently, much attention has been focused on building parent organizing campaigns to create a new change trajectory for public education reform. Yet the theory of reform that distinguishes parent agendas from those of the bureaucracies or privatizers remains largely unaddressed. We do know that campaigns are often organized around those needs parents perceive as compelling, such as the condition of buildings, lack of security, turnover of teachers, size of classes, structure of curricula, and competence of staff. An assumption has been that if one or a number of these features of public education were upgraded, the performance of students would improve.

Consequently there has been a push for targeted investments in public education. Some research suggests that targeted investments in teacher capacity development and recruitment are especially effective. Other findings indicate that learning environments are best improved through greater safety, new buildings, and more capable teachers. These findings have both appeal and merit.

Some part of the ongoing struggle, however, is in making the case—through research findings and community experiences—that specific programs can and do make a difference. What distinguishes parent-led campaigns for public education reform is a shared belief that (1) a revitalized public education is essential to the capacity development of students and the larger community, (2) substantial infusions of new resources must find their way out of the central bureaucracy into local schools, (3) decision making regarding the targeting of new resources must guarantee authentic community participation and honor parent expertise, (4) investment of scarce resources must be informed by the best available research findings, and (5) justice demands a substantial redistribution of resources to public schools in the poorest communities to address specific staffing and programming needs. Although this is not a radical platform, it stands in marked contrast to the policy and practice positions of both public education managers and advocates for privatization. This orientation, however, will be little more than a footnote in the present struggle to reshape public schools unless parents develop an independent base of power. Consequently, nothing less than the fate of public education is riding on the outcome of this continuing experiment in democratic participation and organizing. Such initiatives are increasingly evident and most vividly exemplified in the poorest urban communities. The analysis will now turn to the role New York City, in particular, has played in hosting such an experiment.

Public Education in the Poorest New York City Communities

New York City has often been a hotbed for various kinds of public education reform. As noted earlier, a particularly important struggle for school reform occurred in Ocean Hill–Brownsville in the late 1960s and early 1970s. Subsequent to this failed political struggle by community groups to decentralize the governance of schools, the City of New York reconfigured and decentralized the school system into thirty-two elementary school districts governed by community school boards selected in local elections. The record of this initiative has been mixed. On the one hand, between 1971 and 1981 there was improvement in reading scores for every grade from the second through the ninth. Importantly, these improvements were neither dramatic nor did the analysis disaggregate the differences in scores of the more affluent communities from the poorest school districts. The evidence of a general positive trend during this period is, however, indisputable. On the other hand, equally compelling evidence also surfaced during that decade that a number of the school districts were especially corrupt in their use of public dollars and hiring practices.

However, the director of the IESP, Norm Fruchter, has asserted in Mollenkopf and Emerson's *Rethinking the Urban Agenda*, that it is "a waste of time to argue whether current results in achievement scores represent an improvement or decline." Instead he suggests that the standard should be "educating all of our children so that they are capable of becoming successful college students when they graduate from high school" (208). Of particular importance is the quality of public education offered to students in communities with the highest concentrations of poverty. Data from the late 1990s suggest that New York City's public schools are failing students in the poorest neighborhoods. An analysis of standardized test scores indicates that low-scoring schools are significantly disadvantaged in every category of concern. These poorly performing schools had a disproportionate number of students eligible for free lunches, struggling with English proficiency, enrolled in special education, and having lower than average attendance records. In addition, the schools that underperformed had higher concentrations of students of color. It should be noted that little has changed during the past ten years.

In 1993, a group of New York City citizens filed a lawsuit on behalf of New York City students, which became known as the Campaign for Fiscal Equity. Of particular concern was a just allocation of public resources between suburban and New York City public schools. The plaintiffs argued that the lower funding of New York City public schools resulted in a lower achievement record of poor students of color. As well, they cited state reports that indicated that a strong link exists between poverty, minority status, and lack of achievement. The evidence they marshaled to support the claim that New York City students fared less well than their suburban counterparts was compelling. The brief noted:

> In 1992 . . . 40 percent of the City's grade three pupils scored below the reading SRP, meaning that they were unable to read with comprehension the earliest connected sentences and paragraphs,

compared to 11 percent of students in the rest of the state and 9 percent in the suburbs. . . . By the time the City's public school children reached high school, they had fallen further behind their peers elsewhere in the state. . . . Those high school achievement statistics understate the problem because they do not reflect the large number of City high school students who drop out of school. The annual public school drop out rate for the City in 1989–90 was 7.8 percent as compared to an annual drop out rate of only 2.2 percent in the suburbs. (16–18)

As this lawsuit wended its way through the New York State courts, the public schools in New York City continued to struggle with both underfunding and the significantly lower academic achievement scores in the poorest communities. Data released in 2001 further underscored this point by indicating that over 90 percent of the students in the lowest-performing New York City elementary schools were poor and of color. Equally important, the same report, *Civil Society and School Accountability* by Elizabeth Sullivan, noted that in the highest performing schools, 30 percent of the students were black or Latino, and 40 percent lived below the poverty line.

In 2003, the appeals court of the State of New York concurred with the plaintiffs' argument and awarded New York City an additional four to five billion dollars annually to redress the underfunding of its public schools. This award, however, was not legislatively enacted for a number of years following the ruling. In 2007, funding levels were agreed upon, and new dollars were allocated to New York City public schools. Critically, the issues raised by this lawsuit more than fifteen years ago continue to persist today. This point is underscored by Jonathan Kozol in his most recent book, *Shame of the Nation,* in which he points out that in 2002–3, per pupil spending differences between New York City and five of six neighboring suburbs were between 50 and 100 percent. More specifically, New York City spent $11,627 per student, compared to Manhasset, $22,311; Jericho, $19,113; Great Neck, $19,705; Bronxville, $18,788; and Rye, $16,132. Kozol suggests that what lies directly behind these shocking differences in public expenditures is the relegation of poor students of color to academic failure and dead-end jobs. He argues that this is a dramatic expression of American apartheid, or the continued segregation and sorting of students by race and class. He concludes that little has changed for the poorest, minority communities since *Brown v. Board of Education.*

The Bronx Renaissance

In the 1960s and 1970s the South Bronx became the symbol of "urban blight." The media portrayed the South Bronx as a dangerous urban frontier, spinning into social and economic chaos. A police precinct in the Hunts Point area, for example, was dubbed Fort Apache. The public perception and media representation of this precinct were of a fortress at the edge of civilization.

The social and economic decline of the Bronx during that period is indisputable. Many reports in the late 1960s through the 1970s indicate that the Bronx was "burning." Housing stock rapidly disappeared as fires erupted in numerous neighborhoods. Charlotte Street in the South Bronx dramatically illustrates this epidemic of arson. Jill Jonnes notes in her volume *We're Still Here* that during 1970 "Engine Company 82 made 6,204 runs to 4,246 fires or eleven a day" (234). In a ten-year period, the workload of the company had more than doubled. Critically, the fires began around the area served by Engine Company 82 and then spread south and north. The difficulties experienced by these Bronx neighborhoods were not limited to arson and did not abate. Jim Rooney further underscores this profound decline in his work *Organizing the South Bronx*. He notes that in 1989 baseline data on quality of life vividly conveyed a broad and profound breakdown in health, safety, and education: "There were 484 murders, 604 rapes, 16,220 robberies, 20,659 burglaries, 9,577 felonious assaults, 29,698 cases of grand larceny, and 11,438 other felonies. Of the twenty-five elementary schools with the lowest reading scores in New York City, thirteen were in the Bronx. There were 161,000 children living below the poverty line. In addition, there were 756 cases of AIDS" (63).

Community development corporations (CDCs) and neighborhood churches helped to reverse the physical decay of the Bronx beginning in the 1970s. Tens of thousands of units of low- and middle-income housing were built by South Bronx Churches and community-based organizations including the NSA, and the North West Bronx Community and Clergy Coalition. Over time, the early work of nonprofit developers was augmented and supplanted by private sector initiatives. The consequent resurgence of housing stock caused the *New York Times* to report the period between 1995 and 2005 as a housing boom. The number of permits for new construction more then doubled, from less than three hundred in the mid-1990s to more than eight hundred by 2003–5.

The frenzy of new construction caused many long-term residents to raise concerns about dislocation or gentrification. The Bronx borough president, Adolfo Carrion, acknowledged the legitimacy of the concerns but countered, "It's a good problem to have." The *New York Times* described the transformative consequence of this process: "A few decades after it became a national symbol of urban decay, the Bronx is home to a rash of new construction projects that are changing neighborhoods that have seen little new building in over half a century" (March 19, 2006, 30). Consistent with these trends, the rates of crime and arson have also declined dramatically over the past twenty-five years.

The Invisible, Continued Decay of Public Education

Despite the resurgence of the Bronx's economy and housing stock, its schools continue to fail. More to the point, physical changes in the Bronx have often masked the less visible and persistent problems of its public schools. In "Suburbanization and Urban Poverty under Neoliberalism," Ruben suggests that investment in brick-and-mortar capital projects and continued underinvestment in social welfare projects, such as education, is a hallmark of neoliberal development policy in poor urban communities. In Judith Goode and Jeff Maskovsky's most recent work on new social movements, *The New Poverty Studies,* they suggest that the neoliberal model makes no pretense of directly investing resources and infrastructure in the poor, instead redirecting public moneys and credit away from social welfare provision and toward large-scale private development projects.

This point is underscored by data presented in an IESP report by Zachary and Olatoye, which suggests that the problems of New York City's schools remain acute in the South Bronx. In District 9, for example, more than 98 percent of the more than 30,000 students are African American or Latino, and over 90 percent qualify for free or reduced lunch cost. In 2002, only 23 percent of District 9's students met city or state reading standards. These data are not inconsistent with the achievement scores of a number of districts in the South Bronx.

The recent narrative regarding the renaissance of the Bronx is really a tale of two worlds, one visible and the other more or less invisible. At the visible level of housing, crime, and, to a lesser extent, employment, the Bronx has made dramatic strides in renewing a number of communities. At the less visible level of school achievement, however, the Bronx has been continuing to reproduce academic failure for the poorest youth of color. Increasingly, what is recognized by grassroots groups, many of whom led past struggles for housing development, is that Bronx communities cannot be renewed and the future of its residents secured until the schools are significantly improved. Yet frequently, what parents and community agencies encounter from district decision makers is a lack of shared urgency regarding the need to improve public schools.

Consequently, parents in the Bronx, in partnership with CBOs, initiated a number of organizing campaigns in the 1990s to improve targeted schools. The most notable initiatives were waged by MOM and the NSA. These campaigns experienced limited success. As a result of a confrontational organizing campaign by MOM, a district superintendent with substantial tenure was replaced. In District 9, NSA was able to pressure local decision makers to remove a principal. In both instances, the organizing was prompted by low levels of student achievement and the hostility of public officials to being held accountable by the community. Although parents were successful in removing school officials, they were far less effective in affecting the learning and instruction conditions within the schools. In the aftermath of these changes, both schools continued to underprepare students in both reading and math. Basic competency levels did not improve. Although, individual professionals were held accountable for the failure of the public schools, little else changed.

Parents and CBOs involved in these campaigns, although disappointed, remained committed to forms of accountability that would improve student achievement. An important dilemma they faced was how to shift from a school-based to a systemic change strategy. Simply stated, individual CBOs do not have the capacity to wage successful campaigns for educational change systemwide. It was also increasingly clear that CBOs could not penetrate the learning culture of public schools with singular reliance on confrontational tactics and strategies. Bronx parents were learning through concrete campaigns that although professionals might be replaced, the practices of teachers and the culture of schools that produced and reproduced failure remained intact. Parents were also increasingly aware that reactive campaigns to replace professionals were no longer sufficient. To hold schools accountable for improved learning, communities would also have to develop a proactive change agenda. The question for parents and community agencies in the Bronx was how to use these foundational lessons from earlier efforts of parent-led organizing to build more effective second-stage campaigns.

As parents and agency leadership wrestled with these questions, it was also clear that the circumstances of New York City public schools were in flux. The mayor elected in 2002, Michael Bloomberg, was committed to recentralizing authority for public education. More specifically, his agenda was to wrest decision-making authority from locally elected district boards and transfer it to the New York City Board of Education. A large part of his motivation was the continued failure of the schools, stories of local board corruption, and a firm belief that a centralized board, which was directly accountable to the mayor, would do a better job. The mayor also articulated a commitment to involving parents in the work of rebuilding public schools. For parents, this changing of the guard represented both an opportunity and a challenge. If the mayor was serious about improving public education and involving parents, then a critical space might be opened to leverage the reform necessary to improve schools in the South Bronx. Alternatively, parents were wary. They remembered many broken promises from the past. They also distrusted reforms that increased the authority of centralized decision makers, historically inaccessible and unresponsive to community proposals.

This much was clear: the condition of the schools would not improve unless community groups were vigilant in holding public officials accountable. The renewal of the Bronx and its neighborhoods could not be completed until public schools were transformed. The circumstances in the South Bronx were no different from those in thousands of other poor urban communities throughout the country that also faced underperforming and underfinanced schools. Either they could surrender to neoliberal policies, including disinvestment in public education, privatization, and the allure of testing as an inexpensive solution to the breakdown of public schools, or they could actively reject such an approach as failing to meet the needs of their children.

For an increasing number of parents, the choice was clear. They would have to create alternatives to failed education policies if their children were to have options beyond dead-end jobs. On this basis more and more parents in the South Bronx were affiliating with CBOs to fight for educational justice. Parents' choice to fight is not unusual. What distinguished these community leaders was their willingness to struggle with the lessons of the first wave of parent-led campaigns to invent the next stage of organizing. What follows is the story of these parents, the innovative organizing collaborative they helped to create, and their groundbreaking lead teacher campaign. The ambition of this book, to borrow Goode and Maskovsky's words expressing their hope for *The New Poverty Studies*, is that "by studying and communicating poor people's efforts to organize themselves into coherent politically effective collectivities it can help to reorient public discussion back toward" the essential goal of public education to increase the knowledge and skill capacity of every student (481).

2

The Collaborative to Improve School District 9

In the South Bronx section of New York City a few parent groups had developed education campaigns to improve schools. Repeatedly, however, these organizing initiatives floundered on the shoals of the modest ambition of the organizing agenda and their limited power. Consequently, these campaigns were simply unable to effect either a reinvestment in local schools or contribute to a restructuring of their learning environment.

In the midst of this failure, parents were increasingly aware that their community's housing and economic resurgence was woefully incomplete because of the continued failure of public schools. The urgent need to improve local schools was not lost on a number of the most important agency leaders in the community. For example, Jack Doyle, director of the New Settlement Apartments (NSA), remarked, "When we look at the many problems of the community, people being involved in the criminal justice system, poverty, drugs, some of these problems are fueled by the fact that kids don't get an education. So, I think the schools are an incredibly weak link in a neighborhood that is beginning to show signs of health."

Critically, it was within a context of failed or modestly successful campaigns for school reform that community and professional leaders in District 9 of the Bronx began to consider new approaches that would join local agencies and parents in struggles for educational justice. This collaborative structure was expected to both extend the reach and expand the power of parent-led campaigns. This realization marked the beginning of an effort to build the Community Collaborative to Improve District 9 Schools (CC9).

NSA and Early Parent-Led Campaigns for Public Education Reform in the South Bronx

The rebuilding of the South Bronx can largely be traced to the work of a number of CBOs. One agency with an exemplary record of effectively working with community groups to address local problems is the NSA. Opened in 1990, NSA is a housing development of nearly nine hundred families in the Mount Eden section of the southwest Bronx. It is composed of fourteen fully renovated, previously abandoned buildings within an eight-square-block area that had experienced a destruction largely unchecked from the 1950s through the early 1980s. Its intentionally diverse mix of residents includes a substantial core of working people as well as 30 percent who were formerly homeless. The surrounding neighborhood is part of one of the poorest areas in New York City. In 1996, more than 40 percent of the households had incomes below $10,000, and 93 percent of the children in the local school district were eligible for free lunches.

From its inception, NSA's mission has been not only to rebuild and maintain a significant portion of the neighborhood's housing stock, but also to provide educational programs and community services to all area residents. By 1996, NSA was able to cite a range of accomplishments, including

- providing decent and safe housing to 893 families at affordable rates (typically less than 25 percent of household income),
- enticing the first bank to relocate in the community since the 1970s,
- building and maintaining the only playground for children in the area,
- establishing and staffing a community computer lab,
- implementing a program to combat domestic violence through the training of peer counselors, and
- developing a comprehensive set of youth development programs focusing on arts, academic enrichment, and recreation.

In spite of its many achievements, however, NSA was confronted with schools unable to improve local public education. If one district could represent the ongoing failure of the New York City public school system to effectively educate low-income children of color, it may well have been Community School District 9 in the South Bronx. Since the initiation of decentralization in 1969, the district had earned a reputation for corruption and unresponsiveness to the community. During the 1990s, several New York City Schools chancellors sanctioned Community School Board 9 for numerous improprieties. Academically, the district had an abysmal record, with three-quarters of the district's students reading below the level set by the New York City Department of Education and the New York State Education Department. The gap in reading comprehension scores between the district and the rest of the city during the 1990s had never been less than 15 percentage points. Moreover, the district had shown no substantial improvement. As United Federation of Teachers (UFT) official Herb Katz remarked, "If you could improve District 9, you could do it anywhere in New York City." Research has also demonstrated deep inequities in the distribution of teacher resources. Studies have shown that lower-performing schools with higher-need children in New York City have a lower proportion of teachers who are experienced, lower average teacher salaries, lower rates of teacher stability, and lower proportions of teachers who are licensed.

According to a report issued by New York University (NYU) Institute for Education and Social Policy (IESP), the NSA Parent Action Committee (PAC)

> did some of the finest school-level organizing in the City by the late 1990s. In many ways, PAC's work in District 9 best represented local efforts to organize parents to change the conditions of public schools in the Bronx. While their victory in having a principal removed from a neighborhood elementary school has not resulted in significant improvement of the school, the PAC has had marked success in strengthening the capacity of the community to struggle for its needs and vision. . . . A cadre of leaders has developed with the confidence and knowledge to effectively question and challenge school system officials about school performance outcomes. These leaders feel they have the right and responsibility to contest the prevailing distribution of power in their community.

The PAC's work in the Mount Eden section of the Bronx consistently fell short, however, of influencing either the culture or outcomes of local public schools. For example, the dramatic turnover of teachers in District 9 and its impact on school achievement were not affected by the PAC's work. Additionally, its confrontational tactics to remove principals who failed to improve school performance distanced the PAC from many key institutions and actors, such as the UFT and district administrators. Additionally, the PAC's work was often done in isolation from other community groups. This failure to build alliances limited the power of the PAC and other community groups working on education reform. Finally, the agenda of the PAC was reactive to the breakdowns of public education in the community and did not offer a comprehensive, alternative vision for change to both rally and instruct parents.

By the year 2000, the story of the PAC reflected the overall stage of development in the new field of community organizing for school improvement, which was only about ten years old. Tactics that harshly blamed professional staff and their unions for the failure of public schools in poor communities imposed enormous barriers to building relationships among CBOs, parents, and teachers. Most concretely these tactics contributed to public officials labeling parent activists as an illegitimate leadership, further marginalizing them from decision-making power. This intensified marginalization, in turn, reduced parents' capacity to influence the core learning and instruction functions of the public schools.

It is important to note, however, that the PAC also had a number of significant, albeit school-specific, victories, most notably in removing the principal of PS 64. The school's failure was marked by especially low reading scores. It ranked 657 out of 674 elementary schools in the city. These data caused parents to organize actions to hold the school's leadership accountable for student performance. Such an approach moved beyond the PTA's more defensive posture with administrators. Zachary and Olatoye note in *Community Organizing for School Reform in the South Bronx* that in winter 1997 the parents learned the "astonishing fact that only 17 percent of the students attending PS 64 were reading at grade level." Pressure in the form of a public action was applied at a community school board. Shortly thereafter, a campaign was developed to remove the school principal. The principal's removal as a result of the campaign was a signal victory for the PAC and more generally parent organizing. However, it also underscored the limits of organizing campaigns that exclusively focused on school-based rather than systemic issues.

Jack Doyle, the executive director of NSA, expresses the limitations of the PAC's approach to education reform organizing when he notes:

> We didn't have any preexisting relationships as an organization or as individual members of an organization. We didn't have any insiders with whom we had a relationship that we could build upon. But also we experienced administrators who weren't open to the community participating. She [the principal] didn't know the first thing about talking to, relating to, or being responsive to a community-based

organization or parents' concerns. . . . we were just feeling our way. Some of the things we did were clearly confrontational. I guess we had a naive hope that if things were done we would draw the attention of media, and they would bring additional pressure to bear, and we would have some breakthroughs. But that didn't really happen. We did, though, have some small victories.

Rethinking Parent Power as a Lever for Change

The PAC's approach, although at times effective and appropriate to the stage of development of parent organizing in New York City, ultimately contributed to a low ceiling of possibility regarding education reform. NSA attempted to increase its influence in May 2000 by establishing direct contact with the recently appointed chancellor of the New York City school system, Harold Levy. Parents bought balloons and welcomed the chancellor. He was responsive and warm at this initial encounter. Roz Chambers, a parent leader of the PAC, describes the meeting: "He met with us. We told him we were trying to meet with the district superintendent but were having problems. He said leave it to me and that he would get back to us."

After a short period of negotiation, a meeting was scheduled with both New York City officials and the local superintendent. In the aftermath of the PAC's initial reception, there was a great expectation among parents and organizers that they would have a productive second meeting with Levy. Parents were prepped by organizers on a series of PAC proposals to address the low performance of students. Chambers recalls, "We had a four-point proposal we were trying to get across." Anjelica Otero, a PAC organizer added, "As I heard it before the meeting, we were hopeful that we could get the chancellor to begin to see the learning problems in the district and how our proposals could help to make a difference. We weren't expecting him to accept the proposals but to start a serious conversation about them."

At the meeting, approximately thirty parents and organizers presented a four-point platform to improve student achievement in School District 9. A number of city and district administrators were also in attendance. As one observer noted, "It was neither a radical nor insubstantial set of proposals. They were research based and reasonable." From the very beginning, however, the chancellor signaled his allegiance to district administrators by affirming their recent performance. He was also resistant to the PAC's proposals. A parent in attendance remarked that "it never really felt from the beginning that he was listening. His mind was made up. He was just trying to sell us on him and his people." The four proposals were presented during the course of the meeting, and the chancellor quickly rejected them. Simultaneously, he praised the superintendent of the district, with whom the PAC had a contentious relationship. His response was perceived by parents as both dismissive and insulting. Whatever hope they had brought to the meeting was quickly dashed. Perhaps most important, this meeting squarely confronted the PAC and NSA with the limits of their organizing strategy and power to improve District 9 schools. It was in this moment that parents, organizers, and Doyle began to see their strategy as inadequate to the task of building the kind of power necessary to influence public education decision makers.

Also in attendance at the meeting was Eric Zachary, a staff member of IESP at NYU's Steinhardt School for Education. Zachary helped to establish one of the institute's programs, the Community Involvement Project (CIP), in 1995. From its inception CIP was guided by the belief that the systematic improvement of urban public schools for low-income and working-class children requires both progressive policy reform and the development of powerful grassroots constituencies that can advocate for, support, and sustain reform. Believing that urban public schools fail when communities are disenfranchised and economically and socially marginalized, the program focused on strengthening the capacity of parent leadership and the vision of neighborhood-based institutions in New York City and around the country organizing to support education reform.

The IESP has historically been an influential player in both developing the research and providing the technical assistance necessary to maximize parent participation in New York City public school decision making. Over time, the IESP had developed a strong network of key allies both within and outside the education establishment. Zachary, a highly experienced professional organizer, provided technical assistance to a number of community groups, including members of the PAC. During the course of his work, he had become increasingly focused on the potentially important contributions of CBOs to improving New York City's public schools. CBOs, he believed, were essential to building and channeling parent power. His experience, insights, and leadership would provide a substantial part of the architecture for building a new approach to local organizing and school reform in New York City.

Creating the Collaborative to Improve School District 9

In summer and fall 2000, Zachary met with Doyle to discuss the limitations of NSA's recent school reform efforts. During this conversation, Zachary raised the possibility of meeting with other CBOs "to create something larger with more power." The discussion unfolded gradually. The relatively slow pace of these meetings was strategic, allowing the time to promote a rich dialogue regarding the failure of recent reform initiatives and the exploration of alternative approaches. These conversations, Zachary noted, "led to Jack and I reaching out to several other CBOs to invite them to a meeting in November of 2000. They included the executive directors of the Citizens Advice Bureau, Mid-Bronx Senior Citizens Council, Highbridge Community Life Center, ACORN WHEDCO, and the Latino Pastoral Action Center." Early, in the process, the Latino Pastoral Action Center dropped out because they were interested in starting a charter school and, as Zachary indicated, "it would have been an overload for them to do both." Approximately six months were devoted to engaging leadership of selected agencies in a conversation regarding the educational needs of the community, the similar problems faced by each CBO when attempting to reform local public schools, and a proposal for collaboration.

Both Zachary and Doyle understood that committing individual agencies to a collaborative required patience and a highly participatory conversation. Each agency needed the time to gradually surface its reservations and build confidence in the project. A number of the CBOs expressed concern about the risks of organizing. Zachary explained:

> What organizing is and how it is different from service delivery and housing development is that parents drive it rather than staff, that organizers are out of the office rather than in it and that there was a risk of confrontation with the school system. We repeated this numerous times. Occasionally people would waiver, get nervous. For some of the agencies it was so different from the way they were used to doing business.

The proposal to collaborate was borne out of the disappointing historic record of single-agency organizing campaigns in improving public schools. It was within this context of both critique and strategic assessment that the architecture of organizing to improve local schools in New York City was reinvented. The collaborative was seen as both an alternative public space and a potentially powerful instrument of popular mobilization for school improvement. Critically, proponents of the collaborative advanced the principle that its power would lie not in its donors, its technical expertise, or its administration but rather in the will of the parents. The architecture of the collaborative emphasized the centrality of parents to both decision making and idea generation.

These early conversations helped to spark a reimagining of parent empowerment and community self-determination. Participants agreed that the reach of any single community-based organization to improve public schools was very limited and that collaboration represented a necessary next step. The CBO was seen as a critical nexus between parents seeking agency services and an independent community capacity to reform schools. Organizers therefore anticipated that each of the CBOs would provide access to a large pool of parents and argued as well that the collective power of the CBOs promised specific advantages in leveraging the school system. Critical threads of future CC9 practice, including relationship building through dialogue, leadership capacity development, reflective retreats, and democratic decision making were incorporated into Zachary's outreach to agency executive directors.

Although the executive directors had not made a formal commitment to the collaborative by spring 2001, Zachary noted, there was "sufficient buy-in to proceed to develop a proposal to raise money from foundations." Organizers' attentions quickly shifted to involving parents in the development of CC9. Megan Nolan, an organizer at the PAC, indicated: "We felt it was now time to begin to reach out to parents about the issues they felt were important and begin to lay the seeds of the collaborative in their minds." With this objective in mind, a meeting was convened at one of the agencies— the Highbridge Community Life Center—to promote representative parent involvement from four of the CBOs. In some sense, a democratic web of participation in the early design and thinking about the collaborative was being spun. These tentative first steps in democratic decision making extended into every aspect of CC9's practice.

Building the Collaborative

Parent participation in CC9 was galvanized by the resignation of the superintendent of District 9 in summer 2001, and parents' insistence on participating in the selection of the new superintendent. Additionally, CC9, as

Chambers pointed out, was seen "as the most powerful way for parents to be heard by the board." Zachary observed, "So here we are at a point in our infancy where that is the most important issue probably facing us, but we have no capacity but a moral obligation to act. The future of the district is being made and we have to decide what to do." This event resulted in a meeting in early July at the Bronx Museum of the Arts, which was attended by four or five parents from each of the CBOs. The group sketched out the first steps in the organizing campaign as well as core values of the collaborative. These meetings ping-ponged between the concrete work of organizing and the more abstract work of building a collaborative structure. Zachary pointed out that the group "began to meet early on an almost every week basis with the parents. We did a petition drive and collected almost a thousand petition signatures around our demands. We went to a school board meeting. It was a very busy early summer."

In July, parents began to meet to develop a list of demands regarding the search process for the new superintendent. Participants determined that the selection process had to be open to community review and committed to parent participation. Critically, this was occurring in a district that was often characterized by parents and the media as corrupt and dismissive of parent participation. Thus, organizers were not surprised when the parents' participatory approach was quickly rejected by district decision makers.

With almost jazzlike improvisation, some of the outlines of CC9's practice were borne from the tumult, creative tension, and excitement of the superintendent campaign. The Organizing Committee, composed of parent representatives from each of the six CBOs, began to function as CC9's ultimate decision-making body. This structure assured the centrality of parent voice and authority in CC9 decision making. Additionally, CC9 insisted on parent inclusion in public education decision making. The petition drive to elicit community support for CC9's demands was organized by parents and organizers. A decision was made to act, and not wait, because, as Ocynthia Williams, a parent leader, indicated, "The whole purpose of the collaborative was to support academic improvements for children, and who the superintendent was going to be was the most important factor to impact upon that. We said even if we can't do something major at this point, we've got to do something."

Clearly, substantial demands were being made on the limited resources of a very young organization. And yet it was precisely those demands, made in the heat of an important campaign, that tested the resolve of parents and compelled early strategic thinking about the purposes of CC9. All of these initial activities were carried out without new funding. The work was shouldered by volunteer parents and "out stationed" staff of the CBOs and the IESP. As Zachary noted, "We felt for the integrity of the collaborative we had to do something. How could we just sit on the sidelines and say, 'well we haven't raised any money yet so we can't do anything.' If we are going to be driven by core values, then we had to act on those values." The campaign was a kind of "coming out party" for CC9. Parent actions put an early public face on the collaborative as a serious force for inclusive, districtwide decision making.

In fall 2001, approximately twenty-five parents attended a community board meeting. For the first time, many parents experienced the board's profound disregard for parent voice and participation. At the conclusion of the meeting, board members passed a resolution regarding the selection of the next superintendent of the district without hearing from a single parent or community representative. This resolution identified a final pool of candidates, and the interim superintendent, Stanley Mims, was named as one of the finalists.

Parents continued to press for inclusion as they reached out independently to candidates to schedule informal interviews. However, only one candidate responded. In the midst of parents' efforts to press from the outside for inclusion, word leaked out that the board would select its next superintendent over Easter vacation, when the schools were closed. This seemingly conscious effort to exclude parents was consistent with the board's historically insular practices. A parent leader remarked that "they had no interest in what we had to say. We were ignored."

The board's exclusion of parents, which was, in effect, a lockout, stimulated a rich, productive, and highly participatory discussion among CC9 parents. "Again and again," Williams remarked, "we reminded ourselves we were about what was best for the kids. We weren't about politics. We weren't going to play it safe." Similarly, Anna Maria Garcia indicated that "we have a responsibility to do this for the kids." Parents were guided less by the political factors at play in the selection process than by a sense of obligation.

The collaborative could not reach a consensus about any of the candidates because, as Doyle noted, "we didn't feel that any one of the candidates was so much better than any of the others." Therefore, rather than building a campaign around a candidate, CC9 developed a campaign for parent inclusion. The board's undemocratic process prompted CC9 to schedule an emergency meeting. At that meeting a commitment was made to organize sixty parents to attend the next public hearing of the board. The evening of the board meeting was bone-chilling cold. In spite of the weather, CC9 met its turnout goal. Parents did not just show up, they made certain that their anger was heard as they chanted and marched. Parent presence resulted in the board canceling the meeting. Later, at a hastily reconvened meeting, board members nominated Mims as the next superintendent.

CC9 continued to press the issue of community participation by filing a formal grievance with the Board of Education. The grievance stated that parents' rights had been violated because of inadequate notice. CC9 did not win the battle. However, through this "coming out" campaign, CC9 sharpened its sense of purpose, established credibility by delivering a relatively large number of parents at a public meeting, developed inclusive participatory decision making in the heat and urgency of a campaign, and showed a willingness to confront power to improve the public schools. It was in this campaign that CC9's fighting spirit to do whatever was necessary to improve the public schools was first evident. These events were foundational to CC9's growing reputation as both serious about and effective in working for school reform.

Formalizing Expectations and Standards

In fall 2001, discussions between CBOs about CC9 intensified. A number of directors raised concerns about preserving agency autonomy within the context of a collaborative project. One agency, the Women's Housing and Economic Development Corporation (WHEDCO), was especially troubled about the potential impact of direct action and organizing on funding. WHEDCO had a well-earned reputation for providing quality services, and CC9 perceived it as a valuable potential partner. However, in fall 2001, WHEDCO determined that it could not accept a parent role in the collaborative that might supersede the authority of staff or a member agency. Of particular concern was that parent decision making might lead to actions or events that resulted in the withdrawal of public funding from member agencies. Consequently, it decided not to join CC9.

Throughout fall and early winter 2001, ACORN and a number of CBOs continued to meet, working to identify the core values of CC9 and elaborating a decision-making structure. In December, twenty-six parents and organizers representing five CBOs participated in a retreat at Empowerment

House in Goshen, New York. The pastoral calm of the retreat house was quickly filled with an intense discussion, focused primarily on formalizing the collaborative agreements and continuing to press for needed changes in the school district. The contrast between the setting and the dialogue was palpable. Yet it was the calm of the retreat house and the trust built during six months of dialogue that allowed parents, administrators, and organizers to reach agreement. At the meeting, the group achieved a consensus on its core values, mission statement, decision-making structure, and forms of accountability. The push-pull in the conversation between agency prerogative and collective accountability was a persistent creative tension. It contributed to the development of an Expectations and Standards document that outlined areas of mutual accountability for CBOs, parents, and the public schools.

In the thirteen-page Expectations and Standards document, CC9 emphasized three significant points:

1. a child's right to a quality public education,
2. the need for parents to develop the capacity and power to change the conditions of the schools,
3. the parents' and teachers' need to learn how to work together (and that) qualified caring teachers and parents are the key to better schools.

The collaborative later encoded and elaborated these values in the CC9 platform. Zachary indicated that CC9's general goal was to "develop a community-based constituency with enough power to influence the policies and practices of the schools and district so that the academic achievement of the students of District 9 significantly improves." The long-term vision was to build a citywide movement of parents who have the "capacity to impact each level of the New York City system." Most immediately, each CBO was seen as having responsibility for organizing at the level of the local school and district.

These shared commitments inspired the following six CBOs to join CC9:

- New Settlement Apartments (NSA), which owns and operates almost a thousand units of low- and moderate-income housing in the Mount Eden neighborhood and provides educational and community service programs to area residents. It initiated and continues to provide organizing support to the PAC.

- Highbridge Community Life Center, which has been providing a wide range of educational and social services, including job training programs and entitlement assistance, to families living in the neighborhood since 1979. It helped parents establish United Parents of Highbridge, an independent parent organizing group focusing on CES 73, a public school in District 9.

- ACORN, a national membership organization of low- and moderate-income families with a thirty-year history of organizing for social change. The New York City ACORN Schools Office has developed new public schools and issued policy studies demonstrating racial and economic inequities in the school system. The South Bronx chapter has been organizing parents in Districts 7, 9, and 12 for several years.

- Citizens Advice Bureau (CAB), which has been providing a wide array of services to South Bronx residents for almost thirty years in the areas of early childhood education, after-school and summer programs, adolescent development, homelessness prevention and shelter, and immigrant rights.

- Mid-Bronx Senior Citizens Council, established in 1973, one of the largest CBOs in the South Bronx that is controlled and operated by people of color. It provides a comprehensive range of services, including housing, employment training and job referrals, after-school programs, and child care.

- Northwest Bronx Community and Clergy Coalition unites ten neighborhood groups organizing to obtain and preserve decent and affordable housing, promote safe streets and reduce crime, and enhance the quality of life for all residents. Its Education Committee has been successfully organizing for five years to reduce school overcrowding, improve school facilities, and increase student achievement.

These agencies' decisions to join CC9 were, in part, the culmination of a long history of frustration and a growing awareness that local public schools were in crisis. The risk of surrendering autonomy was offset by the pervasive understanding that the crisis and failure of local public schools threatened the survival of the community. Therefore, organizations were willing to take certain risks in order to engage in a collaborative movement.

The agency leadership of CC9 understood that the work of rebuilding the South Bronx had to extend beyond the brick-and-mortar projects of building housing. As Brother Ed Phelan, the executive director of Highbridge, remarked, "we've done a good job on housing, but the schools haven't really improved in thirty years." The long-term health or viability of the community, he concluded, was tied to the revitalization of public education. This shared insight, along with the promise of foundation money to hire CC9 organizers who would be assigned to member agencies, helped to cement administrators' commitment to the collaborative. The formal statement of Expectations and Standards for each CBO was agreed on and signed in January 2002. Zachary indicates that "the document formalized how the fundamental tension in collaboratives or coalitions, between the need to respect local autonomy on the one hand and to assure collective accountability on the other, would be handled." The moment the document was signed, CC9 was formally constituted, and relationships of mutual accountability and autonomy of the six CBOs were cemented.

A first test in achieving a balance between individual CBO and collective CC9 interests emerged almost immediately. After distributing foundation money to each of the six CBOs, CC9 was confronted with the questions: Who does the hiring, and who is responsible for supervision? Again, CC9 had to navigate a delicate balance between the collective interests of the collaborative and the particular concerns of each agency. To resolve this dilemma, Zachary and a small group of agency executive directors reviewed the entire pool of applicants and forwarded "preferred" candidates to each agency. The CBO then designated its priority applicants. Prior to being hired, each candidate was required to attend a CC9 orientation attended by parents, executive directors, and Zachary. The purpose of the meeting was to communicate to candidates that they would be working not simply for an individual agency but with CC9 as well.

This dual ownership, however, had repercussions. The ongoing push-pull between demands of individual agencies and CC9 often confused and exhausted organizers. Critically, every member agency was granted the autonomy to work within their salary, supervision, and personnel policies when hiring staff. Finally, it was determined that Zachary, the recently appointed coordinator of CC9, had no supervisory responsibility for local school work.

Critically part of the intentional experiment of CC9 was to join the expertise of a university to a grassroots parent-led campaign for education reform. This intentional experiment was attentive to creating the requisite trust and roles necessary for a university–community partnership to flourish. The coordinator role was therefore not simply restricted to technical assistance. Zachary was expected to coordinate and facilitate the work of CC9 only in part through the provision of technical assistance. As well, he was expected to help produce the strategy and tactics of emergent campaigns with parents. Finally, as coordinator, Zachary was responsible for making certain that the organizational capacity for evolving, supporting, and sustaining such campaigns was developed and monitored and that CBOs were held accountable for contributing to districtwide organizing.

As Zachary observed, "At the time, it proved to be a decent compromise that allowed organizations to feel that they were in control of hiring their staff but gave the staff the clear impression right from the start that they were part of something much bigger than any individual organization." Fostering agencies' comfort with the complex, uncharted work of collaboration was an immediate and pressing concern. The anxiety and reservations of surrendering autonomy could only be quieted in this first stage of development by allowing agencies to retain authority in areas they viewed as essential to their operations. In this instance, agencies retained authority over their personnel.

University–Community Collaboration:
The Reproduction of Expertise and Transfer of Access

Much of the initial work of building CC9 was reliant on the resources of NYU's IESP. The institute coordinated early meetings between the CBOs' leadership and helped to deepen the collaborative's commitment to an organizing strategy. As well, initial meetings of parents were convened by IESP organizer Zachary, who was assigned to CC9 and later named as its full-time coordinator. Zachary drew on his substantial organizing expertise to build member capacity and CC9 power.

CC9's early strategic and tactical decision making was developed by Zachary and a number of parent leaders. Zachary helped to stimulate a dialogue by raising questions about specific tactical and strategic choices. These questions stimulated thinking about the potential implications and/or tradeoffs associated with various options. This process provoked members to reflect more deeply and critically about next steps. Over time, these conversations increased the tactical and strategic sophistication of CC9's membership and informed democratic decision making during critical stages of the ensuing campaigns.

The IESP further contributed to CC9 development through fund-raising and providing access to critical public education decision makers. During the first stage of CC9's work, between 2000 and 2001, the group needed to secure financing to hire organizers. The development of increasingly ambitious parent-led organizing campaigns required the support of skilled and dedicated organizers. Zachary developed a concept paper and proposal, which CC9 parents and executive directors refined. Next, with IESP's reputation as a thoughtful advocate of parent-led change, CC9 was able to meet with foundation decision makers. In winter 2002, funding was secured for six CC9 organizers. It is important to iterate that access was gained to critical public education decision makers and activists through IESP. For example, John Kest, the head of New York ACORN, had both a long-standing interest in education reform and a relationship with Randi Weingarten (president of the UFT), Norm Fruchter (director of IESP), and Zachary. He had been instrumental in waging a successful campaign with the UFT to keep the Edison Project and its privatization agenda out of the New York City public schools. Kest and ACORN also shared CC9's strategic and political commitment to building parent power in alliance with CBOs. As the work of CC9 began to take shape, he became an increasingly important ally. This access and shared networks contributed to the early legitimacy and influence of CC9. More generally, NYU, through IESP, transferred a large part of its expertise and reputation to the collaborative. This investment contributed to both the development and effectiveness of CC9.

The People of CC9

A social change partnership, such as CC9, is constituted not only by its formal structure but also by the histories and personalities of those who choose to commit to its mission. Organizing is built across the personalities, ethnic composition, and differences of a community. An integral part of successful organizing is the choice by individuals to fold some part of their life story into the metanarrative of communal change. This choice is complex and difficult to analyze. The sociologist James Jasper, in his article "The Emotions of Protest," describes the moral imperative that individual actors who are embedded in a collective struggle for social change weave into their narratives:

They are actors who are thinking, artfully creating, feeling, moralizing human beings. They are thinking actors who behave strategically and artfully aware of what they are doing, making plans developing projects and innovating in trying to achieve new goals, all the while learning from mistakes as well as from the mistakes of opponents. And, most of all they are moral beings, shocked into action by moral outrage, sustained in their actions by moral commitments.

It is this moral commitment that runs through many of the stories of both CC9 parents and organizers, and a narrative of CC9 would be incomplete without some attention to the individual stories of community residents and organizers who have helped shape and sustain it.

Ocynthia Williams

Ocynthia Williams has been with CC9 since its inception. Her thirty-five-hour work week and pursuit of a bachelor's degree in the evenings have not tempered her commitment to CC9. She has been one of its key leaders, facilitating meetings, speaking publicly, traveling to conferences, and always ready to ratchet up her energy as needed. Her style is nonconfrontational and inclusive. She is part of the welcome wagon of CC9, warmly introducing herself before and after meetings to new parents. Her personality is expressive of a buoyant optimism. At times, Williams questions her avoidance of confrontation. She has observed that it is part of a larger communal predisposition: "The culture of my community, me being a southern person [and] a lot of the folks being from Puerto Rico and the Islands, is not to confront. Even today I struggle with confronting folks. We need, though, to confront each other to do the best we can, we need to try everything that can possibly make a difference."

None of William's four children presently attends CC9 schools. But she notes, "I identify with PS 73 because all of my kids went there." And her identification with a larger community runs very deep:

Sometimes I feel like I don't want to go, but my desire to see children's education improve keeps me going because so many kids in our community are denied what they rightfully deserve. Why should they get the worst of everything? Why should they get the teachers who are least skilled? Why? They deserve better than that.

I want them to be educated. Hispanic and black kids have been
ignored.

For Williams, deep commitment to the community translates into a belief
that "they are my kids. They are. They're mine because they are my people. It
is my community; I'm not leaving, so I have to make a difference."

Denise Moncrief

Denise Moncrief has been one of the central parent leaders of CC9 while
holding a full-time job and raising a child as a single parent. Her contributions have included public speaking, facilitation of meetings, negotiation
with public education officials, and training new parent leaders. Moncrief is
a woman who is often perceived by others, at least initially, as tough, intense,
and fierce in her opinions. But an ongoing relationship reveals a sensitive
commitment not only to the politics of CC9 but to the people as well. She
possesses qualities that may seem contradictory. These pieces, although not
easily assembled or understood as a whole, are all part of her complex makeup.

Some part of what she seeks to gain through her work with CC9 is re-
demption: "I am trying to make up for some things that I did in my younger
days . . . and I will probably pay for them for the rest of my life. . . . Redemp-
tion may come for me if I'm successful in saving just one child. If I get one
child educated the way they are supposed to be."

Moncrief describes the lack of options for the children of her community
as a driving force in her life and recent commitment to CC9. For Moncrief,
the loss of generations of children of color is not simply an abstraction but
part of a daily lived and felt experience that produces both moral outrage and
a desire to find a way to make a difference. She notes, "I was sitting on a sub-
way today and realized that there were about twenty ads for different types
of adult education because we lost that generation of kids. . . . Even if we
lose another generation of kids, it's not going to be because I didn't try to do
something. It's not because I didn't try to fight the good fight. Or because I
let my ego get in the way of doing what needed to be done."

Jamilla Anderson

Jamilla Anderson is a wiry, African American single mother of two daugh-
ters. She speaks in rapid, passionate bursts that are often bookended by long

periods of silence. Anderson has been a part of CC9 for three years and has been quite vocal about the inadequate learning environment of the public schools. Her dissatisfaction extends from the physical decay of the schools to breakdowns in classroom instruction. The critique, like Anderson herself, is pointed and morally indignant: "The bathrooms are a disgrace. No tissue in the bathroom, no running water, papers, or towels. There's inadequacy with books. There's issues with teachers. When they get a little bit more comfortable, they get complacent. One teacher last year was creative. This year she is teaching from the book."

A large part of Anderson's life has been devoted to caring for her disabled daughter. Her ongoing struggle to get her daughter's specific needs met by often inattentive schools absorbs much of her time and fuels an angry, restless energy to change public education.

"Do you know how many times my daughter has been discriminated against because she is in a wheelchair? They think she is retarded. You see a school that is divided between the kids that have special needs and those who don't. So you know what happens? They are not taught as well. These are the unheard. My work is to make certain my child and children like her are heard."

For Anderson, parent apathy violates a deeply felt belief in the mutual obligations of a community: "Because when I am calling a meeting and no one shows up and I'm working for your kids in your schools, that is a slap in my face. Where are you? And if you are working for your kids, what about mine?" Yet despite her resentment, she resists surrendering to apathy: "I've always lived in this neighborhood. My mentality has changed. My desires have changed. So I feel if I am apathetic, what hope is there for anybody?"

Anderson recognizes that her individual efforts are both necessary and insufficient. She understands that parents must integrate their self-interest into a broader community movement for education reform if there is to be meaningful change. "What is the solution? People who are not in power remembering that they are not powerless. People working together to try to work not only for their child, their own issues, but beyond that."

Veronica Rivera

Veronica Rivera is a Latina single parent who recently lost her job as a billing manager for a hospital. Veronica's unemployment forced her to relocate to District 9. She crackles with an energy that is unusual, even by CC9 standards. When speaking publicly, her hands and voice join in a rhythmic dance. Education has been a powerful ballast in Veronica's often turbulent life. "So even when chaos was brewing all around me, I would put my nose in a book. I learned that by reading as a child I had the ability to make my environments more tolerable. I was determined to do well in school, and I am determined that my daughter do well in school."

Rivera's encounters with the public schools, however, have been troubling. She observes that "we don't have the best materials. If you walk around the schools and look at them, which I've done, I am truly amazed that anyone would expect our children to sit in some of these classrooms. There are basic repairs that have to be made, but everything is such a big deal to get done." The conditions of the schools, Rivera believes, are a consequence of both a neglectful education bureaucracy and passive parents. "They're not releasing these funds because we're not screaming and yelling and banging down their doors."

Her civic energy has focused on the condition of the schools and the neglect of their students. She sees herself as a champion in the struggle for educational justice for her child and all of the children of the community. "Since I come from this background, I want to make sure that these kids have somebody to fight for them, not just my own, but all of the children. These children have a champion in their life. And I am not necessarily saying that I am going to be their champion, but I want to be a part of that process."

Ernesto Maldonado

Ernesto Maldonado is a single Latino male who has lived in the Highbridge community his entire life. Maldonado rarely breaks eye contact with members of the group. His intense gaze is immediately evident and part of a searching effort to make contact with individual members. His girlfriend, president of a local PTA, introduced Madonado to CC9 during the lead teacher campaign in the third year of its existence. What is perhaps most striking about Madonado is his infectious laugh. He is the good humor man of CC9.

Maldonado is among the very few males of the community to make a commitment to the work of CC9. His gender, although rarely mentioned, is important to many of the women. This importance is partly rooted in the deeply ingrained belief that leadership should, at least in part, be authored by males. For both the men and women of CC9, however, a leadership role comes at a steep price. "When I don't do something for CC9, I actually feel bad. I had an interview for a job, but I wanted to see Ocynthia speak at Madison Square Garden. I risked the interview because I wanted to see her speak before 22,000 members of the UFT."

He experienced firsthand the breakdown of the public schools in Highbridge:

> You're talking to someone who in the fifth grade was exhibiting behavior problems in a system where teachers had no clue how to deal with us. If I look back to elementary school, I can say who was going to make it and who wasn't. Some were jailed, others are dead. Now how did we reach that point, and why couldn't the schools help make a difference? The thought of college education, it just wasn't there. The failure of the school system is on the parents and the children. If you don't have people make noise about it, nothing will change.

Frances Calderon

Frances Calderon is a Latina who has lived in Highbridge her entire life. She has a deep commitment to improving public education in her community. Her early role as a CC9 parent leader facilitated her later transition into paid organizing work. "My work, it's evolved. I started out as a parent, I wasn't an organizer. I got involved as a parent with Highbridge because my son was in [PS] 73."

Calderon's description of the physical disrepair within the schools is richly illustrative of the difficulties all students face as they try to achieve academically amid a decaying physical environment:

> There is no way you can do math when the plumbing leaks and you have to jump over puddles. There is never toilet paper even in the girls' bathroom. The parents were asked to donate a roll. . . . The walls are cracked, many of the walls have caved in, and they are hazardous. We have one janitor, and he is not good. We're supposed to get new windows, but when? How can you learn in that kind of building?

She does not question the good intentions of teachers but understands that their inexperience, lack of support, and estrangement from the community where they work often lead to substantial classroom deficits.

It is not even the teachers' fault that things don't work in the class-rooms because of the poor working conditions they have to work under. They just burn out quickly. School starts in September, and you see them eager beaver, fresh out of school, spanking new many of the teachers. . . . So here we have these new teachers. The conditions are horrible, and, for example, they don't have the supplies they need. They don't have the time to get this or that done, half the kids may have been just passed on year to year and are behind grade level, and they have no idea how to work with those children. We have lots of kids in every class. No support from the school.

For Calderon, Highbridge is not a geographic space but a place that lives and breathes and is central to her identity. She has seen the decline of the schools, and it is a source of pain that her child and all of the children of Highbridge are being denied the education that they deserve.

I see that so many of our kids don't finish school. So the pain is seeing lives go to waste. These are our children, with no hope or future. For me to give a damn, kids don't have to be from me or of my blood. These are my kids even though I didn't give birth to them. You know all of these kids deserve a chance. I'm going to make sure these kids get a chance so they don't have to suffer any more than they already have.

Anjelica Otero

Anjelica Otero is a thirty-year-old Latina who has lived in New York since emigrating from Ecuador at the age of eight. She has worked as the NSA education organizer since 2002 and often works very long hours, starting early in the morning and leaving late in the evening. Although young, she is highly respected throughout the collaborative for her tactical and strategic contributions.

Otero identifies very strongly with her mother's heroic struggle as a poor immigrant to make ends meet for her family. Her strength and resolve to make a better life were the bedrock on which the family's hopes were built. Otero recalls her mother's essential instruction about what it means to be a strong woman: "I always think about my mom. When we were growing up, she worked two jobs, even though she didn't know English. I always saw her as a strong person. I think that's where my motivation comes from. I need to be as strong as she is. I need to push as hard as she's pushed."

Otero sees organizing as a corrective for both the past injustices in her life and the disenfranchisement that the neighborhood women and children suffer. It is both the moral outrage and the pain of disenfranchisement that links Otero to the women of CC9:

> I was thinking about the schools where we all grew up. How unjust
> it was and there was constant violence. . . . So I am very connected
> to the pain of the children in our community and their parents.
> I think about how hard it is for families to get an education when
> I do one-on-ones, go to people's homes, and the stories people tell
> me moves me and that continues to drive me.

Whenever her commitment wavers, Otero returns to two touchstones. She forces herself to remember what kind of woman she wants to become, and reflects on the inspiration the women of CC9 provide daily:

> I could stop, but I want to be able to grow, it is a challenge. I chal-
> lenge myself to be a stronger woman and to be more centered in this
> work because I really believe in this. My belief has a lot to do with
> the women. The women are very important to me. They're an inspi-
> ration. Just thinking how a lot of the women work all day long and
> yet make time to come to a meeting night after night to change the
> schools. They have such a sense of injustice, and they feel they need
> to do this; they need to be a part of this work. That is an inspiration.

Julia Allen

Julia Allen is a white twenty-five-year-old organizer. She is tall, about five feet nine inches and lanky. Her most striking qualities are a confident poise and sharp intelligence. Her trenchant observations and questions about organizing strategy frequently stimulate rich discussions. Consequently, despite her inexperience, Allen is seen by both parents and seasoned organizers as an important contributor to CC9's work. She was originally hired by the Citizens Advice Bureau (CAB) to do both secretarial and service work. Restless to find more activist work, however, her time away from the job was spent as a social justice volunteer. Her politics and work history with CAB helped to promote a relatively smooth transition to CC9. Allen remarked that "this is something I always wanted to do, organizing and get paid for it, I've been doing this work but as a volunteer." The difference between her history and that of parents, however, weighed on Allen during the course of her year at CC9. She was troubled by racial, economic, and experiential differences that were described as compromising her capacity to make a difference organizing. "I am white and not from this community. Should I really be working to organize this community? A lot of the time I just don't think so. There is a science to organizing work, and I am learning how to do it, but is it fair for me to be learning it on the job?"

Theresa Anderson

Theresa is a Latina in her midthirties. She has three children who have attended public schools in the district. Anderson has been a parent activist and organizer with NW Bronx and CC9. Her effectiveness as an organizer can be traced in part to an ability to translate CC9's platform ideas into a resonant language of family and child-rearing practices. "I put it into very simple terms. . . . I say what we're trying to do here is what we as a culture, especially Hispanic and the African, do." Her work to improve the schools began as a concerned parent and evolved to more responsible leadership roles. Anderson made it her job to know school staff, no matter their status. "When my kids were growing up, I was always an active parent in the schools. The custodian to the principal, they know who I am and can get in touch with me. That is just the nature of the way I was brought up."

Conversation is an essential part of Anderson's makeup. She has used these social skills as an organizer:

> I call some of the parents early in the morning, and it's not just, "Hey, there is a meeting coming up." It's "How are you? How are your kids?" It's a sharing of ourselves. Same with teachers. Bring teachers a cup of coffee, chitchat. Not in a confrontational style. My hope is that, over time, we can all begin to see by getting to know each other we're all on the same side, so let's work together, and have both sides see that this is more productive.

Anderson is very clear about the problems that continue to degrade public education in her community. She knows that "the teachers are overworked, they don't have resources, they're underqualified in the sense that they are brand-new. They don't know how to deal with children in these communities who have so many problems."

For Anderson, CC9 organizing is a calling. It is based on shared wounds, a sense of urgency, collective meaning. Perhaps most important, CC9 offers an opportunity for agency. Anderson views the lives of the women who come to CC9 as intertwined with her past difficulties. As an abused woman, Anderson understands how easy it is to lose large parts of oneself to constant, oppressive fear. She also understands how redemptive and invigorating it can be to regain voice. For Anderson, parent organizing helps to channel the force of shared oppression into a series of escalating actions. It is this part of the organizing work, the mixing of very personal histories with public struggle, that is especially compelling for Anderson:

> I see them as a mirror image of myself because I was in an abusive
> relationship for over twenty years. I never spoke up, I was obedient,
> I tried to make sure that there were no ripples, that everything was
> smooth. And in the end I finally had the gumption to say, no more,
> I can't do this anymore. I ran screaming from that relationship, so to
> speak, with my kids. . . . I got reacquainted with myself, and suddenly
> it is like, I really do have a voice. . . . I matter.

The regeneration of individual strength through communal activism is part of a larger narrative that firmly joins Anderson to the other parents and the organization:

> You are in it to change the schools, you are willing to do whatever it
> takes. That's the way it was for me, and this is what I love to see in
> these women. A lot of these women have been hit very hard by life,
> but they're still standing, still trying. They're getting back their sense
> of worth, speaking up, they kind of lost themselves. That alone is a
> tribute to them. I let them know what an honor it is to work with
> them.

Eric Zachary

Eric Zachary is an organizer with a deep history in New York City and education reform organizing. He grew up in a public housing project in Coney

Island. He remembers how the area declined into a ghetto. The dynamic interplay between housing stock decay, neglect of the schools, and decline of community remains vivid. His roots in New York City community-led public school reform extend back to the late 1980s. He has witnessed both the successes and failures of recent reform efforts:

> I've been involved in this work since 1989 when I became director of the parent leadership project at John Jay College. I've seen and participated in this field almost from the beginning. I've seen the victories, the strengths, but also very clearly the limitations of community organizing for school improvement in New York City. So CC9 was an intentional experiment to build off of some of our experience.

Zachary understands, however, that the work of education organizing is more complex than other forms of community organizing. Improving the schools is, in many ways, more challenging than changing the physical or material conditions of people's lives:

> Education in itself doesn't have one thing where you can say, oh, if we fix it, we can make it work. It's not like there is no heat in the building so you force a landlord to put in a new boiler. It's not as simple as saying we're going to go for a 3 percent salary increase. The importance of school culture is different than in other organizations. When you negotiate a contract, the question of culture is not at the center. When you go for a boiler, the question of culture is not at the center.

Having been a union and tenant organizer, he believes that communities like the South Bronx have simply not gotten their fair share of resources. Zachary sees organizing as building the power to correct past and current economic and education injustices. The problems with the schools, he notes, "are part of a larger political economy." Consequently, he does not see the local organizing of CC9 as an end in itself but as a means for building a social movement to address large-scale inequities in the distribution of public resources. He understands the relationship between degraded public education and neoliberal policies, which have affected economic disinvestment in the poorest communities of color. In sum, Zachary understands the importance of movement building as the best hope in correcting these entrenched and long-standing inequities.

. . .

These brief biographies underscore that CC9 is not an abstraction but rather the sum total of the time, energy, and imagination of the many individuals who have invested in the organizing. Each of these individuals shares a willingness, to quote Portes in "Embeddedness and Immigration," to behave in "ways other than naked greed; such that it becomes appropriable by others or by the collectivity as a resource."

II

A Moral Obligation to Act

3

Creating a Platform for Change

In April 2002, the recently elected mayor of New York City, Mike Bloomberg, announced massive budget cuts to public education. These cuts were in part a response to the economic fallout associated with 9/11. In response, community groups and parents around the city organized various forms of resistance. This struggle, like many struggles throughout the United States as well as in other parts of the world, was about a poor community's fight for sustainability in the face of regressive neoliberal taxation policies that resulted in a disinvestment in all things public and the consequent destabilization of basic institutions such as public schools.

In response to proposed budget cuts, CC9 mobilized a large rally. Until this point, CC9's organizing had been restricted to demonstrations at school board meetings. Over an approximate seven-month period, it had increased parent turnout at key events, from twenty-five in September to sixty at the superintendent finalist forum the following April. Barely completing the relatively modest superintendent campaign, CC9 was now being called on to organize a major rally. In a four-week period (from mid-April to mid-May), the parents of CC9 were expected to turn out between 150 to 200 parents. Parents met regularly in organizing committees, and a core group of leaders began to emerge. Key leaders, such as Denise Moncrief and Ocynthia Williams, planned outreach activities, while other parents distributed flyers and engaged neighbors in discussions about the issue. These activities helped ensure that turnout numbers were met.

Critically, CC9's member agencies opened their service programs to organizers during the course of the campaign. Zachary recalled that "organizations allowed organizers to recruit parents and residents to come to the rally by letting them into literacy programs, after-school programs, and I think that contributed substantially to our success." The campaign also helped to solidify bonds between parents, organizers, and the agencies. As the numbers of parents engaged in organizing for the rally grew, so too did the profile and reputation of CC9.

On the evening of May 12, a rally was convened at the Latino Pastoral Center. The UFT, district superintendent, and local elected officials were invited. The event far exceeded even CC9's expectations. With more than three hundred people in attendance, they filled all available seating. Parents and children, seated and standing, filled all of the empty space in the room. From start to finish, the rally felt like it was about to burst at the seams. Parent leaders and local clergy delivered speeches that electrified an already energized crowd. Parents marched and chanted their opposition to the cuts. The event was purposeful, filled with many expressions of parent voice, and established a new benchmark for CC9 success.

Williams described the rally as "a huge victory." Zachary added, "We were amazed and overjoyed to go from sixty parents to three hundred. That is a real organizing achievement." It was the largest South Bronx parent rally in recent memory. As such, it established a new ceiling of possibility and success. Members were beginning to believe that CC9 could be a powerful instrument for parent voice and school reform in District 9. In turn, many parent leaders began to experience a deepening affiliation with CC9. Finally, the size, energy, and seriousness of CC9 rallies were established. From this date forward, district decision makers gave significant weight to the power of CC9's activist parent base.

Despite the success of this event, CC9 leaders believed that recent reactive campaigns, such as the superintendent selection and budget cuts, had produced little tangible benefit for the community. Too much time was spent responding to hostile situations created by public officials. To break this cycle of unwelcome policies and community reaction, leaders determined that they had to rally around an independent community agenda for education reform. It was within this context that organizers and parents organized planning meetings to develop a proactive CC9 agenda for change.

The CC9 Platform

For CC9, events in winter and spring 2002 had moved very quickly. Consequently, a retreat was planned to refine CC9's vision and identify the most promising reforms for improving academic performance. Critically, this process was also intended to advance a platform and develop the capacity of leaders to think more strategically about CC9's change agenda. Without much notice and due to events beyond CC9's control, the careful retreat planning unraveled. Late on the Friday evening before the retreat, a thunderstorm caused a power outage at the retreat site. In a separate incident, the bus transporting parents to Goshen broke down. As a result, the site quickly shifted back to NSA in the Bronx. Instead of sleeping over, parents gathered for full workdays on Saturday and Sunday. The members of CC9 improvised in a rapidly changed situation. This was not an aberrant adjustment; a particular strength of CC9, and a hallmark of its organizing, has been the consistent capacity to quickly adjust to shifting conditions.

Parent commitment to the work of CC9 was evident on Saturday morning. As Milli Bonilla, an IESP staff person, remarked, "parents showed up, it was amazing. They were up all night on Friday getting back to the Bronx, but still all twenty showed up on Saturday to NSA." Parents agreed that CC9's vision for public education reform had to be concise and bold. They broke into small groups and identified ten things that needed to change in the schools in order to improve student achievement. Parents worked to categorize and prioritize the items that surfaced. Zachary commented that this "was the beginning of the platform for educational improvement that is guiding our work now."

Slowly, a statement of CC9 principles began to emerge that emphasized parent inclusion and professional support as a basis for creating a culture of learning within the district's public schools. More specifically, the platform focused on (1) strengthening the instructional capacity of classroom teachers through investment in lead or master teachers, (2) building a mentor system to enable principals to better guide a school change process, and (3) developing meaningful community school committees to promote partnerships around issues of importance to teachers, parents, and principals. Michelle Cahill, a senior aide to the chancellor, remarked, "the platform recognized that a central impediment to learning throughout the district was the turnover of teachers and principals." This revolving door contributed to a crisis of expertise within the schools and contributed to a chaotic school environment, leaving little space for learning. The first stage of culture shift within the schools, therefore, required a more stable, effective professional staff. To accomplish this, conditions within the schools, which often left principals and teachers feeling isolated and unsupported, had to be changed. CC9's three main objectives addressed these challenges through investments in lead teachers and principals as well as the inclusion of parents. This formative stage of platform development was largely a discussion internal to CC9.

The focus of these discussions was often framed by carefully selected readings on the failure of public education in poor communities. The mining of these reports and publications by parents for a plausible change program, in turn, greatly influenced the development of the platform. In early fall 2002, the conversation was enlarged to include influential public education policy makers, as CC9 understood that its program for change would have no hope for implementation without the support of key education decision makers.

Introducing the Platform to Public Education Stakeholders

A large part of CC9's challenge as a local community group was to create widening circles of legitimacy and support for its platform. CC9 members understood that leadership would have to embrace a cooperative strategy if there was to be any hope of implementing the platform. It is important to reiterate that CC9's approach was a substantial departure from past practices of community groups, which were overly reliant on confrontation to influence decision makers.

Professionals often perceived parents as making demands on the system without identifying the community's responsibility or accountability for changing the educational outcomes. Professional perspective regarding parents hardened over time and created an intensifying adversarial dynamic with no appreciable benefits for the school system or the community. The limitations of prior parent-led initiatives informed both the organizing strategy and education agenda of CC9. CC9's intention was to penetrate the learning and instruction culture of public schools by both building an independent parent power and forging new, more positive relationships with education decision makers. CC9 recognized that, de facto, schools would not change without the cooperation of professionals. Consequently, collaboration with education policy makers was essential to the larger democratic project of parent-led reform of public schools. Williams, remarked, "Look, if we are going to change these schools for our children, we have to be realistic. It just isn't going to happen without getting the UFT and DOE on board."

Similarly, Zachary noted that classic community organizing done outside the system power structure says, "do what we tell you to do and then we will move on. What we are trying to do here is build longer-lasting relationships. The more messy encounters you have that are not well run, that waste people's time, that seem all over the place, that don't have clear-cut outcomes, the more people will disinvest in the process."

A number of meetings between the UFT and CC9 exemplified and tested this commitment to collaboration. Early in fall 2002, Herb Katz, a UFT official who represented Bronx instructors, facilitated a very preliminary conversation between CC9 and chapter chairs to explore the further development of a partnership. These meetings were convened in a restaurant on City Island. He recalled: "We all sat down and had dinner or lunch and talked. So people got to know each other. The organizers, the chairs, the parents were there. What I saw from almost the beginning was the commitment CC9 had to the kids. It was real. This wasn't about them, it was about changing the schools for the kids."

Katz described a moment in 2002 that tested the relationship between the UFT and CC9. After developing the platform, the parents wanted the UFT to support their demand for unscheduled access to teachers in the ten CC9 schools. Katz understood that such a demand would deplete, not build, trust with UFT members. He stated that teachers would perceive unscheduled access as an encroachment on professional autonomy reminiscent of the Ocean Hill–Brownsville conflict. He didn't dispute the legitimacy of the demand but rather questioned its timing.

CC9 and the UFT struggled to preserve their emerging partnership. Katz describes the process:

> The issue is not whether parents should have access, but how. . . . We worked out a way for parents to have access. I know CC9 wouldn't have accepted bullshit! I don't think they would have accepted a lie. I believe the key is in being honest. So we built the trust where they accepted what I said as honest. We worked it through.

The work of CC9 was complex. It needed to build a collaborative powerful enough to hold school decision makers accountable while simultaneously participating in ways that were perceived as adding value or making a difference to the quality of schools' performances. Relationships with the schools had to be perceived as two-way or as promoting a reciprocal exchange.

CC9 was essentially charting a new direction for parent-led school reform in New York City. As Zachary remarked, "the change pressure would come from the top and bottom. That kind of pressure gives us much more of a chance of making the changes that are needed." This new paradigm would borrow from the past by emphasizing parent power and maintaining a commitment to tactics of confrontation when necessary. However, it would also depart significantly from past organizing by struggling to reach beyond parents for other critical sources of support. CC9 was preparing to take the leap of faith necessary to depart from past parent disappointment with school officials, the teachers unions, and politicians to create new partnerships necessary to change the schools. The first step had been taken with the partnering of six CBOs at CC9's formation. A critical next step required that CC9 have a public event to express its interest in working with key decision makers around elements of the platform and flex its growing muscle of parent support.

The Platform as a Tactical Tool to Illuminate Convergence of Interest

In fall 2002, a new group of DOE and regional administrators was assigned the responsibility for reforming the New York City public education system. As noted, part of their agenda was to centralize decision making and wrest control from decentralized boards. These boards were often corrupt, and they tended to marginalize parents. In 2003, the New York State Legislature, in a landmark piece of legislation, returned authority for the public education system to the mayor of the city. Consequently, the new managers of the system assumed office with far greater influence and power than their immediate predecessors. This shift in the locus of power, although troubling to many community leaders, offered CC9 an important new opportunity to advance its change agenda.

In this moment of transition the new leadership was more prepared than their predecessors to work in collaboration with community groups. As Michelle Cahill, a senior advisor to the new superintendent, Joel Klein, remarked, "This was a moment of opportunity. District 9 before Irma Zardoya, the regional superintendent, had a pretty sad history. As far as beginning to move forward on a collaborative agenda, there's a tremendous leadership for doing that." Cahill also noted that CC9's platform was compatible with the chancellor's agenda as articulated in the DOE report "Children First." In an interview, Cahill described this convergence of reform interests: "We are focusing on the key levers of change. . . . I want to change schools to have more capable leadership and high-quality instruction. Having teachers that learn and develop and to have good family–school relationships. We're using multiple strategies to get there. That is important to me."

The DOE viewed CC9's "theory for change" as both sophisticated and pragmatic. DOE decision makers considered the stabilization and upgrading of public school instructors in the neediest communities as an especially critical lever for increasing the achievement of students. This point is underscored by Cahill, who explained that "the issue is how to get highly qualified teachers in high-need neighborhoods and high-need schools. We need a 'grow your own strategy.' We are not going to be able to import many of them. We can import a few teachers to mix in with the others. . . . We need to build teacher capacity. So it is a theory of change." More generally, Cahill concluded that "their platform was probably the most sophisticated presentation from a community collaborative hitting on the four levers for change in school reform. They would be focusing on leadership, teaching, quality teaching, and family–school connections. That is also key to our Children First Reform, the key levers of change, so we are highly aligned."

This alignment of the change agendas was not simply a product of serendipity. It can be traced to CC9's intensive work to balance achievable goals against the urgency of a shifting school environment. Out of this work, a solid, legitimate platform with clear and attainable objectives was created, and the space opened up for collaboration with the city's DOE.

Early conversations between the UFT and CC9 suggested union receptivity to the lead teacher proposal. Little difference existed between CC9 and the UFT on the need to develop a more expert cohort of classroom teachers. The UFT had a long-standing desire to create a career ladder for classroom teachers. Lead teachers, with a new tier of expertise and salary scale, could achieve just such an outcome. CC9 understood that this new stratum of teachers was an instrument for mentoring new instructors and, in turn, stemming the tide of out-migration from the poorest communities in the city. As noted earlier, the platform was developed with one eye on the kinds of reforms most likely to change the learning environment within the schools and the other on developing a change agenda with a potential trajectory of partnership or collaboration.

A Focal Point for Organizing a Wider Collaboration

As noted, the platform was developed during a moment of political opportunity within the New York City public school system. The reform agendas of the new chancellor and CC9 converged over a short period of two months. This opportunity, however, was weighed in relationship to the readiness of parents to undertake this next step. Were parents sufficiently fluent with the platform to discuss key issues with New York City education policy makers? Was the CC9 parent base strong enough to effectively press key decision makers on needed change? The answers to these questions would be tested during these first-stage encounters with DOE. It was clear, however, that such political opportunity would not be replicated in the near future. Consequently, CC9 would have to take the risk of moving too quickly or beyond the capacity of its parent base if it was to capitalize on the opening offered by this transitory moment.

To solidify and deepen both DOE and UFT commitments to the platform, CC9 initiated a two-pronged strategy. They scheduled private meetings with key decision makers, such as Cahill and Michelle Bodden, a UFT vice president. They also organized a public event to include a cross section of public education decision makers. Throughout the early fall, CC9's efforts were focused on presenting and "selling" the platform to powerful stakeholders in public education. Zachary noted that "in managing this top-of-the-system process, you have to make sure that they are focused, that they're invested in us, otherwise the momentum will get away from us. They can get distracted by the one hundred and one other responsibilities."

Gaining and maintaining the attention of public education policy makers with many counter pulls, while never easy, are especially difficult for local groups outside the system pushing for change. There is a tendency to minimize local parent-led initiatives by presuming that they do not see the larger picture, that they have insufficient expertise to fully understand problems or solutions, and that they are not powerful enough to matter. These have been substantial obstacles to focused and sustained conversation between parent groups and policy makers. CC9 had gained preliminary legitimacy through its recent work and relationship to the IESP. However, this early legitimacy simply produced access. At this point, there was no assurance that CC9's platform would gain the fuller attention or commitment of decision makers. The next stage of events that CC9 developed was tactically intended to both engage officials in a sustained conversation regarding the platform and generate at least an early public commitment to its change agenda.

A Rallying Point for Educational Justice

The Organizing Committee began to plan a rally for October 2002. The goals of the rally were to energize and mobilize the parent base of CC9 as well as press education officials to publicly sign a pledge of commitment to the platform. Parents immersed themselves in the details of planning every aspect of the rally. They identified speakers, selected a site, established turnout goals, developed an agenda, and agreed on the tone of a festive gathering combined with a seriousness of purpose. Parents were clear that at the conclusion of the event, public officials must offer tangible evidence of their commitment by not only signing a pledge but also agreeing to followup meetings about the platform. Throughout this process, parent voices dominated the discussions.

Upon entering Christ the King's gymnasium, both festivity and seriousness were evident. Parents signed in before entering the gym, and they were handed flyers announcing, "It's a New Day in District 9 and Time for Real Change." Every item distributed during the rally was translated into Spanish, a powerful sign of welcoming for the many Spanish-speaking parents in attendance. The walls of the gym were decorated with bouquets of multicolored balloons and CBO banners. The six CBO banners were a physical representation of the communitywide strength and membership of the collaborative. The CC9 banner offered a sharp message of purpose, stating "Organizing for Educational Justice." Before the official start of the rally, the room pulsed with the rhythmic chanting of parents orchestrated by two facilitators and a translator. The rally opened with a children's choir from a local elementary school. Their performance as well as the opening remarks by the leader of the choir ("we need to get the resources that the children deserve") grounded parents to the purpose of CC9 and the event. The parents, speakers, and clergy were impassioned in their calls for education reform and repeatedly received extended, feverish applause from the audience.

At the conclusion of the rally, education officials and politicians were asked to publicly sign a poster board pledge of commitment to the platform. Bodden indicated that "the UFT completely supports the platform, and we will sign on and make a commitment to the platform and action." Cahill added, "I am here to support the platform. I am also here to pledge Joel Klein's support for high-quality education for every child in the neighborhood." A commitment was made by parents and public officials to form a planning committee consisting of CC9, Cahill, Bodden, and District 9 representatives. The rally had produced an agreement to convene more serious, sustained discussions of the platform sought by CC9 and was, on that basis alone, a significant success.

This was another critical moment in establishing a public legitimacy for CC9. To begin with, parents were acutely aware of the powerful members of the educational establishment who were not only in the room but signed the pledge of commitment. For parents, then, there was a growing recognition that CC9 leadership was capable of reaching and influencing important public education decision makers. The substantial and growing parent support for CC9 was also not lost on public and union officials in attendance. The union, the Department of Education (DOE), and district representatives repeatedly commented on the size of the crowd.

This was an opportunity for CC9 to flex its muscle publicly, and it did so to great effect. Step by step, the power and influence of CC9 were growing. However, the process of building alliances with both the union and the board was fraught with both historic and present obstacles. The success of CC9 would depend in great part on its capacity to persuade powerful institutions to invest in a new and groundbreaking partnership. This would not be easy. The UFT continued to be wary of community groups. For decades, the UFT leadership understood community reform as a synonym for struggles that had occurred thirty years earlier in Ocean Hill–Brownsville but that echoed loudly for many members. The new leadership of the DOE, although steeped in a verbal commitment to collaboration, was nonetheless suspicious of the potential struggle and consequent fallout of working with community groups. A message often repeated by CC9 was that their primary commitment was to work with the schools and union to promote student achievement. As Zachary noted, "We demonstrated to all of these people that we weren't going to just try and beat them up, that we were focused on one thing and one thing only and that was school achievement and that we were professional, and that means essentially that we were organized, focused and that we gave respect to achieve it." The trust necessary for these institutions to invest in CC9's platform emerged not in a single moment but over time.

The UFT's and DOE's deepening engagement with the CC9 platform occurred during a series of planning meetings held in winter and spring 2002–3. In the wake of the rally, it was agreed that meetings would be convened with key public education officials to discuss CC9's change agenda. Organizing such meetings, however, posed certain difficulties for parents. In the past, parents had minor roles when sitting at the table with public education officials to discuss the neglect and needs of the schools. From the outset, however, CC9 parents were determined to shift this balance. It was with this in mind that parents announced that they wished to lead the meetings. Other stakeholders assented to CC9's leadership role. More specifically, other participants agreed that CC9 should "drive the process." A powerful symbolic expression of an increased parent influence was that the first meeting occurred at NSA, or "CC9 turf," and not at the offices of the DOE. At this meeting on December 10, 2002, participants were divided into working committees to discuss each of the platform's three planks.

The intensification of work for parents as they straddled the demands of the working committees and CC9 reaffirmed their central role in the process. Zachary explained that

> Three working groups emerged, one on teachers, one on principals, and one on family–school partnerships. A parent runs every meeting, formulates the agenda. We talk to people in between meetings. Parents come to meetings during the days. So that has taken up a lot of people's time and energy. We've got to prepare and drive the process. This structure and work of the work committees is being led by the same leaders coming to the organizing committee meetings. The challenge over the next six to eight weeks is to get the CBOs to connect to large numbers of people so we can expand participation.

An implicit tension for CC9 was that the expertise and number of parent leaders were not keeping pace with the mushrooming work demands. As Zachary explained, "We've got to figure out a better way of expanding our base around the platform." Neither of these dilemmas would ever be fully resolved by CC9, and in this moment a conscious choice was made to trade off wider parent participation or base building in favor of focusing CC9's resources on fully exploiting an unusual moment of political opportunity.

Meetings of the larger planning and smaller work committees continued throughout the academic year. Regular participants included the superintendent of the region, Irma Zardoya; the superintendent of the district, Stanley Mims; as well as Cahill, Bodden, Katz (the district representative of the UFT), and Arthur Forresta (a key figure in the nonprofit organization New Visions for Public Schools). Faculty from the schools of education at Lehman College and NYU also participated. Over time, the work groups developed reports that laid out a framework for change that had greater specificity and increased "official" support. The commitment of decision makers, however, remained verbal and tentative. As an internal CC9 memo distributed on April 4, 2003, noted,

> The planning committee is working well. The two big hurdles which are critical are the cluster issue and money to support the lead

teachers. . . . Irma Zardoya said there is no money but she did offer to set up a meeting between CC9 and Caroline Kennedy, the DOE's chief fund raiser with the private sector. . . . Clearly CC9 needs to increase its organizing to influence both issues.

Systemic Change and Local Opportunity: Campaigning to Formalize the CC9 Network

Sweeping structural reform (i.e., centralization) of public education in New York City in fall 2002 posed both great opportunity and difficulty for CC9. The schools associated with CC9, although entirely located in Region 1, were in jeopardy of being moved to new networks or clusters. DOE was proposing to reorganize the school system into ten regions, which would contain formal clusters or networks of schools. This reorganization plan threatened to redistribute CC9's schools into a number of networks within the Region. More specifically, CC9 feared that the ten schools with which it had been working would be gerrymandered into different "clusters," thus further fragmenting their work and making it increasingly difficult to build on the accomplishments of the past two years. Therefore, support from the new superintendent of the Region, Zardoya, to formalize a cluster relationship between the ten schools was critical to CC9's future work. In early February 2003, CC9's leadership sent letters to Cahill, Klein, and Zardoya outlining their interest in creating a formal cluster relationship between the ten Region 1 schools. In the letter, they wrote:

> In preparation for upcoming meetings we thought it would be useful to outline how CC9 and the schools it is organizing fit within the new administrative structure. . . . we expect these ten schools to share not only the systemic reforms but also the points outlined in the platform. At the heart of the platform is the relationship that grows between CC9 and the schools. To facilitate both instructional and organizational coherence the schools should constitute a CC9 Cluster for Educational Excellence within Region 1.

Zardoya was the target of a systematic organizing campaign intended to pressure and engage but not alienate. Walking the tightrope between winning her support and not angering or further distancing her from the CC9 agenda was difficult. Tactics had to be combined in ways that reminded her that she was critical to moving an important community change agenda forward but not perceived as an enemy. Throughout spring 2003, CC9 employed tactics of engagement and gentle confrontation. CC9 sent petitions to her to convey parent support for a CC9 cluster. Flowers congratulating her were also delivered to her office. The flowers were a message of personal affection while reminding her of the importance of the cluster to the larger community. Later, hundreds of parents called the district superintendent's office asking her to support the CC9 network. Simultaneously, CC9 parents were present and vocal during Zardoya's public appearances. While these multiple tactics wore the superintendent's patience thin at times, in the end she indicated support for CC9's goals. In spring 2003, the CC9 cluster was formally recognized by both the Region and Board of Education. As Zachary remarked,

> We saw the opportunity of systemwide reorganization, and we drove a truck through it. We were the only community group organizing to establish a network of schools during that fluid moment. Our agenda was unique but so was our accomplishment. We are the only network in the whole city that straddles two districts. That happened because of our organizing.

CC9 effectively pushed its agenda to formalize a cluster relationship between the ten schools without becoming publicly combative. It was, as Zachary indicated, a good example of how "we straddle that line, create the balance between confronting power and working toward collaboration." Critically, during this early formative stage in CC9's development, the organization strategically employed tactics of both confrontation and collaboration.

CC9's primary message of education reform through collaboration was tempered by recognition that if community will and the CC9 agenda were ignored, more confrontational tactics would have to be employed. However, in the selection of such tactics, leadership was always mindful of the calculus between short-term gain and longer-term damage to critical relationships and the larger CC9 agenda. This caused leadership to carefully weigh both the moment and available options.

In June 2003, a rally was held that announced through flyers that "it was a new day in District 9, and it's time for real change." The recent victories of creating the cluster and pledges of commitment to the platform offered hope that a next stage—one of more fundamental change in the conditions of the schools—was at hand. The celebration was vibrant. Nearly four hundred parents and community residents attended. They hung banners, and colorful combinations of balloons adorned every wall. Once again, passionate, rhythmic chanting by parents announced the power of CC9 and was a palpable expression of solidarity, critical mass, and celebration. As is consistently the case at CC9 events, the primary speakers were parents, who described both their excitement at recent progress and their impatience to move on to the very difficult work of improving the public schools of District 9. The meeting agenda was tightly conceived and executed—the entire event lasted a little more than an hour. The tone of the rally, Williams remarked, "was not on the basis of attack but on the basis of the fact that it is time for real change and we can do it together. . . . We were mobilizing people on the basis of hope."

Deep Democratic Practice and the Engagement of Parents

The most critical source of power for CC9 is its base of committed and competent parent leaders. The relationship of organizers and parents to each other as well as to the platform was consciously constructed through democratic practice, a primary feature of CC9 culture. As noted earlier, the central role of parents in decision making was encoded in the Expectations and Standards document, in which the CC9 Organizing Committee was identified as the central decision-making body.

Democratic practice is neither static nor one-dimensional. It thrives and grows in environments that actively promote participatory processes and structures. Access is an especially important precursor to inclusion and democratic participation, as it provides the necessary beachhead space to participate. At CC9, support systems are put in place to facilitate access for as many parents as possible. For example, monolingual Spanish-speaking parents are given the tools to participate through translation services. Additionally, free meals and child care are provided, allowing single mothers to concentrate for a time on the public work of changing the schools rather than the immediate needs of family.

The engagement of parents through democratic practice was not restricted to enlarging access. Democratic practice extended to a welcoming of and respect toward parents' voices. Parents indicated repeatedly that what they had to say was acknowledged, often affirmed, and never shouted down. The ground rules developed by CC9 regarding group discussion promoted dialogue, not monologue or speeches. Dialogue was a thread that ran through every aspect of CC9 practice. In both formal public and private meetings, the professional organizing staff listened to parent leaders. And most importantly, they acted on community members' recommendations. Parents also indicated that the organizing staff worked to narrow the social distance that often separates professionals from low-income communities. Many members remarked that organizers' willingness to share parts of their own histories and acknowledge their own mistakes strengthened their connection to CC9. These remarks suggest that effective democratic practice has both a structural and interpersonal dynamic. For parents to sustain participation, they must experience both professional and interpersonal forms of support. Critically, such practices are a counterpoint to the school system's historic silencing and marginalizing of poor parents.

As the social theorist Arjun Appadurai notes in "Deep Democracy," it is on the basis of such dialogue that discussion is structured to prompt participation as "a mode of exchange based on seeing and hearing rather than of teaching and learning; of sharing experiences and knowledge" (31). Consistent with this framework, preparatory sessions were developed to increase parent capacity to create an agenda, facilitate a meeting, and think through the trade-offs of strategic and tactical choices. Training was created to explore the organizing techniques and knowledge necessary to advance specific education reform initiatives. These preparatory sessions increased parents' abilities to participate effectively. They also enabled some parents to gradually assume greater leadership roles.

The Trade-offs Associated with CC9 Organizing Decision Making

No community group in recent memory had penetrated the learning and instruction conditions in the New York City public schools. CC9's goals and early achievements were an important first step in rewriting the still young history of parent-led organizing in New York City. A point raised repeatedly during planning meetings in spring and summer 2003 was that CC9 power needed to grow substantially if the organization was to have any hope of running an effective campaign around parts of the platform. CC9's base, although substantial when compared to other community groups, did not have deep roots in the public schools. Until this point, CC9 emphasized districtwide, rather than school-specific, issues in order to establish a wider reputation, formally stabilize a base of schools, and begin a conversation with regional and city decision makers about the CC9 platform. Much of the early energy of CC9 was invested in codifying expectations and standards and creating an agenda for change. The rhythm of the work was fast and focused on specific kinds of outcomes critical to building a districtwide visibility.

This decision, although appropriate to the collaborative's stage of development and responsive to specific kinds of immediate opportunities, did not come without a cost. By focusing attention on district issues, the six CBOs had less time to develop parent leaders and reform goals at the school level. But what may have worked at one point in CC9's life cycle became less appropriate within the developmental arc of CC9's organizing. In its next stage of work, CC9 would have to focus on organizing in each of the ten schools. Only in this way could CC9's base of parent leaders grow to meet the demands of the next, more ambitious campaign for school reform. Such sustained attention to local school or base organizing, however, had not been a norm and would require a shift in both the attention and commitments of each of the CBOs.

The turnover of organizers also posed a threat to the continuity and effectiveness of CC9's work. This "churning of staff" can, in part, be traced to decision-making trade-offs in forming the collaborative. As noted, early understandings reached through the Expectations and Standards document codified areas of agency autonomy, including salary, benefits, and supervision of organizers. The role of the IESP was to coordinate and support organizers through training and technical assistance but not to supervise their day-to-day school-level work. The turnover of organizers, however, caused CC9 leadership to question the viability of these arrangements. Organizers in four of the six agencies turned over at least twice between fall 2002 and 2003. The reasons for the turnover were complex and varied. They included daunting job demands, lack of supervision, frequent isolation of organizers in agencies with service cultures, especially low wages in a number of the CBOs, and the lack of fit between the capacity of specific staff and CC9 work demands. For some of the agencies, these positions remained open for months. A consequent concern of parents and remaining organizers was that the continuity of work with the schools and parents suffered in the meantime.

It was clear that these trends had to be altered if a stable cohort of organizers was to be developed. Simultaneously, it was understood that a collaborative effort like CC9's is fragile and therefore requires flexibility. As Zachary pointed out, "Differences in contribution are built in. That is a given. But then the question is how to get groups to live up to what they said they would do. That is where it becomes uneven." The tension between enforcement of uniform collaborative standards and the variable investment, contributions, and cultures of individual participants is endemic to any coalition project. This dilemma would remain a site of important, but difficult, practice struggle for CC9 parents and staff.

The start-up work of CC9, although complex, was poised to move to even more difficult and uncharted terrain. CC9 leadership, particularly the co-ordinator, Zachary, understood that the organization was a "change experiment." It was created to address a number of organizing questions, such as:

1. How can a culture of solidarity be built between parents from different neighborhoods to advance a coherent, unified agenda for changing the schools?
2. How does one build social capital that bridges local community organizations that are often competing for funding?
3. Can a grassroots collaboration such as CC9 expect to "scale up sufficiently" to influence citywide actors, such as the teachers' union and DOE?
4. As a group's primary organizing strategy moves from conflict to cooperation, can it maintain the same degree of pressure required for sustained reform?
5. Can the CC9 platform, or more specifically the lead teacher proposal, make a difference inside the schools that positively influences student achievement?

The complexity of the work was daunting. It required that CC9 struggle to build relationships and ultimately accumulate power across many different types of organizations and groups of stakeholders. Such an effort demanded a grassroots leadership cohort that was capable of working with rapid tactical changes, intimidating power brokers, and the often arcane language of education policy. It also presumed that there was the capacity to create a sequence of goals and activities that promote an accumulation of power, a nimble responsiveness to new opportunities, and a willingness to take risks in the midst of uncertainty.

To address the often shifting and always dense realities associated with organizing choice(s), the most effective organizations create a "learning space," or opportunities to think more deeply about the work. CC9 has struggled to meet the challenge of complex organizing by situating its work within a culture of learning. To begin with, Zachary and others have described the project as an experiment. These are not empty words. Effective collaboration requires a willingness to experiment and find the best strategies for maximizing partnerships/relationships. Additionally, the effort to create a new paradigm for education reform organizing, which relies less on confrontation and more on collaboration, has caused CC9 to consciously explore the implications and impacts of this strategic shift.

The learning culture of CC9 has also helped to incubate the struggle to find new ways to improve public education. To achieve improved learning outcomes in the schools, members often had to challenge long-held beliefs or attitudes. Zachary indicated that the process of opening up to new ideas can be painstakingly slow:

> In CC9 we've gone through periods where the idea is put out and because it is fairly new and breaks the paradigm, the first period of time is really spent trying to get used to it, batting it around. Then you hit a moment when something breaks through and it becomes more comprehensible and integrated as a part of the work.

The first phase of CC9's work emphasized internal organization building, which allowed for the development of an infrastructure capable of assembling the necessary power to improve the learning conditions within District 9 public schools. A second dimension of CC9's practice looked outward to stakeholders in and beyond the community who had the power to translate parent ideas into school programming. With this in mind, the collaborative formalized the cluster relationship between CC9 schools, announced its platform to the larger world, organized small meetings with key decision makers to enlist their support, and held public rallies to maximize the visibility of CC9's growing power. This flurry of activity between 2001 and 2003 put CC9 on the map. Both in New York City and nationally, CC9 was establishing a reputation for marrying the language of community-led collaboration to a practice and power that had the potential to effect substantial change in local schools.

4

Attending to the Base and
Consolidating Alliances

As CC9 began to plan for the 2003–4 school year, fault lines in its practice were evident. CC9's work rhythm during the past year often had been hectic and frenzied. The fast, outcome-driven pace had strained its leadership resources. CC9 would be able to expand parent leadership only if it slowed the pace and shifted the work focus to local school-based issues. Critically, CC9 needed to recruit more members from each of the ten schools in order sustain its legitimacy as a representative of parent interests. Finally, attention also had to be paid to further developing relationships with the teachers and administrators in each of the schools.

If CC9 was to have any hope of organizing an effective lead teacher campaign in the coming months, the ranks of parent leaders would have to grow. "The hope," Zachary noted, "was that somehow we could combine local issues with the platform to build all kinds of new relationships with the schools that will make CC9 stronger, more powerful. What is the right balance? It's complicated, it's not simple; there's not a formula we can plug into." During summer 2003 parent leaders and CBO administrators reached the same conclusion: CC9 needed to shift its focus from the district to local schools. A commitment was made to build family–school partnerships and organize local campaigns. In doing this, they needed to find a new equilibrium. As Milli Bonilla, the IESP's trainer, noted, "the local work identified with each CBO could not allow the districtwide work for the platform and expansion to suffer." The organizers always needed to be mindful of achieving a balance between the development of a deeper, more extended, school-based system of parents and the larger imperative to create districtwide change.

Inside the CC9 campaign, school-based organizing was never viewed as an end in itself. To the contrary, local organizing was viewed as a prelude to the districtwide campaign in winter 2004 for lead teachers. To successfully wage this fight, CC9 needed to grow its base of parents throughout the community. Although the work of school-based organizing has an independent integrity, for CC9 it was always tied to the larger purpose of building the parent power necessary to change learning and instruction conditions throughout the cluster. In effect, the local work was consciously understood by both parent leaders and organizers as a short-term strategy as well as a long-term investment. In the short term, CC9 was readying itself for an unprecedented campaign to leverage fundamental changes in the size, composition, and functions of instructional staff throughout the district. This reform over the longer term was considered a part of the necessary scaffolding for improving student achievement.

Stepping Back and Slowing Down, Revisiting Local School Organizing to Expand the CC9 Base

Greater emphasis on school-based organizing work was systematically discussed and implemented by CC9 staff in fall 2003. Training sessions were held to develop organizer skills and knowledge. For many of the organizers, even the more experienced ones, door knocking and, more generally, outreach were a source of great discomfort. As the most seasoned of the organizers, Anjelica Otero remarked, "many of the staff, at times myself included, just didn't feel comfortable going up to people cold and starting up a conversation about the schools." In response to this, CC9 organized training sessions with the organizing staff, offering a forum for parent leaders to discuss their discomfort as well as to learn specific scripts and approaches that they might use. This base-building work was not limited to door knocking in apartment buildings. It also involved distributing flyers and engaging in conversations with parents near each of the schools. This general outreach was augmented by house meetings in apartment buildings, which were hosted by parent leaders. Finally, organizers were expected to contact parent associations to recruit new parents. It was understood that outreach would have to be done with great care to avoid a turf war with the parent associations regarding who represented community interests within the schools. Over time, the success of the outreach would be judged according to specific outcomes, such as the development of new parent groups in the ten CC9 schools. One of the concrete goals to facilitate this was to have each CBO recruit three parent representatives to attend organizing meetings. It was understood that collaborative relationships also had to be built with district, regional, and local school officials.

CC9 leadership viewed family–school partnerships as the basis for engaging teachers, principals, and parents in a dialogue to identify and solve school problems. The Family School Partnership Committees were expected to promote an exchange of ideas and mutually conceived programs to improve academic achievement. Most generally, the committees were expected to enable parents to enrich school programming and conversation. Such collaboration, however, represented a leap in thinking and practice for both parents and organizers.

Historically, many parents in poor neighborhoods viewed teachers and principals as adversaries. They were perceived as often blocking community initiatives intended to improve the schools. The harshest and most stark parent assessment was that the failures of the schools were directly and singularly traced to school professionals. CC9's platform and strategic emphasis on collaboration, however, assumed that school-based reform could only be achieved in partnership with professional staff. Accountability of schools to the communities they serve was understood by parents as indispensable to meaningful reform. The community's aspiration for mutual accountability involved not only teachers and principals but parents as well. This is a critical point. Often times, school professionals viewed parents as critical of their work but not committed to the nuts and bolts work of improving school conditions.

As CC9 went about the work of reaching out to parents and professionals in fall 2003, it encountered numerous obstacles. Parents often expressed confusion about the content of the platform and how it could contribute to school improvement. Frequently, there was a disconnect between the CC9 platform and parent concerns. For example, many parents talked to CC9 organizers about the lack of safety in and around local schools. Most upsetting were threats and acts of student-on-student violence that created an unsafe, untenable learning environment. As one parent remarked at an organizing committee meeting, "How can our children learn when they don't feel safe? Every day my child goes to school and wants to learn, but the place is so tense, so unsafe, it's just not possible." Although this concrete parent concern was affirmed and integrated into a discussion, seasoned leaders felt that an emphasis on school safety in this initial campaign was strategically misguided. Earlier, local campaigns that focused on school safety had floundered because of the complexity of the issue and the consequent difficulties of creating an alliance to solve it. Equally important, many parent leaders and organizers had chosen to focus on an investment in school professionals as both a bridge to create alliance and a theory for improving student achievement and safety. The translation of this goal into a robust campaign, however, required that a growing number of parents understand the potential importance of lead teachers to their children's education.

Consequently, at organizing and other committee meetings, time was taken to orient and reorient parents to the platform. Despite this effort, many parents, disproportionately those who spoke only Spanish, remained confused about the content and relevance of the platform to their children. Julia Allen, a CAB organizer, stated, "I think it would be hard for a parent who is only prepared to take responsibility for where the kids cross the street to go to school to somehow be able to criticize how prepared the principal or how prepared the teachers are." The transition from focusing on very concrete local safety concerns to more abstract and subtle learning and instructional conditions would prove especially difficult for parents new to CC9. To ease that transition, Zachary noted, "The bottom line in organizing is you start where people are. I think it is very important not to get hung up on the platform. As they get more involved, bring in the platform. Just because safety is not on the platform, there is no reason not to use it. Don't make the platform the be-all and end-all in the organizing work." This flexibility was one of the hallmarks of CC9's organizing work.

The Local Organizing Work of the CBOs

The school-based organizing work of CC9 did produce modest early results. Parents with children in CC9 schools were increasingly attending organizing committee meetings. Average attendance increased from fifteen to twenty in spring 2003 to twenty to twenty-five in fall 2003. Equally important, a number of the CBOs, most notably NSA's PAC, the Highbridge Life Center's United Parents of Highbridge (UPOH), and the CAB's parent group, began to develop committees in five of the ten CC9 schools.

The performance of the CBOs, however, continued to be uneven despite the prioritization of the local organizing work. The different contributions of member agencies, over time, began to wear on the morale of some of the staff. As Anjelica Otero noted, "I get frustrated, I feel that myself and the NSA organizers have made a very deep commitment to CC9 work. I am not sure that the other organizations are investing as much as we are. So for me it is frustrating, and I feel somewhat resentful because we are all in this together, and we are all going to benefit from it." But Otero also noted that this resentment was tempered by an appreciation for the larger importance of CC9's work: "I said to Frances the other agencies need to be struggling to achieve their goals. But she said, well, it really doesn't matter because it is about the kids. It is really about the overall goal. I realize she is right . . . but I am still resentful because we could be so much stronger." This return to the fundamental values driving CC9's work, education justice, was a touchstone that repeatedly helped parents and organizers work through and cope with emergent difficulties. This conscious practice frequently enabled members of CC9 to diffuse or solve conflict and, as Zachary noted, to "keep their collective eye on the prize."

Developing a base of committed parent leaders, while an essential ingredient to the future success of CC9, had to be accompanied by relationship building with professional staff in the ten public schools. The absence of such relationships would eliminate any hope of implementing reform. Also, the insularity of teachers and principals would relegate parents to marginalized roles. The compelling need to break through the walls that separated the schools from the surrounding community occupied much of CC9's attention. A large part of the work of building understanding and trust between parents and school staff required a process of reintroduction. The staff frequently dismissed parents as lacking the expertise or commitment to make a difference either for the school or their children. At the same time, parents often perceived teachers as having only the most superficial commitment to the community and the students. These stakeholders' dismissive impulses could only be changed through new forms of exchange that, over time, stimulated a reformulation of long-held beliefs. The exchanges would need to begin to challenge understandings of expertise, the resources of poor communities, commitment, and, perhaps most important, the value of community–staff collaboration in strengthening the work of the schools. It was on this basis that a program of parent-led community tours for teachers was initiated.

Community Tours

Creating new forms of engagement between parents and professional staff of the ten schools posed a daunting challenge to parents. Over the course of many months, CC9 parents discussed ways in which they might systematically expose teachers to the daily experiences of their community. Such exposure was seen as at least a partial corrective to the "distance" of teachers from students and the community (and the teachers' consequent choices to leave the schools). Parents recognized that in order to succeed, any structured "forays" by professional staff into the community would have to be sanctioned and supported by the UFT. This tacit partnership was expected to further cement the relationships among the UFT, the DOE, and CC9. This concrete collaborative project offered a basis of building social capital among these institutions. More to the point, its promise was that information sharing and a coordination of activities might lead to more robust social networks and over time to an accumulation of social capital.

At a very early point, the UFT and the DOE signed off on the "tours," thus signaling to chapter chairs and principals that the initiative was important. They reached an agreement that accorded a portion of staff development time to this project. CC9 scheduled meetings with principals to identify mutually agreeable times and dates. However, active and tacit forms of resistance on the part of many principals often delayed implementation. The complex task of simply getting all of the stakeholders on board for a specific tour date and time was daunting. The arrangements were made within the context of overwhelming demands already pressuring principals and teachers. Over the course of the fall, however, most of the schools conducted a tour led by parents.

The tours exposed teachers, frequently for the first time, to community resources like libraries, cultural centers, and social service agencies that could directly benefit classroom work. Community landmarks like parks and historic buildings were also included in the walk. The tours helped to expand the narrowly circumscribed relationships of professional staff to the communities they were serving. To begin with, the walks served as an outreach tool intended to get the teachers out of the classroom and into the community. As one organizer remarked, "For too many of the teachers, their only experience with the community is going from the school into the parking lot and then into their car."

The tour was also intended to provide teachers with a more proximate knowledge about the daunting challenges that their students often faced outside the classroom. The organizers hoped the experience would, in turn, catalyze teacher commitment to engage and struggle with some of these issues. The walk through the community also represented an opportunity for school staff to experience parents as leaders. It was the parents who directed the tours. They introduced teachers to specific landmarks and helped them to understand some of the communal difficulties they experience, difficulties that may be only faintly evident in the classroom. In effect, parents were assuming the roles of instructors. This shift in role and perception was critical to the development of more equal and reciprocal relationships. Finally, students and residents were able to observe teachers outside of the schools, walking their streets. This was a startling and exciting moment for many community residents. Frances Calderon remarked, "the children were so excited when they saw the teachers walk by. They yelled to them, the teachers stopped to talk, it was so great, such a connection."

The tours were also perceived by many parent leaders as improving the prospect for teacher retention and learning. Calderon elaborated on the anticipated relationship between community tours and the retention of novice teachers:

> There are new teachers all of the time. I'm not saying they are good or bad, I'm saying they are not around enough for us to get to know them. They just come and leave; they don't bond with the children. . . . Sometimes it feels like they were just there physically, they don't want to overextend themselves, they come and after school get back into the car and go back to the suburbs. . . . But it is a whole different thing to work with kids whose parents have AIDS or are drug addicts or alcoholics. And the teachers are trying to make a difference in the classroom without knowing all of this. But since the tour, it's changed a bit for the teachers. I guess it hit home to them. One of the teachers said she didn't know that Allen had worked this garden, he's such a difficult kid in class. But he was proud of his patch of earth and talking about it, he never showed interest like this in school. If you're a teacher, you have to know something about kids you are teaching, and these young teachers are learning that through the tours. As they learn, we are hoping they will also choose to stay.

The tours were a success. To begin with, they heightened CC9's visibility with teachers, chapter chairs, and principals. The tours also substantially increased the teachers' knowledge of the community. The collaborative was increasingly perceived as capable of bringing parents and school professionals together in new ways to advance mutual interest to improve the learning conditions within the buildings. Perhaps most important, the tours helped to promote the perception of CC9 as adding something of concrete value to the schools.

There were instances in which principals provided critical leadership that benefited the tour; this, however, was the exception rather than the rule. In general it is fair to say that, with a few exceptions, principals generally seemed indifferent at best. However, they ultimately supported the work of CC9 because regional administrators signaled their support for the tours. During their meetings with both CC9 and principals in fall 2003, Irma Zardoya, the regional superintendent, and Yvonne Torres, Zardoya's deputy, indicated that the tours were important to their reform agenda. It was because of this that the vast majority of principals cooperated. At times, the support of regional administrators for the work of CC9 was especially far-reaching. Zachary remarked,

> There was a meeting a few days before school started with ten principals, Yvonne Torres, and four or five CC9 people. Yvonne had endorsed the CC9 platform. She was clear that the CC9 platform was congruent with their vision and that the principals had to work with us. Then a principal asked, there is a lot of stuff in the platform, should we expect you to evaluate us? It was directed at CC9, but before any of us could respond, Yvonne jumped in and said, no. Nobody is evaluating you but me. I will evaluate you. Does that mean I will talk to CC9 about your performance in relationship to them? Absolutely.

Consolidating the UFT Relationship

Similar meetings were held between CC9 and Herb Katz, the district representative of the UFT, who had instructed his chapter chairs to cooperate. Katz described the tours as one ingredient in the growing collaboration and trust between CC9 and the UFT. "They came in with a conceptual idea that in order to succeed they had to work with the UFT. We already had a conception that in order to succeed we had to work with the parents. The tours were one way we began to work together to build relationship between teachers and parents."

Collaborative projects with local schools were strengthened when regional and UFT allies signaled their support for the CC9 agenda. As Zachary noted, one of the potential strategic advantages of collaboration is that it "can build pressure from both the top down and the bottom up to change conditions within the schools." This intensifying pressure, however, did not diminish the need to simultaneously engage school-based professionals as allies. On the one hand, the intention was to "scale up," or create external pressure to promote district-wide change. On the other hand, CC9 needed to build local or school-based momentum for improved learning conditions. This was a complex undertaking that became even more difficult due to the ambivalence that many organizers felt toward building alliances with teachers and principals.

A number of organizers echoed Allen's viewpoint "that the principals really want to co-opt our work, or to convert us into employees of the schools." Torres reinforced such suspicion when she noted that "everything CC9 puts out should be seen by the principals first." As Zachary indicated, "there is no way that CC9 would agree to that because it would compromise our independence." He added, however, that "for the younger organizers who didn't participate in the first ten years of education reform in New York City . . . for whom organizing is fairly new, it is more difficult to grapple with the complexity. So they are just struggling to keep their heads above water in terms of the parent organizing. So, then, trying to figure out how to build relationships with teachers and principals has been difficult. . . . I think some part of the problem is that they're uncomfortable being in a relationship with these people who have authority like the principals and UFT."

CC9's movement toward collaboration was seriously impeded by the historic conflicts and distrust that divided poor communities from the school system. Yet parents, organizers, the UFT, and DOE administrators were slowly coming to understand that their interests in improving the schools were interdependent. As Appadurai notes, no local group can improve public institutions without the support of powerful allies. In line with this, CC9 continued to struggle to find common ground with potential allies as it readied itself for a major campaign.

Moving from the Words to the Actions of Collaboration

Throughout fall 2003, parent leaders and organizers met with UFT and regional administrators in small, private meetings about the CC9 platform. Parents pressed these officials to voice a more public support for the ideas and program agenda of the platform. At the heart of this conversation was CC9's insistence that key decision makers commit some part of their resources and reputation to a parent-led reform agenda.

The Challenge of Building a Joint Project with the DOE

CC9 convened meetings in fall 2003 with regional administrators and DOE officials, most notably Cahill, Zardoya, and Torres. The meetings were generally productive. As Cahill noted, "There was a lot of evidence that that's what needed to happen. This is pushing the department for resources for particular things. This is pushing the department toward the kinds of service change, high-quality leadership, high-quality teachers that is a pretty plausible theory of change that is going to get them better schools."

The DOE's new leadership had a history of valuing parent involvement in public education. Cahill in particular had a demonstrated commitment to both school reform and maximizing parent participation. She also shared CC9's understanding that the community needed allies to advance an ambitious change agenda. For a community initiative to penetrate the culture of the schools, teacher and principal expertise had to be honored, and their participation valued. Only in this way could parents have even a faint hope of improving public education. It was within this context that Cahill noted, "What you need for any complex change is leadership, change, and expertise. I believe that. I've written about it many times over the years, and I think it has to be multidimensional in all of these categories. You need community leadership, you need school leadership, and you need leadership for change. You need a variety of expertise, and parents have a particular expertise. I'm using expertise to include specific kinds of information. Parents have information about how the school operates. They have information on how that may impact on the children. They have insider information in lots of ways as surrogates of their children."

Cahill viewed CC9 parents as a "capable leadership, bringing participation and expertise." She went on to note that it was the long-term dedication and effectiveness of CC9 parents that left a lasting impression: "They're very dedicated, and they've gone this very long way in understanding what can get the children in the neighborhood a much better education." For Cahill, both the viability of a platform, with which she already agreed, and the accumulating evidence that CC9 could help to deliver changed learning conditions within the schools were of critical importance during fall 2003. CC9's recent record persuaded her that they could effectively transition from the conception of a reform agenda to its execution.

Perception of effectiveness or competence was, if not everything, at least a very compelling reason to experiment with new community partners. For

Cahill, the next logical step was to work with CC9 to implement parts of its platform. Simultaneous to the small meetings with institutional partners, CC9 convened a community dialogue with Zardoya in December 2003. The meeting took place at NSA and included about twenty-five parents, organizers, and school administrators. The parents were prepared for the meeting. They had been challenged to think about ways in which regional administrators might resist or challenge the three proposals contained in the platform: (1) the principal mentoring program, (2) the lead teacher proposal, and (3) school-based partnerships in education decision making between parents and professionals. Almost as soon as the discussion began, Zardoya and Torres indicated a very strong resistance to CC9's principal mentoring program, which relied on an outside agency to provide the mentoring service. In contrast, Denise Moncrief, Ocynthia Williams, and other parents strongly advocated for a partnership between the Region and an independent, widely respected agency, New Visions, which had substantial experience developing such mentoring relationships.

Zardoya and Torres countered that the Region had already developed and implemented an internal support program for principals, which offered a mix of training and mentoring. They were emphatic about the merits of the program. CC9 leadership conveyed its concern and skepticism about a mentoring program embedded in the accountability structure of the Region. They suggested that this tight chain of command would produce substantial fear among new principals that candor regarding problems might affect evaluations. Parents responded to every argument that the regional administrators put forward with a spirited resistance and a well-informed defense of their alternate proposal. After much prodding and with great reluctance, Zardoya agreed to follow-up meetings to discuss further the merits of the CC9 and Region proposals. This impasse represented a victory for parents simply because regional administrators were forced to concede that the conversation with the community regarding the structure of the mentoring program needed to continue despite their substantial investment in an "in-house" proposal.

CC9's leadership, however, quickly shifted its attention to the lead teacher proposal. In general, this proposal was well received by both Zardoya and Torres. These public officials raised questions, but the Region agreed to work with CC9 to raise money to finance a lead teacher program. This was a critical moment; it was the culmination of many private and public meetings to enlist the active support of the Region to help implement parts of the CC9 platform. The administrators of the Region agreed to publicly support the idea of lead teachers, a necessary first step in moving the proposal up the education chain of command. Additionally, Zardoya and Torres promised to lend their credentials and network in the search for private and public funds.

The relationship between CC9 and the Region was bumpy at times. Differences of opinion regarding the roles of principals, the urgency associated with the change agenda, and the roles of parents in the schools were but a few of the areas of tension. As Torres remarked, "The rally was very energetic, but I had mixed feelings about it. My mixed feelings were, wow, they're very energetic, but they sounded almost political and ready to move forward regardless of who they stepped on." Over time, her comfort in working with CC9 increased. In part, this could be traced to the same factors cited by Cahill: parent competence and commitment. Cahill remarked, "The parents are prepped. But you can also hear the flavor of their own passion around the work and really believing that they're supporting their school to support their children. There was a real mixture in there. But I feel now there's a real comfort level there."

CC9's collaboration with the Region and the DOE, although critical to later success, was consistently less robust than with the UFT. In part, this is a consequence of the endemic tension between the "insider role" of regional and DOE administrators and the "outsider" work of community groups like CC9, and to a lesser extent the UFT. The DOE and Region control increasingly tight public education purse strings. Consequently, they are often targeted by community groups to redistribute and increase allocations. Critically, neoliberal policies of reduced public investment stimulate a spiraling tension between professional managers of scarcity and parents interested in heightened, targeted expenditures on local schools. The tight strictures that are often imposed on public education administrators—such as expansive federal and state regulations, a destabilized teaching force, ever more scarce public dollars, and decaying physical plants—contribute to a sense of ongoing crisis management. This makes it difficult for administrators to focus on the proactive reform work of groups like CC9. Finally, the education bureaucracy, despite staff's personal or ideological impulses to work with parents, frequently relegates community residents to junior partner roles at best. The bureaucracy fails to accord community groups anything but a marginal role in policy or practice decision making. It should also be noted that the work of DOE administrators was also complicated by the Bloomberg administration's major restructuring initiative.

For all of these reasons, the trust developed between education administrators and CC9 was cautiously constructed. It is within this context of cautious partnership that the Region endorsed the CC9 lead teacher proposal.

From Collaboration to Solidarity with the UFT

The relationship that CC9 was developing with the UFT rapidly evolved into an especially strong community–labor partnership. This is particularly noteworthy given the lingering tensions of Ocean Hill–Brownsville. This development is also notable because it signifies an increased understanding that community–labor partnerships can effectively challenge neoliberal policies of deregulation, disinvestment, and privatization.

However, Katz admitted that he was distrustful of CC9 at first: "I was at a first meeting, and that meeting did not go exactly smoothly. There were marked differences between CC9 and the UFT . . . but at the same time I thought it was remarkable that they made the effort to work with us considering what was going on in New York City the last thirty years." Both Katz and Bodden, a UFT vice president, shared a commitment to parent involvement in the schools. For Katz, his commitment could be traced to a belief that

> I'm with the students x number of minutes a day. I need a partner to help those kids beyond the walls of that building. I don't think that anybody thinks that you can educate children in six hours and they go out for another eighteen without it having an effect on what goes on in the schools. So I've always felt that it is important for staff and parents to get together.

For Katz, the reason for greater parent involvement was simple: "Learning conditions can't be changed without the active participation of parents." Bodden also saw the parents as a powerful ally in helping to stabilize the school environment: "The people who are constant in the schools are the parents and the teachers. The administrators change all of the time. So if we could get the teachers and parents to work together, that could survive no matter what administrative changes were to come. The work between teachers and parents could be bulletproof to God knows what kind of organizational changes."

She described Katz's particular contribution to this community–labor partnership:

He is very clear about wanting to work with community because he wants his schools to be better. . . . I cannot say that is the view of all of our district reps. We have some people who were around from Ocean Hill–Brownsville, so they are very suspicious about working with community groups. So I think that the hard part is to convince some of us that the community groups are trustworthy, that they are not going to try to stab you in the back. That they are not coming in to tell you everything you are doing is wrong. Nor can we go with the approach that everything that we are doing is right because it isn't. . . . If Herb didn't want to do this, it wouldn't work. I don't care how much I wanted to do this or Randi [Weingarten]. There are too many ways to kill it.

The rancor and reverberation of the decentralization battles of the late 1960s and early 1970s were still fresh for many in the UFT. Consequently, there was little will for or trust in the value of joint projects with parents. Slowly, this began to change as UFT leadership and teachers found themselves under attack for the failures of New York City public education. This line of political attack, orchestrated by politicians and the media, effectively rendered the major structural issues—such as underinvestment in public education and the consequent impact on teacher–student ratios, instructor supports, salaries, and the decaying physical plants—invisible. These pressing issues, which were related to funding, were barely mentioned. Consistent with neoliberal ideology, union work rules were considered by many politicians and professional managers to be the single most critical variable in reducing the effectiveness of public institutions. Resource scarcity was presumed to be an intractable part of the fiscal landscape.

In keeping with this line of thinking, the City Council Education Committee convened hearings in fall 2003 to explore and heighten the visibility of the relationship between the failure of the public schools and union contracts. A number of groups attended. Their testimonies tended to merge the failure of the schools with work rules that protected "incompetent teachers." The public politics of the city council hearings in 2003 reverberated with the more private politics and themes raised by management in negotiations.

Critically, the UFT found itself relatively isolated from the communities its membership served. At this moment, the UFT made a strategic decision to ask for CC9 support. In this context CC9 made a public statement at the council hearing about its collaborative work with the UFT. Williams eloquently described the emergent partnership between CC9 and teachers to improve the schools. This act of public solidarity cemented and extended the relationship between the UFT and CC9. As Bodden noted:

> They were magnificent. That was a parent voice that was speaking. Not because we told them to, not because we told them what to say. . . . The council hearings attacked the contract, it was kind of attacking the way teachers function. So the council talks about firing teachers. I mean schools are a place continually losing teachers. Firing people is really not an issue. . . . And so it was a wonderful feeling to see someone stand up without prodding or pushing.

Bodden suggested that this public support caused many teachers attending the hearings to rethink their assumptions about parents. "For other people to see this kind of connection with parents was a real eye-opener. They had heard a little about CC9, but to see them and see how they presented themselves was, you know, this is a different group of parents. Again there is a residue of distrusting parents. So there was some reticence, but this cut that completely." Williams added, "We spoke about our relationship with the UFT but didn't get into the contract fight with the city. We purposefully stayed away from that. We wanted to show our support for the UFT without taking sides on the contract."

CC9 and ACORN were the only groups to step forward and defend the UFT's recent record in working with the community to improve public education. In its internal discussions, CC9 struggled to craft a public statement that, on the one hand, supported an ally and, on the other, did not antagonize the DOE. Consequently, parents chose to discuss the union's growing, positive relationship with the community but not to raise the subject of its contract with the city. It was an important public gesture of solidarity and Katz noted that it

> impressed the UFT central headquarters and others within the union. It's easy to say "yes, I'm with you" when you're at a table, but to go public in one of the most publicized hearings in the last ten years, to stand up and do that took courage and determination. They didn't have to do that to prove themselves because they had already done that. What they did there was remarkable.

Shortly after the city council hearings, the UFT requested that CC9 organize parent support for a budget rally in Albany sponsored by the union. This was not a simple or small request. It required that parents give up a substantial part of a weekend and that CC9 redirect much of its attention, in the short term, to organizing for the rally. CC9 agreed and organized about fifty parents. Katz commented on the accumulating evidence of CC9's seriousness and trustworthiness as a partner:

> They didn't just go up there. They went wearing bright red outfits telling people who they were. . . . They showed up; they were able to get the numbers. It tells me they deliver and know the importance of state funding for their kids' education. When I go to talk to other people, teachers, people in the UFT, about CC9, who they are and why we need to work with them, I let them know you weren't there, they were.

Through both its solidarity and capacity to deliver numbers, CC9 accrued legitimacy with the UFT. CC9 had a growing reputation of "delivering." Such "delivery," whether in the form of political support, mobilizing parents, or productive dialogue, was the source of CC9's expansive currency with education policy makers. In turn, these sources of legitimacy, trust, and reciprocity were fibers that sustained the larger fabric of collaboration.

This emergent relationship of solidarity could also be traced to a growing recognition within the UFT of the limitations of unalloyed union power. UFT leadership had concluded that new forms of solidarity between the teachers' union and community groups would be required to stimulate the public investment necessary to retain, nurture, and adequately reward teachers. Members and leaders of the UFT continued to question the wisdom and value of such a partnership. However, it was precisely such a partnership that the UFT was testing with CC9. This experience of solidarity also had a more personal dimension. For example, Katz indicated that some part of the trust between CC9 and the UFT could be traced to a belief in the sincerity of leadership:

> If Eric, Ocynthia, or Denise were phonies, I hope that I could catch that. If I was a phony, I think they would catch that. So the key is you have to build a relationship between core people, you must do that first. If you start off moving helter-skelter, there is no trust to go

back on. But if you trust the other person, that is the way you look for ways to make it work, you don't pull away so fast. . . . You have to have that layer. I happen to like the people in CC9. You can't build trust among groups unless you have trust among the individuals.

Katz expressed his respect for parent leaders: "This is not the union's platform, this is not Herb Katz's platform. They are the ones who proposed it, except for maybe one or two lines. It is great. They did the work, they did the research." Katz also understood that "whatever the meeting is, the parents are the ones who run it, and we contribute as opposed to dominating it. I think that's why the trust has built up, because none of us has tried to dominate it."

As Jasper points out, in "The Emotions of Protest," this joining of collaborative work to affective personal relationships is elemental to an enduring solidarity and movement work. The dynamic might be described as building a community to change community. Zachary remarked at the time, "We've had our differences with the union, but there has been enough mutual respect that we've been able to navigate our way through it." The conversations with the UFT leadership during summer and fall 2003 also clarified their shared commitment to the lead teacher proposal. The UFT had a longstanding interest in creating a career ladder for classroom teachers. CC9's proposal was seen as a pathway for creating such mobility. Additionally, the UFT had an interest in stemming the rising tide of turnover among teachers in the poorest neighborhoods of New York City. The lead teacher proposal was specifically intended to address this crisis of teacher retention. In sum, a growing stock of trust and convergence of interests caused the UFT to pledge active support for the CC9 lead teacher campaign, which was planned for early 2004.

During the process of building alliances with the UFT and key public education decision makers, it was increasingly evident that the lead teacher proposal would be the centerpiece of the winter campaign. In part, CC9 made this decision because of the signals of support that the proposal received from powerful institutional actors, such as the DOE and the UFT. Additionally, CC9 determined that improving classroom learning and instruction was an essential starting point for changing the culture of the public schools. Other elements of the platform would, in the short term, be subordinated to the larger need to develop a lean and clear organizing campaign around a single compelling issue. One short-term challenge facing CC9 was the need to commit new parents to the lead teacher proposal. As noted earlier, for many of the new parents, the role and potential contribution of lead teachers to their children's education were confusing. A far more compelling issue for them was safety. Addressing and negotiating these tensions were, of course, critical if CC9 was to have any hope of success in the coming campaign.

5

Building Community to Change Community

Based on the experiences of past education reform efforts in New York City, CC9 parents understood that going it alone was simply not an option. This was especially true given the ambition of their goals. Consequently, much of CC9's work focused on building partnerships for the lead teacher campaign. These external partnerships proved critical to CC9's organizing. However, CC9's specific internal practices in building both solidarity and an activist community of parents were also fundamental to its work. While this discussion is not intended to suggest that CC9 is the only community organization engaged in such work, it is apparent that similar efforts to create democratic public space are both uncommon and undocumented.

To succeed in both the long and short term, CC9 practice would have to consciously build bonds of solidarity between parents. This would be difficult to accomplish, particularly in the heat of a campaign when urgent demands for participation are in competition with the compelling familial and work obligations of parents in a daily struggle to maintain their fragile subsistence. The challenge of producing bonds of solidarity is at least as daunting as organizing a successful campaign to change education policy. Much of the literature acknowledges the complexity and importance of the task but pays little attention to the processes and practices of creating relationships of solidarity. But at least this much is clear: such a praxis, as Paulo Freire notes in *Pedagogy of the Oppressed*, demands a strong effect of organizational or collective ties in sustaining participation.

For many of the parents of CC9, the struggle was to move from the margins of citizenship to the center. This struggle is tied to their anger and distrust of public institutions; many parents are angry about the injustices they experience regularly, and distrustful of organizations that have promised much but delivered little. For example, poor people are regularly frustrated when they visit public agencies to seek redress, and leave with little assurance that anything will change. Such encounters with the public sector foster disillusionment and rob citizens of a sense of power and dignity.

But such experiences also provide a reference point for alternative models of citizenship. Those who reject public institutions may feel a stronger attraction to settings that value and develop their voices, expertise, and authority. As Jasper notes, in *The Art of Moral Protest*, the search for alternative experiences is, in part, animated by parents "shocked into action by moral outrage and sustained in their action by moral outrage." Jasper suggests that moral protest "provides individuals with a rare chance to probe their moral intuitions and articulate their principles" (4). The space in which parents experiment with these principles and practices of citizenship is, in effect, an alternative public sphere. It is a space in which they can forge collectivity, nurture solidarity, and develop organizing campaigns. That is precisely the kind of public sphere that CC9 created. Its daily practice offered a counterpoint to parents' prior citizenship experiences of individualization, impotence, and invisibility by developing forums for democratic exchange that promised new forms of parent power. CC9's capacity-building and organizing work touched much deeper issues, such as the meaning of citizenship and the struggles of a single community to subsist in the midst of a neoliberal political economic shift. It was within this context that strong democratic practice was the seed from which parent power was grown.

Despite obstacles such as ethnic tensions, cynicism, and scarce time, CC9 succeeded in developing an expansive cohort of parent leaders who formed bonds of solidarity. It is one of CC9's most enduring and important achievements. How was this accomplished? What practices engaged parents and caused them to deepen their commitment to CC9? How are solidarity and collective forms of mobilization joined?

Breaking Down Barriers to Democratic Engagement

Drawing parents into campaigns to improve their communities is impeded by both (1) the absence of a collective movement/activity that residents can "join," and (2) the everyday barriers to participation that many individuals face (child care, time, resources, etc.). As Doug McAdam and Ronnelle Paulsen indicate in "Specifying the Relationship between Social Ties and Activism," without structural attention to promoting participation or opportunities that facilitate activity, the individual will remain inactive. These obstacles to engagement have been systematically addressed by CC9 through both its development of effective campaigns for educational justice and its efforts to lower the access costs that often prevent broad citizen participation in social change projects.

The neighborhoods and schools that CC9 is organizing are increasingly populated by monolingual Spanish-speaking parents. For CC9 to engage these parents, it must find ways to communicate. This sounds like a simple requirement, but in fact it is quite complex. To begin with, organizers must either be bilingual or find others who can translate. CC9 has placed a premium on hiring bilingual organizers. However, despite its best efforts, many staff members do not speak Spanish. Consequently, intermediaries have been drafted to provide translation services.

Step by step, CC9 has found ways to make language less and less of an obstacle to democratic participation for parents. During outreach, bilingual staff members are always deployed with monolingual English-speaking organizers. This is not easy given conflicts in scheduling and substantial workloads, but it is always at the forefront of planning. The difficulties of communicating across languages at CC9 meetings are especially complex. The complexity is largely a consequence of sheer numbers: twenty to forty people, for example, wanting to speak in languages that are incomprehensible to a large segment of parents attending a meeting. CC9 has retained a translator and equipment to promote communication and dialogue during meetings. The technology provides individual access to translation and facilitates participation. This investment has not gone unnoticed, especially among Spanish-speaking parents, who comment on their discomfort communicating in English. Anna Guzman, a parent from Highbridge, recalls that "this was when I was just learning how to speak in English. They helped me to speak in Spanish also. They make you feel comfortable, that you are not a stranger. The translation helped. I think if the translator wasn't there, I would have just been quiet."

Language is a lightning rod for fears and feelings of inadequacy frequently associated with transitioning to a new and strange culture. In general, this fear was realized during painful encounters with the school system or other official agencies. CC9, however, was described as a safe harbor, in part because of the concrete availability of translation services and in part because of the meaning parents attached to this gesture of hospitality. A parent leader from NSA, noted: "People will get embarrassed speaking in English and not want to make a mistake. . . . Sometimes they have a good idea, but they don't want to present it. They won't take the risk. . . . People will take the risk at CC9 meetings because of the translator, but also because they begin to see this is a place where they can take a risk."

CC9 has also tried to reduce access costs to participation by providing both dinner and child care. This is especially important for CC9 leaders, who are mostly women and heads of single-parent households. For these parents, the demands of finding babysitters to care for children or preparing a meal are often prohibitive to full or even partial participation. Many of the parents are juggling multiple familial and work responsibilities. A failure to address these needs would have compromised both recruitment of new parents and the continued participation of more seasoned leaders. As Ocynthia Williams noted, "We have food at every meeting, we have child care at every meeting. Even carfare for some folks. Always we have translation. So, the stage has been set where there is no reason you can't be a part of CC9, unless you just don't want to be."

These supports also convey a message that participation requires investment. The meaning that parents ascribe to such investment is that their presence and voice are valued. CC9's attention to the subtle requirements of participation is recognized by many members. Veronica Rivera, a parent relatively new to CC9, remarked that "food, child care are so important. This is what makes it so different from anything that I've ever been involved in. If you want parents to participate, you have to help them, you need to make them feel welcomed and included. And that is so important and speaks volumes about CC9. The smallest detail is covered."

Promoting Participation through Practices of Leadership Capacity Development and Discipline

CC9 meetings are structured to have parents lead and not rely on professional staff or organizer expertise to direct decision making. The commitment is to methods of organization, mobilization teaching, and learning that build on what the poor know and understand. Some part of what distinguishes CC9 practice is its willingness to invest resources in the development of parent skills and leadership. This capacity-building work is a part of the reciprocal exchange and a source of growing trust between CC9 and new parents. Despite the many pressing demands on organizers to deliver numbers, leadership development remains a priority. For example, staff are queried at staff meetings about time spent prepping parents to facilitate meetings, deliver speeches at public events, do specific kinds of research, or present at meetings with education policy makers.

Prepping is an essential element of CC9's capacity development practice. It helps to germinate self-confidence in parents that, in the recent past, may have seemed out of reach. Anna Maria Garcia stated that "in CC9, like everywhere else, you start at the bottom, and with the organizers taking you under their wing and pushing you and training you, then eventually you become a leader." Williams offered a fuller explanation of the dynamic relationship between preparation and parent development:

> Basically, the training, the preparation gives you confidence, knowledge. I guess the knowledge gives you the confidence, and just knowing that someone else believes that you can, reaffirming what you've learned by telling you that you did a good job at a meeting, or by helping to prepare you for a meeting. In our conversations we discovered certain things by looking at the data. The data says a, b, and c schools have been at this level for a long time, and then it makes you think, Why? Why hasn't there been any improvement? And then I guess you have this awareness, not just the academic part. We can now suggest reasons for the data and the school failing.

Two elements of the preparatory sessions were "reps" and "what ifs." The reps, or repetitions, anchored parents to particularly important parts of potential future discussions. Organizers repeated points until parents were able to incorporate them into their repertoires. This exercise is not unlike conditioning an athlete to develop a specific technique. Over time, repetitions promote muscle and mental memory for sprinters, fencers, or basketball players. For parents, prepping through repetition of critical ideas or talking points has contributed to an evolving fluency with education issues and vocabulary. As well, "what if" questions were frequently raised by organizers and parents to challenge leaders to think more deeply about an issue or question. The exercise of posing questions and developing "best responses" helped parents to project themselves into future roles and, perhaps most important, prepared them for discussions with powerful education decision makers. By preparing for the unexpected, parents were less likely to be intimidated or freeze in critical moments of a public meeting or event.

CC9, however, continues to struggle to balance the pressing, immediate demands of a campaign against the essential work of developing parent capacity. Creating this equilibrium in day-to-day practice is not always easy or neat, but it is always a priority. Williams described the concrete payoffs of the prep work: "I am able to speak as well in public because of all of the training that Eric gave. He said prepare, prepare, and prepare and project when you speak, project." Roz Chambers, a parent leader from NSA, remarked that the preps made her feel more confident in speaking to the media: "I've been chosen to be a parent spokesperson for the media and didn't know anything, I just wasn't prepared. That does not happen with CC9; you are prepared, maybe at times overprepared, but that is okay. Because I am more in control when I go into a meeting."

Importantly, what ifs and reps were also used during CC9's internal, private work developing a platform. The content of a change agenda that might begin to fix the schools was not immediately apparent to parents or staff. Instead, it emerged out of extended dialogue, posing questions, and exposure to a literature dealing with recent approaches to reforming urban schools. This process demanded patience, discipline, and flexibility of thinking. Ultimately, however, it yielded a platform with a coherent theory of change that was respected by a cross section of policy makers. This deep understanding and ownership of the platform would prove critical during the earliest stages of the lead teacher campaign, when it became apparent that many new participants did not understand the content or importance of the proposal.

Over time, seasoned leaders graduated to the roles of facilitator and trainer, helping to explain, for example, the lead teacher proposal to new parents. In this way, preparatory work was essential to a cycle of learning and teaching, as well as producing and reproducing the conditions for change. This growing mastery often translated into an improvisational capacity to work effectively with new situations and information. To transition to such roles, however, parents often needed emotional support from organizers and seasoned parent leaders. The nurturing enabled many parents to risk taking on new roles and responsibilities.

The convergence of preparatory work and leadership development is most evident when parents assume important public roles. For example, a parent facilitates every CC9 meeting. Organizers are expected to work with leaders to help them develop an agenda, to understand the role of facilitator as catalyst, and to gain a basic fluency with the issues. Many parents are initially reluctant to take this leadership step. Rotating this responsibility across CBOs and parents, however, forces organizers to identify and work with often reticent candidates. Guzman noted, "I used to just go to meetings, but now I am able to facilitate meetings. I learned how to facilitate by watching others. I don't usually volunteer to do anything, I'm the kind of person you have to stay on. But by watching and being pushed, I stepped up to do it, and it made me feel, well, like there is even more that I can do." Another parent leader, Jamilla Anderson from the Mid-Bronx, spoke about how access to relevant information is essential to both her confidence and performance as a facilitator:

> Eric was really knowledgeable in prepping me. He would take
> me through what I needed to know step by step so I wouldn't be
> confused. He got back to me when I asked for things. But I always
> wanted to be fully versed because what if they asked a question?
> What would I say? That I would give them an answer at another
> time? It made me feel more comfortable because if you are well
> versed in what you are doing, you're going to feel more secure,
> because you know what you are talking about.

Perhaps the most powerful and frightening role for parents is that of public speaker. For many, it represents a rite of passage, a moment that dramatically underscores increased capacity to use language to persuade and move others. As Arjun Appadurai notes in "Deep Democracy," "by addressing an audience . . . the poor enter a space of official recognition and technical legitimation" (36). Public speaking is, however, especially frightening for parents. Often there is a push-pull for parents, who may have dreamed of speaking publicly on issues such as education but are afraid of failure. Overcoming these fears is critical to the development of confident citizen leaders. As Denise Moncrief explained, "My self-confidence since coming to CC9 has skyrocketed. I never knew I could speak to people and get them to listen, speak to people and move them, and speak to people and impart knowledge that wasn't trivial." Moncrief suggested that CC9 helped her develop skills and have the courage to make independent decisions:

> When we did the first rally, and they wanted me to do a speech and
> the mission statement, I had thirty seconds of stuff written out. They
> said you have to make it longer. They encouraged me, and Eric
> walked me through the entire thing. By the second rally, it was
> "Leave my speech alone! Don't touch it!" No matter what I have

wanted to do, I have always felt supported by them. They have shown extreme confidence in me being able to do whatever they need me to do. And that makes me want to produce all the more.

The shift from early engagement to a stronger, more permanent relationship with CC9 can be traced in part to the emotional attachments that are spawned and grown during the leadership development work. Strong, deep interpersonal relationships among CC9 members are less easily achieved in organizing campaigns, when the task-driven work often eclipses the need to build and sustain more personal attachments. Emotions, Jasper notes in *The Art of Moral Protest,* are the glue of solidarity. While the tasks of an organizing campaign are necessary to building solidarity, they are simply not sufficient. Over the longer term, the abstract pull of communal change is frequently not strong enough to overcome the counter pulls away from activism generated by the concrete needs in other areas of parents' lives. Rather, over time it is often the emotional and relational connections that are built between people in a common struggle that create the kind of commitment or identification that can withstand demands in other corners of a parent's life. As Garcia noted, "what connects me is, it's the human relationship aspect of CC9."

CC9 is consistently mindful of how the relational and more formal programmatic demands of developing parent leaders are often intertwined. From the moment a parent enters a CC9 meeting, she or he is exposed to specific kinds of welcoming. Seasoned parent leaders will often reach out to new parents during the course of a meeting. This is an intentional part of CC9's culture of solidarity and deep democracy. The formal and informal structure of each meeting is organized to promote affiliation, parent voice, and leadership. Every meeting begins with an icebreaker. This is a device used to narrow distance between old and new members by enabling people to introduce themselves to each other through an introductory exercise. In this way, favorite pieces of music, heroes, dance steps, and jokes are shared. It is a first and brief step in creating a level playing field among members and in revealing private parts of each participant's life that would otherwise be hidden in public meetings. In a sense, these icebreakers signal to parents that what is private can also be shared publicly, that sharing and trusting are risks that are necessary to building complex relationships, leadership roles, and a sense of community. A statement repeatedly and ritualistically chanted at the close of each meeting—"Who are we? CC9"—is also intended to reinforce feelings of membership and collectivity. The opening and closing of meetings help to dynamically create points of emotional connection between participants and, over time, contribute to a more general identification with CC9. After a brief time working with CC9, Rivera observed that "the openness, the respect is amazing. I've been involved three months, and it feels like I have been involved forever. Everyone has welcomed me and my daughter with open arms. . . . This is my favorite phrase: this is our family."

Family as a Symbol of a Hopeful, Healthy Community

This experience of family is not tangential but central to both leadership development and democratic practices. The parents who are involved in CC9 experience the organization as a family because it offers the supports and nurturing that are often unavailable in other parts of their lives. As noted, parents are not simply told to facilitate meetings, present to officials, or speak at public events. They are offered the substantive and emotional supports that enable them to make such leaps. CC9 organizers do not see capacity as a simple product of pouring information into parents' heads, but rather as a part of a supportive dialogue that increases both skill and confidence. The dialogue enables parents to democratically cocreate agendas and speeches.

The experience of CC9 as a family was transmitted not only through staff-to-parent exchanges but also through parent-to-parent exchanges. This often occurred through acts of kindness that parents extended to each other in the midst of their own, often dire struggles. It is in these individual exchanges that parents, perhaps paradoxically, root themselves most deeply to CC9. This web of relationships is the very fabric of the organization. The mixing of personal, political, and professional relationships is an essential feature of organizing intended to promote change by building a democratic leadership-centered community that coheres into solidarity over time. As Moncrief explained,

> When George's wife died, the support from other CC9 parents was tremendous. They gave money, sent cards. It was just an outpouring of love. I've watched these people and there is just so much love.

Or as Garcia put it,

> At first maybe it was like a job for me. But then there is that family part—parents call, organizers call and want to know why I haven't

come to a meeting. I am missed by other parents. It is a warm feeling for other people to worry about you.

For many parents, the CC9 family offered forms of respect that are less available elsewhere. Guzman noted, "Your ideas are respected, no matter what. That is something important for the parents. No one is better than anyone else." Some part of this respect is traced to members listening to each other. This may seem like a simple, self-evident point, but it is significant. Often at community meetings, participants are so focused on being heard that they will shout over other speakers, raise their hands aggressively, and distract from a presentation, or simply engage in cross conversations.

As Ruby Santan, a parent leader, noted, "Here, we listen to each other. Everybody states their questions, or their ideas, or comments, and everybody listens to each other." Jamilla Anderson suggested that they "work through the agenda, and everyone has a voice. If you sit there and speak up and ask a question, you are well received. No one says, well, why don't you speak to so and so, and no one says it. Even if a person may deserve to hear that kind of answer." Along these same lines, Moncrief indicated that "no one in the CC9 family has ever belittled me if they disagreed or thought that what I was saying was stupid. There was always that respect for each other, and that makes you feel safe. Then you can say whatever you want to say." Rivera described the relationship between patience, the experience of being nurtured, leadership development, and family: "CC9 has helped me become a leader by nurturing me. They nurture me by answering my questions and sharing their experiences. Never, never saying, that doesn't make any sense, that is nurturing, that is family."

Listening, however, is not only interpreted as attentiveness in the moment. Parents also understand that CC9 leaders and organizers are listening when they act on a member's ideas. Through this process, parents understand that the promise of being really heard in the CC9 family is authentic, not simply empty rhetoric. As Garcia indicated, "What I say as a parent is heard. I know this to be true because as time goes on, my words and the words of other parents are acted on."

Parents' representation of CC9 as family, although idealized, was clear. They characterized the CC9 family as having a sense of common purpose and therefore being "close." It was in the "closeness" of shared aspiration and mutual respect that parents found a basis for believing that they could safely grow their capacity and change public schools for their children. This back and forth between the political and the personal, however, was part of a whole fabric of capacity building, for parents and public education. Williams richly described how these threads cohere:

> So the connection is powerful, it is unbelievable. When people come together around the table, we are strategizing about how we are going to do this and that, but in the back of our minds is the fact that this is going to make things better for all of our children and for the future. So the talking, the crying it all stays in the room. It feels like a family. . . . Everyone was dancing and laughing and drinking together. It felt like a family reunion.

Similarly, Moncrief indicated:

> There have been rough patches like with any family. Everything I've done has been kind of trial by fire. They throw me into the lion's den. But I've never seen a group function as well or as efficiently as this one. How many groups do you know that can come up with a platform and there is no trail of blood? Because of CC9, I know what a well-functioning group looks like, I know what needs to be done. I knew where the problems were, and how to constructively go about trying to correct them.

CC9 as family is a multifaceted, complex experience for parents. Two recurrent themes raised by parents regarding the CC9 family are the trust-worthiness of other members and the deeply held belief that individual interest is consistently subordinated to the shared, collective needs of the group. Rivera described the trust of knowing that what is said in the family stays in the family:

> It is a family in the sense that I can call any one of the parents or organizers and tell them what's happening to me, I'm having a problem paying a bill, something has happened, and I need to talk about it, and there is no embarrassment or shame, or any fear that the information that I divulge will somehow be used against me in the future. That lack of fear is what makes me feel so comfortable and, I guess, willing to be a leader.

Chambers also described the collective culture of the CC9 family: "To me a family is where everyone is able to sit down and talk. There are no big I's.

At CC9 you ask the newcomers about who they are as they come through the door and explain this is what we are doing, this is what we are trying to achieve, and ask about their backgrounds. It is about we, not I."

This ideal, romanticized understanding of CC9 was tested. No matter the challenge, however, CC9 parents always returned to shared values and dialogue as a way of working through difficult differences. Theresa Anderson indicated, "I know it is not perfect. We have had our differences. What gets us through, though, is talking it through, finding where we agree and how we can keep working together. Often what helps is not losing sight of what really motivates us, changing these schools for our kids."

From Individual Empowerment to Membership Identity

Democratic, group-centered leadership development is woven into the practice of CC9. For example, rotating the leadership roles among parents is an important component of this practice framework. The intention is to create a fluid leadership group while safeguarding against the development of a permanent parent elite. This design has effectively maximized inclusion. Importantly, the democratic practices of preparatory work, access, attentiveness to voice, and respect for parent expertise were part of an earlier body of work on group-centered leadership developed by Zachary while working at John Jay College. He transported this training protocol and practice to the IESP and CC9. The pollination and flowering of group-centered leadership practices within CC9 have in large part been accomplished through role modeling by Zachary and other IESP staff.

For many parents, the choice to grow into leaders is closely tied to the risk and vulnerability inherent in a public, activist work. In risking public vulnerability by raising their voices and activist profiles, parents begin to test their leadership capacity. For many community members, this is the first time that they have experienced an activist, public role. The experience of being more fully utilized has a potentially powerful reverberation. To begin with, the benefits of CC9 participation are perceived as accruing not only to the community but also to the individual. As suggested earlier, individual benefit is critical because it provides parents with the most tangible evidence that collective work is not simply about sacrifice. The importance of individual benefit was repeated by a variety of respondents. What they noted, both explicitly and implicitly, was that CC9 practice enlarged their understanding of what it means to be fully utilized and empowered.

As Jamilla Anderson remarked, "I don't feel that a lot of people are being fully utilized, because they are not being heard or seen. You come and hear a politician speak. When have they even taken the time to hear what our concerns are, except when it's an election year? Now I'm being more fully used. Let's put it like that. I am able to give speeches. I've always spoken up at community meetings. Now people are asking me to speak. That helps me to speak up for the unheard."

Similarly, Moncrief said, "This is the only place in my life where I feel anything is growing. The growing that I am doing here is starting to bleed into other areas of my life. . . . I never knew that I could telegraph and communicate information back to other people, speak to people and move them. And speak to people and actually impart knowledge that wasn't just trivial stuff you see on *Jeopardy*. I've always been a kind of lone wolf, a by-myself kind of person. I've learned a sense of working in a group that I didn't possess before. . . . Before CC9, I always considered myself a kind of workhorse person. Tell me what you want done and I'll go do it. Now I am actually in a position where I can show people."

Embedded in the experience of being more fully utilized is a reciprocal exchange between parents and CC9. As parents experience an enlarged sense of individual possibility, they are often also reworking their relationship to CC9. Frequently, they begin to join their individual hopes, ideas for change, frustration, and energy to CC9's collective campaign for educational justice. More to the point, parents cross the divide from individual participant to collective member of CC9, and more largely to a solidarity with others who are engaged in the fight to improve public schools. Importantly, new parents step up to more and more significant roles in large part because leaders and organizers help to nurture belief in their potential and capacity. In return, these acts of faith and investment promote a deepened affiliation and identification with CC9 and campaigns for change.

Critically, the internal practice work of CC9 has, in part, been about helping parents build new relationships to their own potential, each other, and the larger community. Each of these three dimensions is incorporated into the deep democratic practice of CC9. This work is expected to grow a cohort of parents whose relationship to CC9 moves beyond engagement and participation to membership identification and a solidarity of common struggle for educational justice. The work of leadership development is always threaded through the demands of building campaigns for education reform. As noted earlier, every step of the way, organizers and parent leaders have to carefully balance capacity development and other demands that must be met to wage effective organizing campaigns.

Joining Individual Empowerment to a Collective Legacy of Educational Justice

As noted, the growing solidarity between CC9 parents can only partially be traced to a growing sense of their individual potential. It is also a consequence of identification with the collective struggles of CC9 and intimate ties to other members. This is a dynamic, multifaceted process. The opportunity to influence public education not only in their community but perhaps throughout the Bronx invigorates many parents to remain engaged with the challenging work of education reform.

CC9 has enabled parents, many for the first time, to believe they can help improve the quality of their children's education. This is not a surprising finding; every textbook indicates that effective organizing promotes such beliefs and inspires this energy. However, as every organizer understands, there is a substantial chasm between the textbook promise of organizing and the day-to-day struggle to promote hope and change. But the practices of CC9 have turned this abstract promise into a concrete reality. Parents perceive CC9 as the best possible instrument for improving the public schools and the life choices of their children. Perhaps most important, participants have come to believe that they are critical agents in a larger change process. As McAdam and Paulsen note in "Specifying the Relationship between Ties and Activism," bonds between individuals and organizations have a "special force and significance when the tie is embedded in a broader collective context linking to" movement change (663).

The empowering experience of leadership development in combination with the growing collective power of CC9 are what emboldens parents to imagine that they can leave an important legacy or rewrite history. As Frances Calderon explained,

> We want to see the changes. This community, I have lived here my whole life. This place, it means a lot to me. Our schools, we need to better the education, make it work. We want to see the changes. We're not just standing by and making comments about what needs to be done. Here we are able to do something about it in an organized manner with other people.

Jamilla Anderson described the legacy that she wants to create through her work with CC9:

> All the things that I've wanted to do and am doing on a lower level is now being brought to a broader level. So it makes me feel connected. I feel like I'm part of creating a larger thing. Part of me is thinking, did we start this? And in ten years we may see the effects. So my pride is in seeing the end results. What we are doing now, what we are trying to change will maybe be here in the future, and my kids will look back and say my mom helped to create that work.

The intersection between individual values and collective work for change was powerfully conveyed by Williams when she stated:

> I identify with this community. I feel like I am destined to do this work. This is a beautiful community, but it doesn't get what it deserves. At CC9 it is about making certain our kids get what they deserve. If I'm able to participate in a project that is going to make a difference for the community, then I have to participate whole-heartedly. This is a calling for me, and CC9 is just the vehicle.

Moncrief richly described the hope that she attaches to her work with CC9 when she said,

> We've lost a whole generation of kids. We can't get them back, they're just lost. I don't want to lose another generation of kids, and I don't want to just sit back and watch it go. CC9 can make a difference; it is making a difference. Whatever happens next it is not going to be because I didn't try to do something. It is not going to be because I didn't fight the good fight.

Maintaining a consistent focus on the educational needs of the children through a subordination of individual egos is not, however, easily achieved. Critically, community-based collaborations have, at times, foundered and broken up because of turf conflicts or jealousy between community residents. From its very inception, however, the culture of CC9 was to inculcate and reproduce, through both message and action, the importance of the children. The focus is always on what the children need to improve their academic performance. Key organizers and leaders share this understanding. This perspective is encoded in the platform and articulated during meetings. When tensions inevitably arise that are tangential to the primary agenda of CC9, they are directly addressed but rarely allowed to deflect the attention of the group from its primary agenda.

More to the point, when a meeting moves "off course" because of either conflict or confusion, parent leaders are expected to step into the discussion and reset direction. If they are unable to independently refocus, the organizers invariably step into the process and remind everyone about the need to keep one eye on the clock and the other on the meeting's larger purpose. On occasion, when a particular member continues to deflect the conversation, convey disrespect to the facilitator, or struggle for control of the agenda, parent leadership recommends scheduling a separate meeting to address the points being raised. Harsh expressions of disrespect that violate CC9 norms, however, are addressed in the moment and directly. When such conflict surfaces, the agenda is suspended, and the violation of group norms is discussed. In general, such discussion focuses on the reasons for the norms and concludes with a reaffirmation of specific group expectations regarding individual behavior during meetings.

It is important to note here that parents' relationships to CC9 were not uniformly positive. Many parents complained that there were too many meetings. For example, as Jamilla Anderson noted, "between the meetings with CC9, STEPs (a parent advocacy group), and the subcommittees, and other things that are going on, it is very difficult because a person could get burned out." Other parents were sometimes discouraged by the turnover of organizers. They repeatedly remarked that the instability of organizers affected their connection to the local and districtwide work. Anderson indicated that "I am having a really hard time with the turnover of organizers. It disturbs the continuity. It is really hard to keep the ball rolling. Plus you have to deal with all of these different personalities over a short period of time. It is really hard."

Similarly, Moncrief described how organizer turnover influenced the work of specific CBOs: "A couple of the organizations have had major organizer transitions. They have issues in holding on to organizers. Another agency has the organizer doing a whole bunch of things so that her focus is not on CC9 too much of the time." Victories in education organizing are a scarce commodity. Chambers talked about the challenges and frustrations of trying to get even simple things accomplished: "Even getting small things like speed humps is so hard. So much stands in your way. It is never easy. It is a tough fight day to day."

Moncrief and other parents felt that CC9 is sometimes less inclined to challenge decision makers in ways that "rock the boat." They indicated that as CC9 collaborated more closely with institutions like the UFT and DOE, it was less willing to forcefully push parent perspectives.

None of these frustrations, however, catapulted parents out of the gravitational pull of CC9. To the contrary, parents described a dialogical, democratic environment that allowed them to voice such concerns without fears of reprisal. Perhaps most important, their experiences indicate that parent critique was valued as staff struggled to incorporate what they had to say into the work of CC9. These responses further illustrated CC9's ongoing effort to create a dynamic, flexible learning environment, drawing directly from experience to rework practice.

The Practice of Building Solidarity

Solidarity is a complex product of what, at first glance, may appear to be the magical cohering of different strains of political work and personal interests. For CC9 parents, the experience of solidarity is less about magic and more about a practice that creates and nourishes democracy out of the carefully cultivated ingredients of deepening expertise, political will, and interpersonal relationships. What parents repeatedly noted was that the work and people of CC9 had an authenticity that promoted attachment. For many parents, authenticity was perceived as synonymous with "being real." It expressed itself in many ways as parents became immersed in the work of CC9. From preparing or training parents to more fully participate, to the lowering of professional and personal barriers, the CC9 experience is perceived by parents as "real" in its intention to share power, build capacity, and change the schools.

For CC9, the political dimensions of solidarity that emerged out of shared struggle, which were consistently tested during campaigns, endured because of the foundational blocks of interpersonal solidarity that were consciously built through daily practices. As described earlier, the democratic practices of CC9 were attentive to the many ways in which parents can be either inhibited or encouraged to participate. Participation was not limited to public or private meetings around a campaign; it was also evident in smaller, informal moments when frank discussions were opened between parents and staff

about how their histories influenced the decision to organize for school reform. The frustration, hope, pain, shared commitments, and joy that were
often central to these discussions created a solidarity that cannot be achieved
through larger, more formal meetings. It was in these moments that participants, through the safety of small-group discussions, risked vulnerability to
create the strong, multidimensional solidarity necessary to effective organizing campaigns.

Building the parent power necessary to change the public schools demands
that the political struggle be undergirded by strong webs of interpersonal
relationships. It is relatively easy to pull away from shared social or political
commitments. After all, the very act of participation is not required but voluntary. Why, then, would citizens, or in this instance, parents, continue to
stay in such a demanding, intense project? The answer lies only partially in
the larger vision: changing the schools for their children and the children of
the community. Shared vision is necessary to the project of democratic participation and effective organizing work, but it is simply not sufficient. In
the lives of so many parents and organizers, other pulls, such as family, job,
money difficulties, and unstable housing, can cause people to rapidly disinvest in such hopeful activities, no matter how deeply felt.

What sustains democratic participation in a larger change campaign is
more often than not a shared experience of trust, respect, and perceived
authenticity among members. In this case, CC9 provided a safe space where
people could air and resolve differences. Out of CC9, a new public sphere
emerged—a public sphere in which people are able to join their individual
development to a larger community struggle. No matter the counter pull,
the experience of community membership makes it more difficult to pull
away or limit participation. Developing organizing campaigns infused with
a culture of democratic participation is an especially complex undertaking.
It requires a practice that pays attention to the critical links between building and changing community. CC9 has consistently struggled with these
pieces as it assembles and reassembles a dynamic and volatile puzzle, align-
ing the necessary solidarity and strategic sophistication to launch effective
organizing campaigns. Ultimately, however, it is in the shared, protracted
struggle for vital necessities, such as education, where relationships of solidarity are tested and deepened. Peter Evans has suggested in "Government
Action, Social Capital, and Development: Reviewing the Energy on Synergy"
that "poverty puts poor communities in the front lines of battles for sustainability and that these struggles are not only essential to their immediate

survival and interests but also the general interests of the larger society." It is in that battleground for sustainability that CC9's mostly women leaders deepened their solidarity and extended the role of mothering into the terrain of political activism. As Theresa Anderson remarked, "My connection to these people, these women, is about the fight for our children. If we don't succeed in changing the schools, well, let's face it, we fail as mothers. I have such love for them because we are all sacrificing so much to make it better not only for our own children but for each other's children."

6

Launching the Lead Teacher Campaign

As CC9 prepared for the lead teacher campaign, much time and energy were invested in shoring up its base. This work largely occurred during fall 2003. What became evident during the outreach, however, was that the parents, union, and CBOs did not yet have necessary levels of commitment from their bases to effectively implement the ambitious lead teacher organizing agenda. To invigorate each of these groups, CC9 planned outreach events. This initiative was expected to deepen stakeholder commitment to lead teacher reform and, in turn, increase the probability of a successful campaign.

The campaign goal was to create a new job title, lead teacher. These seasoned, expert instructors would spend half of their time in the classroom and the other half mentoring young, inexperienced teachers. The intention was to both draw expert instructors to the poorest communities in the city and simultaneously to provide an expansive cohort of young, inexperienced teachers in neighborhood schools with essential classroom supports. The lead teacher program linked recognition that the single most important factor in student achievement is instructor capacity with a specific intervention to improve the classroom skills of inexperienced staff. The campaign demands were that the city create a lead teacher job title and invest the resources necessary to fund a substantial number of lines in the ten CC9 schools.

Enabling Parents to Appreciate the Value of Lead Teachers

The outreach work in local schools during fall 2003 resulted in many new parents joining CC9. However, many of the new parents tended to focus strictly on the most evident forms of breakdown in the schools. As Julia Allen, the CAB organizer, noted, "The issues that parents are most concerned about is what they see. If you talk to parents, they will immediately begin to nod their heads when you talk about traffic safety. Things like safety on the streets, lead paint, safety in the cafeteria, these are the things that parents immediately want to change."

Although these issues were important to new parents, they were not included either in the CC9 platform or the campaign that CC9 was planning for the spring. As noted earlier, the campaign departed from past practices of parent-led community groups by not focusing its attention on visible issues, such as safety. Rather, they chose to focus on the subtle, relatively invisible instruction and learning issues within the schools. The platform was built by a first generation of parent leaders through extended dialogue and research. The next generation of leaders, however, did not have this historic, foundational experience. Consequently, they frequently could not see how the platform's proposals would lead to an improvement in their children's education. Discussions regarding the lead teacher proposal were a consistent source of confusion and estrangement for new parent leaders.

Although efforts were made to explain the importance of this initiative, the presentations were shoehorned into meetings that already had demanding agendas. Allen described the difficulty of bridging this divide:

> I think it is a challenge because CC9 goals and agenda have already
> been formed. They sort of grew up together, and parents who were
> part of it have an understanding of the platform and what it means.
> It's something that has already been figured out and has a history.
> Our new parents don't really understand how it is meaningful to
> their lives.

Some organizers explained the importance of the lead teachers to parents during the course of local organizing work. Theresa Anderson, the organizer at North West Bronx, noted:

> They [the new parents] got it because I put it in very simple terms.
> In relative terms. I say when someone has a baby, they may look
> to an elder aunt or sister for advice. But you don't go to your
> mother-in-law, because she is just going to criticize. This is what we
> are trying to do with the lead teachers, create that environment of
> support from someone who is a peer and eliminate the supervision
> part of it. That is how I am selling lead teachers, and for the most
> part it has worked.

For Allen, selling the platform to new parents was necessary but not sufficient. She wanted to help new parents understand how their safety concerns were part of a larger breakdown in the public schools: "I would argue that it is a personal step. . . . it would be hard for a parent who is only prepared to criticize and be angry to be able to discuss proposals to support the principal or teacher. What I struggled with in the beginning was how to bring these two things together. That takes time. People grow into this a little bit at a time." Allen indicated that for parents to invest in CC9 proposals, they must first rethink their anger toward teachers and principals for the deficiencies of local schools. "There is an urgency to catch people up to where they want to be invested in the lead teacher proposal while they're still talking about the conditions of the schools. They're really angry with teachers and principals and not necessarily in a position where they want to sympathize and put themselves in their position."

For CC9, however, time was running out. It needed to quickly educate new parents about the importance of lead teachers to their children's academic achievement. An early pressing organizing demand was to gather ten thousand signatures in support of the lead teacher proposal. CC9 leaders anticipated that they would present the petition to the chancellor at a strategic moment. To carry out this part of the campaign, an army of new and old parents had to be recruited to participate in community outreach. Enlisting new parents for this outreach work, however, remained a challenge. To accomplish this, they planned an event for early January 2004 to train new parents in the content of the platform, with specific attention paid to the lead teacher proposal. The training would also prepare parents for the outreach work in the first stage of the campaign.

The training was successful on many fronts. The materials that were distributed explained why and how the lead teacher project would be a partial corrective to systematic underinvestment and underachievement in low-income schools. Consequently, the presentation enabled many parents to more fully understand the lead teacher campaign as an investment in their children's education. Additionally, every aspect of the training emphasized participation, from its planning to the improvisational acting associated with a role play to specific forms of chanting. Finally, the parent-run meeting began and ended on time, which signaled to busy parents that their time was valued.

Each of these practice principles was in play during this meeting, and they facilitated both parent ownership of the lead teacher proposal and interest in returning for follow-up meetings. Such an outcome was not an accident or a product of parent predisposition, but the actualization of a disciplined, reflective, participatory practice. This is but one concrete example of how practice choices influenced the reach and effectiveness of the lead teacher campaign.

Anna Santos, a parent, remarked that "when I saw how many teachers had come through my children's school in the last few years, how much turnover, I began to see the connection to the lead teacher work. It really opened my eyes. If teachers come and go like that, we need to do something to keep our best teachers, to make them better." The data presented to parents by CC9 richly illustrated the connection between principal and teacher turnover and the academic performance of students. As well, the substantial gap in per capita student investments between neighboring suburban communities and District 9 was vividly conveyed to participants. During the course of the training, new parents, like their predecessors, gradually concluded that improved academic performance was largely dependent on stemming the tide of professional migration out of the community. As well, new parents were angered by the different levels of investment in public education in low-income and upper-middle-class communities. As parents came to understand the underinvestment in education in poor neighborhoods, many concluded that an investment in lead teachers could serve as a partial corrective. A number of new parents were sufficiently aroused by the training to make a commitment to both CC9 and, more specifically, to the petition campaign. The particular flavor of the event is conveyed through this exchange between organizers: Anjelica stated, "The parents I brought enjoyed it. They enjoyed the learning and the skit. They want to come to more meetings like it." In turn Eric Zachary noted, "I thought it was a good combination of inspiration and substance." Allen concluded this exchange by suggesting, "I thought the strengths were the facts, that facts were broken down for people, and they kept repeating it, chanting it, and hearing it. They owned it. Also the skit involved parents, and it was fun."

The training clearly conveyed an urgency and reasoning for the organizing campaign. As well, it heightened parents' sense of injustice and fed their anger about the conditions of the schools. As Jasper notes in "The Emotions of Protest," "responses to moral shocks vary greatly in the emotions that ensue. Most people, in most cases, resign themselves to unpleasant changes, certain that governments . . . do not bend to citizen protest. But others . . . channel their fear and anger into righteous indignation and political activity" (409). The collective support, platform, and strategic direction offered by CC9 enabled new parents to choose an activism tethered to hope rather than withdrawal out of fear.

Reaching into the UFT Rank and File to Create Solidarity with the Lead Teacher Campaign

To wage a successful campaign for the lead teacher proposal, there would need to be a growing sense of solidarity, or at least partnership, between teachers and parents. Although CC9 leadership had worked effectively with UFT officials on specific issues, the sense of partnership was at best limited to a very small cohort of parents and union staff. Also, many of the organizers continued to harbor a distrust of the UFT's intentions. They questioned the union's commitment to working with parents as equal partners.

In an effort to mend this breach, Herb Katz suggested that the UFT sponsor an event to honor the work of CC9. Such an event was unprecedented. The UFT, which had a history of enmity with parent-led education reform initiatives, was publicly acknowledging the work of a community group led by black and Latino parents. The importance of the event to the UFT was signified, in part, by Randi Weingarten's interest in attending and speaking. Teachers from each of the CC9 schools would be in attendance to hear the concerns of parents. Katz suggested that as a sign of respect teachers should serve the parents dinner. "Eric said to me the parents would serve the meal, and I said 'absolutely not.' This is not what we are coming for. First of all, I said that this would be disrespectful and that we would serve the food. All of my colleagues served the food. When I first suggested it, I thought it would be a way of breaking down barriers." Katz also suspected that a party or celebration might promote new forms of relationships between teachers and parents: "I always believed that if you can get people together in a social atmosphere, you can get them talking and seeing each other differently."

Zachary saw the celebration as a boost to both CC9 and the impending campaign. When asked how he thought the event would add to the legitimacy of the lead teacher campaign, he responded:

It adds legitimacy across the board. They gave us a feeling of power. And with the teachers involved, it obviously gives the union's stamp of approval. And then you have their institutional players there, like the local instructional superintendent and people from the Department of Education. It just sends a message that the UFT is

> prepared to have its words and actions synchronized. It gives every-
> body a shot in the arm and a legitimacy when a major institution
> like the UFT goes out on a limb and sponsors a reception like this.

Zachary also noted, however, that he didn't want the event to appear oppo-sitional to the DOE. He indicated that the campaign needed to reach for a triumvirate partnership for education reform "led by CC9 but with the sig-nificant collaboration of the UFT and the Region." It was with this in mind that invitations to the event were changed at the last minute to include regional administrators of the DOE as sponsors. This change, although a small detail in the development of the event, illustrates a consistent, strategic focus on building collaboration and not slipping unconsciously or unneces-sarily into oppositional tactics. This last-minute change, and the flexibility of the UFT, was viewed by Zachary as richly illustrative of "the relationship between CC9 and the UFT. There is a level of give and take, there's a level of risk taking, there is a level of proactivity, all of which are the ingredients of a serious collaboration." Importantly, Zachary saw the UFT event as "a kickoff for the lead teacher campaign."

At the event, the UFT regional representative, Vince Gaglione, spoke about "the need to create new learning though teacher and parent partner-ship." Katz publicly reaffirmed the UFT's commitment to a partnership when he noted, "For all of these years we have been apart it makes no sense. A child can't learn if the two most important adults in his life are not communicat-ing or trusting each other. . . . They need us to be together." He then went on to more specifically affirm the important work of CC9 parents: "There are real heroines and heroes in the CC9 collaboration. You have done some-thing that they thought couldn't be done. You have brought CBOs, parents, the UFT, and principals together in one room."

Yvonne Torres, the regional representative, echoed Katz's remarks in her speech. "This is a unique moment. Every constituency is here, and they are all concerned about the children. A lot of us talk about collaboration, but I never recall it happening." She further remarked, "This is one more step toward being more passionate and making the schools work, having a team and many of us not feeling so all alone." Weingarten, president of the UFT, offered important support for the campaign:

> The UFT pledges that on the platform, we will help you drive the
> agenda, a shared agenda. . . . We are with you on resources coming to

the Bronx, on assuring that every teacher is terrific in front of their class, on safety and sufficient supplies. If there are stresses and strains, well, we will have to struggle to walk in each other's shoes so that we can stay in this together.

Parent speakers emphasized both the historic gravity of the event and the task at hand. Ocynthia Williams noted:

As a parent I am overwhelmed by the respect and commitment that the UFT has shown to the parents of CC9. I want to say you are the first group to hear us and treat us as partners. We have gotten support from our collaborators, but we need even more support. We want this celebration to kick off our lead teacher campaign. We are going to collect ten thousand signatures to show our power to Bloomberg and Klein.

Denise Moncrief added, "This is historic. We are giving you a weapon to fight for our children, a piece of paper in the folder. It is a petition. There is an assignment for each of the teachers and parents. We are asking each of you to take one of those sheets and get it filled out."

Many parents remarked that the UFT celebration was a turning point for them. They began to see the teachers less as the obstacle to their children's education and more as a potential partner in need of support. The UFT event reinforced for parents the importance of the lead teacher initiative to their children's education, while simultaneously recasting teachers as approachable, human, and potential allies. As Carmen Jerez noted, "That UFT meeting in January was really great. It was really good—the teachers and parents really need to get together and have real conversations. Many of the teachers are parents too. So we as parents need to know how the teachers think." Roz Chambers added, "What was different was that the principals and teachers were at the table for the first time with us. It made me feel like a partner sitting at the table. It created a lot more trust, and that hasn't always been there between parents and teachers."

As discussions between parents, teachers, and UFT officials occurred on a more or less equal footing, members of CC9 began to see that their own experiences with the schools had merit and were integral to improving public education. This realization did not occur in a single moment but rather unfolded through a series of events that affirmed and developed parent expertise. The UFT event was particularly dramatic and meaningful to parents precisely because professional teachers had chosen to publicly honor their work. CC9 parents began to reshape these relatively static understandings of expertise as they effectively applied and refined what they knew to alter the professional discourses regarding neighborhood schools.

CBO Accountability and the Persistent Strains of Collaborative Work

Consolidating both parent and teacher support for the campaign was, of course, critical. However, a dilemma that compromised CC9 parent organizing was the continued unevenness of the six CBOs' contributions. Each CBO developed and committed to baseline expectations of increased parent participation in spring 2003. These expectations of expanded, consistent participation were not consistently met by all of the CBOs. Zachary described his concern:

> I see a kind of lack of fire, kind of verging on good or mediocre
> work, which simply isn't sufficient for the outcomes we are shooting
> for. There is a critical back and forth between local and CC9 wide
> work, and that is why we are at such a critical juncture now. We're
> rebuilding the local bases or building them up at the same time
> we are preparing to really launch a sophisticated and complicated
> CC9 campaign on lead teachers. We all have to escalate our work,
> or we will fail.

A number of executive directors recognized the problem and struggled to explain it. Brother Ed Phelan of Highbridge Life Center noted that "each organization has a different investment in this project. How close to the heart of the organization this is. So there are varying degrees of participation. Maybe with more money on the table there would be greater participation . . . funding is always close to the heart." Brother Ed also remarked that some groups appeared to have less commitment to the very local school work because their orientation to organizing is different from CC9's:

> Some groups, I think, feel we talk about things too much; they want
> action. They are more heavily into organizing broader, bringing out
> a lot of people, showing your power. It is just a different mentality.

So that may explain why at times they may have less enthusiasm for the smaller work that can lead to the bigger work. Maybe they are just impatient.

Jack Doyle acknowledged that the contributions of member organizations varied substantially. He wondered if some of the CBOs were in this for the longer run:

> I don't know if we are going to reach a point where some of the groups are going to tire of this and decide it is not what they want to do. Having one organizer out of a staff of eighty or a hundred people just doesn't make this an integral part of an organization. Some of the organizations are saying $55,000 is nice, but they are not going to add another dime. Organizers' work is hampered because they don't have some of the things they need, like access to a photocopy machine.

He also questioned member agencies' depth of commitment to the project by noting their unwillingness to invest some of their own resources in CC9: "All of the organizations are different. I don't know how many, if any, of the organizations have decided that this work is so important that they're going to devote some of their fund development capacity to try to give them more of their resources. I don't know."

Zachary cites agency culture, life span, size, and leadership as powerful variables in explaining the differences in agency contributions. Some of the distinctions that separate even the strongest agencies are richly described in the following passage:

> The most successful of the groups have an agency culture that is not bureaucratically encrusted. If it is not as large an agency, for example, they can work more flexibly, and parent organizing doesn't get lost inside it. And then you put on top of that a visionary leader, and you can see why it works. With some groups I think part of it is personality. The director is not a bureaucrat, there's an openness, a fluidity there, and even though it is an older agency, it is not encrusted. They have other organizers, they operate out of a store-front, and they are doing similar things, so they are not as isolated.

In contrast, other groups much larger and much older, are more encrusted without perhaps the visionary leadership I described. Although because of the talents of the organizer they are building something in the local schools. But still I wonder, is this the type of agency to enlist for this organizing work?

The Complexity of Establishing and Enforcing Collaborative Standards

Organizing work is, by definition, messy. It is especially messy when it involves agencies with distinctive histories, records of accomplishment, and work cultures. This delicate tightrope between flexible standards of accountability, on the one hand, and uniformity of both purpose and contribution, on the other, is difficult to walk. This tightrope is particularly precarious because agencies, when pushed too hard, can always choose to exit from a collaborative arrangement. This was an especially vexing problem with a looming campaign that required substantial agency commitment, a circumstance that CC9 faced in early 2004. Zachary feared that if the campaign proved unsuccessful, the viability of community organizing as a principal strategy to reform public education would be damaged. Zachary described the consequent need for CC9 agencies to recalibrate their commitment to the work and the campaign:

> We're at a new juncture . . . where the CBOs' investment has to be
> raised to the next level for CC9 to be successful. If CC9 is successful
> in the next stage, then it will strengthen all of the organizations. If
> CC9 fails, there will be added cynicism concerning the possibility of
> community organizing to be a successful strategy to improve local
> public schools in New York City. So, it's in all of our interests for
> CC9 to succeed. The CBOs have to put more emphasis on CC9 for
> their own organization's self-interest as well as CC9's.

It was with this in mind that Zachary challenged member agencies to meet specific standards of parent involvement, both within their assigned schools and in CC9 during early winter 2004. He proposed a tentative structure of accountability, and each of the CBOs agreed to meet these new standards in rather short order.

Although verbal commitments were made during a relatively cool meeting, the test would come in the heat of the organizing work as agencies were challenged to up their ante, even as other demands intensified. Critically, Zachary understood that the CBOs would respond to the challenge differentially. By setting a clear bar of expectation and accountability, however, Zachary's intention was for each member agency to more equally bear the CC9 workload during the lead teacher campaign. The ongoing struggle of holding individual agencies accountable for collaborative work would remain a persistent area of tension and struggle for CC9. Zachary underscored how this dilemma, if disregarded or unchecked, could undermine the very essence of the CC9 experiment:

> My job is to keep our eye on the prize. My job is to facilitate mutual accountability. The things that I'm putting out here are things we committed to two years ago, that we agreed to again back in July. So, I'm not asking anything that we as a group have not already committed to. I'm saying the performance has not met the expectation. We don't want to end up like the school system where accountability becomes a meaningless term. We're trying to model a different kind of accountability.

The Campaign for Lead Teachers: Organizing for Educational Justice

The sources of pressure to advance the lead teacher proposal were threefold. To begin with, community support was heightened through the petition campaign. The goal was to collect ten thousand signatures. Also, CC9 was engaged in foundation fund-raising to demonstrate that a community group had both the will and capacity to raise some part of the budget necessary to implement a lead teacher program. CC9 believed that if it could raise substantial dollars privately, it would intensify the pressure on the city and, more specifically, on the DOE to invest public money. Zachary anticipated that the legitimacy of the campaign would grow as foundations invested their currency, literally and figuratively, in the lead teacher proposal. Finally, private discussions were also taking place with political leaders and members of the education establishment to develop "insider" networks of support. These three elements were often referred to by organizers as the "three-legged stool" upon which the campaign rested. Each of the legs was expected to create the requisite pressure from parents, the UFT, politicians, and foundations necessary to move the proposal forward.

The Three Sources of Tactical Pressure: Foundation Investment, External Political Support, and Parent Mobilization

It is important to reiterate that CC9's theory of change suggested that lead teachers would begin to provide the supports necessary to upgrade the performance of classroom instructors who were often very young, inexperienced, and prone to turnover. In addition, advocates of the lead teacher campaign hoped that this would begin to change the culture of support within the schools and, over time, result in less turnover. Repeatedly, both the DOE and the UFT cited the turnover of teachers as a particularly destabilizing influence on learning and instruction within the poorest schools in the city and as a primary explanation for the low achievement scores of students. In sum, CC9 perceived lead teachers as a critical tool in promoting the retention necessary to upgrade the performance of both teachers and students.

No community group in New York City had ever successfully undertaken an organizing campaign focusing on core learning and instruction issues. Clearly, this was a very steep hill with an array of obstacles that CC9 was attempting to climb. Even Zachary was initially cautious in describing the outcomes such a campaign might produce:

> We are hoping to raise about $2.2 million. If CC9 can raise half a million of that, I would be very excited and happy. . . . The overall budget is $2.2 million; the fallback is $825,000, so there is lot of variability there. The important thing for CC9 is that we see this program by September. To be frank, I think that logistically it will be very complicated and difficult to do the whole program by September. It would require an incredible number of lead teachers and interviewing a very large number of applicants. If we are able to recruit twenty teachers, two per school, it will be an amazing victory. And that is the realistic outcome I am hoping for.

These anticipated levels of investment were redefined during the course of the campaign. After preliminary queries were made through the IESP, a number of foundations asked CC9 to submit a lead teacher proposal. These foundations included Booth Ferris, The New York Community Trust, and the Carnegie Foundation. By March 2004, Booth Ferris had made a commitment to the lead teacher proposal. Over the course of approximately five months, CC9 raised $350,000 of the estimated $2.2 million budget that was described as necessary for full implementation of the project.

The foundation's decision to fund the proposal was well timed. It occurred as the campaign was picking up steam. This convergence was not accidental. Members of the IESP staff, most notably Zachary and Norm Fruchter, had projected a timetable for submission that coincided with the earliest stages of lead teacher organizing in January. Zachary developed the written material and contacted some of the key decision makers at each of the foundations. Again, the IESP's role was significant in helping to marshal the access and expertise necessary to raise resources and, in turn, ratchet up the organizing pressure. The support extended by the foundations, although quite welcome, was not entirely anticipated. As Zachary noted, "In my mind we needed a foundation champion. Booth Ferris shocked me by so quickly offering to support it and with the amount of money they were thinking about."

Another leg of the campaign was mobilizing political support. As Zachary indicated, "In my mind we needed both a foundation and a political champion." The search for a political champion naturally led to the president of the Borough of the Bronx, Adolpho Carrion. A critical point of access to Carrion was the executive director of the Settlement Housing Fund, Carol Lambert. Again, access was not accidental but a product of the political and social networks that CC9 had developed over three years. Lambert was familiar with the work of CC9 through Doyle. A first meeting with Carrion went very well, according to Zachary, and concluded with the Bronx Borough president "basically giving his full support. Other than committing his money, he committed to writing a letter of support, being at a press conference, and brokering relationships with the Bronx City Council and New York State delegations." Subsequently, CC9 would reach out to a cross section of politicians and gain their endorsements for the lead teacher proposal.

The organizing plan was moving forward in an almost seamless manner. As Zachary remarked, "It was working. The strategy has been grassroots support through petitions, foundation support, and politician support, all of which we would then bring to bear in trying to leverage money out of Klein and Bloomberg, as a private–public partnership to start a model." The campaign, however, would succeed or fail on the basis of the support it received from parents.

The creation of a parent army to support the lead teacher proposal was the most essential element of the campaign. It involved an expansive number of parents needed for the day-to-day work of the campaign: planning strategies, attending meetings, and participating in outreach to the larger community. Parents were also needed to collect the petition signatures of members

of the community. From the very beginning, the goal of ten thousand signatures seemed out of reach. According to Anjelica Otero, "In the beginning
when we said ten thousand, it just felt like such a big number. When they said
ten thousand, I was totally skeptical. I said, 'Is this realistic?'" As the petition
campaign got under way, however, the goal appeared increasingly attainable:
"People have risen to the ambition of the petition campaign, and some of the
groups have taken this on in a very serious way."

The unevenness of coalition members' contributions continued. Nevertheless, CC9 leadership proved flexible. Zachary remarked, "Certain groups
have done so-so with the petition work, but that's the way it usually works
in a coalition. It's never going to be perfect in each part, but the whole point
of CC9 is that the whole is greater than its parts. And then you hopefully
strengthen these parts as the whole gets bigger."

Otero described how the parent energy associated with the petition
campaign grew. "As parents got out into the community really talking about
the lead teachers, they really began to embrace and to begin to understand
it." Otero noted further that "everybody took petitions, and everybody signed
up to collect one or two sheets. There was a lot of commitment from community members to make this happen." Frank Correa, a Highbridge organizer, described the intensity and breadth of the outreach to community
members: "We assigned parents to do their buildings. . . . And then we went
out in front of the schools, out to churches and community centers." There
was also an anticipated multiplier of pulling new parents into the work of
CC9 through the petition campaign. Correa underscored this point when
he explained that "our primary target was all parents. We wanted to involve
the parents. . . . I think the fact that you had people signing something, we
were able to follow up to make a phone call. . . . So for me this was not only
a petition outreach campaign, but it was also a good source of outreach
period." By March 2004, CC9 had met its goal of ten thousand signatures.

Public and Private Endorsements from Key Players

Throughout the early stages of the campaign, these three streams of organizing work were augmented by private conversations with critical decision
makers from both the UFT and the DOE. The UFT leadership was prepared
to stake some part of its reputation, both with rank-and-file membership
and in the larger world, on the development of a lead teacher program. For
the UFT, the project represented an opportunity to begin to create a career

ladder for the largest segment of its membership, classroom teachers. CC9 was proposing that lead teachers spend half their workday teaching and the other half supporting classroom instructors. Moreover, CC9 recommended a salary differential for lead teachers. The content of the proposal emerged out of conversations among CC9 members and in a series of meetings between parents and the UFT as well as the DOE leadership.

The UFT commitment to the campaign moved from a general agreement about the idea to a deepening partnership regarding the specific elements of the proposal. This partnership was bolstered when the UFT agreed to involve part of their membership in the petition campaign.

CC9 also cultivated other relationships with critical players to create momentum for the lead teacher proposal. Parent leaders scheduled a meeting with the DOE senior official Michelle Cahill. She asked a member of the Department of Human Resources to attend because "DOE was already beginning to think about the translation of the lead teacher proposal into a formal job title." At the meeting, she offered tacit support by describing how the proposal and the objectives of the DOE leadership were consonant. Cahill indicated that

> their agenda is aligned with ours and with our Children First Reform Agenda. We have an alignment of interest. Whatever is happening in their particular schools or the level of leadership in the department, we are aligned with them. They also have a certain level of access which is beyond the school, beyond the regional superintendent. So they could call me, for example, which they did all of the time. This helped to move their agenda.

Simultaneously, CC9 convened meetings with Ellen Frazier, the chief of staff for the Bronx Borough president. These sessions led to Carrion's unqualified support for the proposal. Finally, meetings with the regional leadership of the DOE, including Superintendent Irma Zardoya and her deputy, Yvonne Torres, were organized by parent leaders. Although concerns were raised by DOE managers about lead teachers being released from classroom work half of the day, these early reservations faded over time.

Importantly, CC9 consistently employed a critical tactic: to first have small, private conversations with the DOE and the UFT decision makers about its change agenda before organizing more public events. These early private meetings provided the scaffolding for later public and private work with the DOE and the UFT. The intention was to first create a common language between groups, a foundation of trust, and an early shared understanding of particular ground rules, for example, prior warning before going public with the media. This prohibition of public disclosure was essential to private conversation, building the trust necessary for candor, risk taking, and a potential trajectory to agreement(s).

Rather quickly, actors offering private expressions of support were asked to lend the lead teacher campaign more public, concrete forms of political currency. For example, representatives from the UFT, DOE regional leadership, and CC9 attended the meetings with Carrion. A critical fund-raising meeting with Booth Ferris in March 2004 also included members of the UFT and the Region. At an earlier CC9 rally, key politicians, UFT leaders, and DOE administrators signed a public pledge of commitment to the lead teacher proposal.

Step by step, CC9 organized a collaboration between the UFT, the DOE, and community groups that gradually began to displace a historic, wary distrust. Zachary indicated that collaboration with the DOE was based on mutual power. "It's not a collaboration first and foremost because we like each other. It's a collaboration because we've been able to create the perception and the reality that we have significant power." Cahill, while acknowledging the importance of power, also pointed to the quality of CC9 work and the respect it engendered. She said, "I admire them because they are very dedicated. They've gone this really long way to understand that they can get the children in their neighborhood a much better education. And they work extremely hard to get that. They are very good organizers, and they're very capable. And you can trust that they are going to do what they say they are going to do."

The process unfolded in a developmental cycle that spiraled outward from private negotiations, which clarified stakeholder positions and concerns on lead teachers, to public positions that were expected to cohere around a single lead teacher initiative. The negotiation was very time sensitive because it had to elicit DOE support during the spring if there was to be any hope of implementation in fall 2004. If CC9 pushed too hard too quickly without first creating a solid foundation, the DOE might simply walk away from the table. Therefore, CC9 leadership needed to vigorously push its agenda to meet specific deadlines while remaining attentive to DOE leaders and any wavers in their support. Finally, and perhaps most important, parents and organizers needed to sustain a level of energy and commitment that was often daunting.

The intensifying campaign produced cascading demands that led to parent leaders putting other parts of their lives on hold as the campaign moved through its stages of organizing public rallies, privately garnering support from key players, and intensifying private and public pressure on the DOE to support the CC9 proposal. These steps occurred over a brief period—essentially four months—and every meeting with public officials demanded multiple preparatory sessions. Almost without exception, the leaders of CC9 met the challenges, pouring large parts of their time and energy into the campaign while simultaneously surrendering part of their private lives. As Moncrief remarked, "All of those nights coming home late, all those nights sitting up writing stuff, all those days off from work and fighting with my boss, all those evenings looking up information on the computer. It is like living through the civil rights movement." Veronica Rivera noted that "my time at CC9 is too important to give up. I will work part-time at a very well paid job to keep doing this."

Intensifying Pressure on the DOE

CC9 successfully executed the first stages of the campaign by the end of March. As noted, parents collected ten thousand signatures on petitions, the coalition raised private dollars to finance the proposal, and political support among Bronx politicians was growing. All of this occurred as the drumbeat to reform the New York City public school system was growing louder and louder. For example, the Campaign for Fiscal Equity (CFE), a nonprofit that developed a legal challenge, had been making steady progress to increase the financing of pubic schools. Their work resulted in a landmark legal decision to reallocate substantial public dollars to the New York City public schools.

Zachary described the convergence of the CFE, the political environment, and CC9's organizing:

Fortuitously, for CC9, two days before we met with Klein, Bloomberg gave a speech saying here is my vision of how the CFE money should be spent. And he talked about lead teachers, he talked about financial incentives to attract teachers to struggling schools, all of which is what our lead teacher proposal is all about. So the political stars have aligned themselves. I'm under no illusion that it's because of all of our grassroots organizing alone that has resulted in this moment; it is a combination of our work, the alliances we've built, and political opportunities.

In late March, a letter was sent by parent leaders to Chancellor Klein requesting a meeting. When the chancellor did not respond, parents made phone calls to his office. Almost immediately, the chancellor's office contacted the CC9 leadership office with a proposal to meet at DOE headquarters or the Tweed building on April 2 in the late afternoon. They requested that five representatives from the DOE meet with five representatives from CC9. CC9's counterproposal was that nine representatives from CC9 be at the meeting, one parent from each CBO, as well as Zachary, Otero, and Doyle. As the negotiation proceeded, however, CC9 was informed that the chancellor was excluding the UFT from this preliminary discussion. Zachary was in communication with both UFT and DOE officials on this point.

> Michelle Cahill says, "I really don't think the union can be there because they've requested bargaining on this issue, and this is not a bargaining meeting, so legally they can't be there." I then called Michelle Bodden and relayed that message. We both commiserated that this is fucked up, but we have to figure out a way to resolve this because we don't want to let this meeting go by.

What Cahill was alluding to was the UFT's request for an impact bargaining session on the specific job title of lead teacher in the ten schools. Impact bargaining takes place when either of the primary parties who have reached a collective bargaining agreement wishes to reopen negotiations over a salient issue. With CC9's support, the UFT sent a letter to DOE requesting impact bargaining over the lead teacher proposal. Perhaps for the first time in its history, the UFT request for bargaining on a collective bargaining issue was signed by a community member, a parent, Ocynthia Williams. This was another bit of evidence of the growing strength of the collaborative bond between CC9 and the UFT. Their mutual trust, however, would be severely tested in this moment.

Once the DOE intention was relayed to Weingarten, she essentially indicated that the arrangement for the meeting was untenable. According to Zachary, she also indicated "that if CC9 goes ahead with the meeting, it would seriously impact the collaboration." The following day, Zachary, Williams, and Bodden discussed the situation. Bodden reinforced Weingarten's message that CC9 should not move forward with the meeting. CC9 leadership was concerned about the steep costs likely associated with canceling. Zachary said to Bodden, "We can't afford to lose this meeting. If we lose this meeting, we're not going to get another meeting with Klein very easily at all this year, and then the lead teacher thing goes down the drain." He then raised the critical question, "Can't you trust CC9 not to betray your interest?"

This was a moment of crisis for CC9. If its leadership could not create a mutually agreeable compromise, the work of the past year would likely go up in smoke. This crisis had other reverberations for CC9. For example, ACORN, a member agency and a historic ally of the UFT, registered its concern about the impasse. Late in the evening, Zachary called Katz because "he understands what is at stake with this meeting. Also he trusts CC9 the most, based on his direct experience. . . . And so I said, 'Herb, I cannot speak for CC9, but what I can say is that if the union absolutely doesn't want us to go, we won't go. . . . But as you know, here is why I think we should meet, and you know we won't make any decisions.' So he says, 'Let me call Randi.'" Katz described his conversations with Zachary and Weingarten:

> Eric called me, and at that moment I knew exactly what would unfold, and I knew everything was fine. To tell you the truth, I never thought for a second they would go without us. I had faith in the relationship based on our collaboration. So I called Randi and said, "Eric said if you are insistent that they not go without us, they won't go." I knew exactly what she would say. She said, "OK, then they can go." Because the question was not, do they go, but under what conditions. She said they have to go, but then they have to insist that we be at the next meetings.

In retrospect, Zachary felt that the matter was poorly communicated to Weingarten, and that Katz as well as ACORN's John Kest helped to clarify CC9's continued commitment to the UFT: "Somehow, Randi got the notion that CC9 was going to the meeting with or without the union. That's never what I said or what I intended."

The prep discussion the night before the meeting with Klein was thorough. Materials were distributed on the lead teacher posting, and notes provided on key talking points by staff. As well, parent speakers were identified and prepped by key organizers. A number of precautions and questions informed parts of the discussion. Otero indicated that "everybody warned us;

Klein likes quick presentations. He is a quick read. Do it short and to the point. So we went over what if he doesn't come? What if he is ten minutes late? What if he comes for five minutes and leaves? What if he says there's no money? You know . . . back and forth, back and forth." At the conclusion of the meeting, parents were prepared to negotiate with the chancellor. Attendance at the prep session was declared a prerequisite for meeting with the chancellor.

As parents and staff entered the physical space where negotiations were to take place at DOE, they were surprised by the lack of privacy. They entered a spacious, open room where many meetings were occurring simultaneously. Otero explained, "It was one of these large rooms where there are many tables and there is no privacy. There were four groups meeting at the same time in this big open space. I felt a little put off, but then I remembered that the chancellor wants everyone to work in a bull pen—that is his attitude. That is how business is conducted." Otero indicated that from the beginning, the meeting did not go exactly as planned: "I noticed with some of the parent speakers they try to speak from the heart . . . and what happens is they move away from the prep and some part of what we are trying to accomplish gets lost."

Despite the loss of focus, the chancellor remained open and respectful. Moncrief remarked,

> I was very surprised. The meeting was very cordial, very friendly.
> I would admit something, I actually liked the man. He came across
> as very intelligent. I didn't get the sense that he was trying to blow us
> off or belittle us, or that he wasn't taking us seriously. . . . He heard
> us out, we heard him out. It was a very different, dynamic. Other
> politicians tend to underestimate the parents. . . . And he never
> walked in the door with that assumption.

Williams added: "He treated us with respect. He made parents feel that he was listening to what they had to say. He was friendly and funny and very welcoming."

After CC9's presentation, Klein quickly agreed that lead teachers were needed in District 9. That was an unexpected response, followed by another: "I don't want to sound like a big shot, but if you can make this work, I will give you the money for it. Continue with your fund-raising and whatever you don't meet, we will find it."

At this point in the conversation, the focus shifted from funding to the structure of the lead teacher program. Klein had a number of concerns. The chancellor did not want to overrecruit lead teachers from the instructional staff of other Bronx public schools. Zachary summarized the chancellor's point of view:

> He said the talent pool of teachers in the Bronx is limited. He wanted to make sure that we don't drain the best teachers from other struggling schools in the Bronx to come to our schools. So, he wanted to design this in a way that highly skilled teachers from more effective high-performing schools in New York City will be interested in coming to the South Bronx.

Of particular importance to the administrators of DOE was the time that lead teachers would be out of the classroom, and the distribution of lead teachers by grade. These issues had both economic and pedagogical implications. The more time out of the classroom, the more expense associated with the lead teacher program because other instructional staff would have to fill those vacancies. Equally important, the estimated number of lead teachers the project could afford was between thirty-six and fifty. Consequently, a decision needed to be made in defining the number of lead teachers needed to maximize impact. Throughout the discussion it was clear that the chancellor's remarks were casting one eye on the CC9 experiment and the other on a potentially larger, citywide lead teacher initiative. The CC9 effort was perceived as breaking new ground. The DOE wanted to put in place a local experiment that, if successful, could be transported to other parts of the city. Finally, both the chancellor and CC9 recognized that the lead teacher initiative required the support of the UFT. At the conclusion of the meeting, Klein explained, "I have union issues to work on. The UFT has requested impact bargaining."

During the course of the meeting, parents appeared overwhelmed and a bit disoriented. This resulted in a number of parent performances that organizers perceived as substandard. This is not a small point. No matter the preparation, effective community engagement with power brokers is a developmental process, and there are no performance assurances. Setbacks are an inevitable part of this complex dance between the historically dominant and dominated. At any given moment, differences in power, status, and confidence, and the attendant emotional fallout may prevent parents from fully expressing their fluency with the issues. In this instance, the aura of space and credentials caused some parents not to trust themselves or to forget what they had learned, recede, and allow professionals to dominate the conversation. Otero observed, "I don't know if they were intimidated or what. I kept saying to them, 'You guys have to jump in.' I kept pushing them, because I know they know the stuff." Zachary was disturbed by seasoned parent leaders' wavering on a specific point:

> He asked, is there a salary increase for the position? And one of our parent leaders played it wrong. She said, "Well, the money isn't really important . . . we want teachers who really love kids and want to take the position as new kinds of teacher leaders." We had gone over that point, and she just missed it. I knew immediately that he wasn't looking at it from that angle. He wanted to know, is this something that highly skilled teachers will gravitate to? So I knew this is a critical moment, and I jumped in immediately. I said that the proposal has a salary adjustment from the beginning.

Subsequent to the meeting, CC9 staff and parents celebrated and quickly moved to next-stage negotiations with the deputy chancellor, Carmen Farina. At that meeting, it became clear that the DOE wanted to revise parts of the CC9 proposal. Zachary summarized the meeting with Farina:

> She raised questions about how much time outside of the classroom lead teachers should have. We have been proposing 50 percent. She was proposing less than that. She was proposing money per session or variable salary adjustments as opposed to permanent salary increases. We were growing increasingly concerned that the department was going to move farther away from our original CC9 lead teacher proposal and that we would be in a significant fight.

After the meeting with Farina, CC9 felt that essential elements of the proposal were in jeopardy. Equally important, CC9 understood it could not impose its will on the DOE without allies. At this juncture, CC9 convened a meeting with the UFT. Five parent and staff representatives from CC9 met with Weingarten, Bodden, Katz, and Vince Gaglione. Here, Weingarten pledged her support to pressure the DOE to invest in the CC9 version of the lead teacher proposal. The form of pressure that Weingarten had in mind was a joint press conference, if "it came to that." The growing solidarity between CC9 and the UFT was especially evident during this meeting. Zachary noted:

> The atmosphere was warm and friendly. All of us at CC9 have built warm, very positive relationships with Michelle, Herb, and Vince. We've been working together for a year and a half. There's lots of camaraderie and chitchat back and forth. . . . I think everyone was fortified knowing that the union and CC9 would join forces to see this through.

In the middle of April, CC9 went on its annual retreat and spent time considering Farina's counterproposals. After an extended discussion, parents were willing to reduce the number of lead teachers from fifty-six to forty-five. They felt strongly, however, that to make a difference, lead teachers would require 40 to 50 percent release time from the classroom. Finally, parents were unanimous in their belief that a salary adjustment for lead teachers, negotiated with the UFT, would have to be part of any settlement. These responses to Farina's proposal were e-mailed to Cahill. A third meeting with the DOE was scheduled. The meeting included representatives from the Region, CC9, the UFT, and the DOE.

Like every other meeting with the DOE on lead teachers, the element of surprise was defining. It was almost immediately evident that the DOE was going to "fast-track" the CC9 lead teacher program. Zachary noted that "Farina opened the meeting by indicating that there was a cap of money that would be committed to our program, it was 1.6 million dollars. I think right up front it shocked the shit out of us." Farina, with very little prodding, agreed to a salary adjustment for lead teachers. She specifically indicated that there would be a guarantee of $10,000. Farina also signaled to the DOE lawyer in attendance, Dan Weissberg, that the impact bargaining sessions on salary adjustments needed to proceed immediately. Then, when reminded about the CC9 demand to have two lead teachers in a single classroom to preserve continuity and split time, she responded, "if that is what you want to do, then start with that as your model." Otero's summary remarks were apt: "She gave us almost everything that we were hoping for."

The discussion quickly moved to matters of implementation. DOE officials, particularly Farina, believed that the quality of training provided to lead teachers would substantially affect the success of the lead teacher program. The DOE and CC9 agreed that both attracting and retaining lead teachers would represent a significant challenge. Salary adjustments would provide only part of the incentive necessary for teachers to migrate to some of the poorest schools in the city and remain there. Instructional staff would also need to experience both the school and the lead teacher role as important to their professional development. A training component for lead teachers was part of DOE's larger intention to build a model program, with potential replicability. In a short period of time, CC9 had moved from an outsider community group with the unprecedented agenda of changing the instructional dynamics of South Bronx public schools to a partner with the DOE and the UFT in implementing its own agenda. The importance of this moment cannot be overstated.

Nailing Down the Agreement

Throughout the lead teacher campaign, CC9 had set September 2004 as the target date for implementing the program. Time was rapidly running out. For the program to be up and running by September, CC9 organizers and parents believed that prospective lead teachers needed to be interviewed in June. They had many tasks and decisions in the month and a half ahead of them. Again, CC9 pushed to achieve a daunting set of objectives in a relatively brief period of time. This created a pressure cooker environment for parents and organizers. As Allen remarked, "We had so much to get done and so little time to do it, at times it felt as if it was just going to be impossible to get it all done before September."

The next negotiating team meeting between the UFT, DOE, and CC9 was scheduled for May 13. Two weeks had passed, and little progress was made in developing a job description for the lead teachers. The department was represented by Dan Weissberg, chief labor attorney, and Betsy Arons, director of Human Resources. Weingarten's proposal echoed earlier understandings. She essentially proposed a $10,000 increase in salary for lead teachers and that 50 percent of the lead teachers' time be dedicated to working outside the classroom to support other instructors. At that point, Moncrief said, Weissberg indicated that "he would have to think about it."

Zachary recalls that "those of us from CC9 were astonished because we thought the department understood our urgency about this. We needed to post the position quickly, and Carmen Farina had said in our April 30 meeting that she hoped this would be concluded by May 3." Furthermore, the response of department representatives indicated that they had not seen the summary of prior agreements e-mailed by CC9 to Farina. This was a frustrating moment, raising serious concerns about the DOE's commitment to the project. Zachary was puzzled and disturbed: "What is going on? One arm of the department is negotiating without the knowledge of what the department had agreed to."

Alternatively, CC9 could see that the UFT shared its basic sense of urgency. As Williams remarked, "They arrived to the meeting with a proposal, and their president, Randi, was at the table. You don't have your president there unless you are really wanting to get things done." Williams and Moncrief voiced their disappointment with the DOE at the conclusion of the meeting. Moncrief recalled, "And then we were angry. We were able to give our opinion and say, 'Look, you are bull shitting. This is a stall tactic. You have already said what you are willing to do, and the UFT has said what they want, CC9 has said what we want, and it is all in front of you. Why do you have to take this back to DOE?" The parents understood that the slender thread of hope that the lead teacher program could be brought to life by September was breaking. Williams concluded that "the concern is that they're not going to come to an agreement in a timely fashion for us to get this thing going. And then it's not going to happen in September 2004."

Immediately after the meeting an e-mail was sent to Cahill, Klein, and Farina describing CC9's disappointment with the meeting. They raised questions about the reasons for the delay. The response from the DOE was to remain patient: "These things take time." Officials indicated that the Office of Management and Budget (OMB) was now an active participant in the decision making, and they had their own timetable for working out the details of the agreement. On the one hand, CC9 understood that part of the delay was located outside the DOE, with the OMB. The total of lead teachers, proposed salary increases, and budget allocation had yet to be calculated. This snag, however, was largely explained by Zachary as "the department not having done its homework. They hadn't worked the numbers. Also they were in an unproductive back and forth with the union on the same issue."

Although this was a dominant perspective, other explanations for the slow pace of DOE decision making also were expressed. CC9 parents and organizers recognized the sheer size of the bureaucracy, understaffing in key areas of the department's operations, and multiple pulls on executive staff involved in lead teacher negotiations as impediments to a more rapid DOE decision. Although they acknowledged these conditions, they did not accept them as reasonable explanations for the delay. The urgency of directing new resources and programs to the historically neglected schools of District 9 outweighed any real or imagined constraints experienced by the DOE. Parents and organizers were not willing to countenance any further delay. As Jamilla Anderson explained, "Providing an education that gives my kids the same kinds of opportunities as kids in the suburbs has been delayed too long." Delay was not an option. The lead teacher program was perceived as a down payment for years of neglect that required immediate redress. It was within this historic context of underfunded schools and underachieving students that CC9 was unwilling to tolerate delay, no matter how rational the explanation.

CC9 organizers recognized that by intensifying the pressure on the DOE, they would risk future collaborative ventures and, more immediately, the fate of the lead teacher program. To date, negotiations had proceeded privately and were more or less cordial. As the fight for the lead teacher program became more public and contentious, however, the good will necessary for collaboration was in jeopardy. It was within this context that CC9 struggled with a number of pressing tactical questions: How high do you raise the ante to speed up the process? What are the thresholds of confrontational tactics that, if passed, may boomerang and hurt the long-term prospects for school reform and the lead teacher program? How long could CC9 wait before the very possibility of implementing the lead teacher proposal by fall 2004 disappeared? These were but a few of the most important questions that CC9 parents had to quickly address in order to move forward in the campaign.

Again, CC9 was setting a course in essentially uncharted waters. No other community group had as effectively balanced advancing an agenda for school reform from the outside while maintaining a respected insider voice during negotiations. The DOE's unwillingness to use its authority to finalize a settlement pointed to the need to intensify pressure on key decision makers. Zachary elaborated:

> Obviously the balance you are trying to strike and always wondering
> if it is the right balance is with DOE. The balance is most compli-
> cated by the education bureaucracy because they are the decision
> makers. They have the power to do these things, the union does not.
> And I think a bureaucracy truly doesn't know how to be a partner. It
> is not part of their culture to be a partner in a meaningful way. And
> so they are the target, especially as things are delayed because they

have the authority to change policy in a way that nobody else does. That's the nature of being in authority.

What CC9 struggled with was whether or not to challenge the DOE publicly. As impatience mounted, many parents suggested going to the press or staging a very militant demonstration that would attract media attention. Others were not persuaded that tactics should move so abruptly from negotiation to public confrontation. After an intense discussion during a late evening meeting in May, a decision was made to employ more confrontational tactics. Parents agreed that it was necessary to signal a significant change in tactics to the DOE while still leaving the necessary space for ongoing negotiation. Otero described this balance when she noted, "we need to keep the lines of communication open and nontoxic so that the relationship can grow while pushing them in new ways to get it done."

Of particular concern was preserving as much trust as possible while changing course. It was determined that every step of the way the DOE needed to be apprised of CC9's actions and its disappointment. CC9 would delay calling a press conference, which was essentially a declaration of war, until the very last minute. Zachary described CC9's thinking at this moment:

> You give them a heads up and say we talked to you a week ago and nothing has happened. We changed our strategy accordingly. You can't expect people from the South Bronx, given the history of government neglect and lying, to wait indefinitely. Then you have to take some risks, but even then we decided not to go to the press. We need to have some kind of direct action without going to the press yet. Once we go to the press, the whole relationship with DOE shifts.

DOE administrators, particularly Cahill and Farina, were concerned that CC9 would take actions that would harm the process. When e-mails and faxes flooded Tweed, the building where the DOE is headquartered, after the last failed meeting, Cahill reached out to CC9 leaders to assure them that the process was moving as fast as possible. She also indicated that because the agreement would have citywide implications, decision makers were slow in signing off. As Zachary explained, "That is why we backed off a bit and didn't do a press conference." Cahill and Farina again reminded parents that they needed to be both judicious and patient. Farina also warned CC9 not to move to public actions, because they would threaten the negotiations and funding for the project. After a three-week lull, however, CC9's patience was rapidly evaporating.

CC9 planned an intermediate action for May 21. On that date, parent leaders delivered the ten thousand petition signatures in support of the lead teacher proposal to Klein, Cahill, and Farina. Shortly thereafter, on May 26, CC9 decided to stage a quiet action at Tweed. CC9 called DOE officials to, as Moncrief put it, "let them know we were coming." A group of about twenty-five parents and organizers gathered on the front steps of the building and asked to meet with either the chancellor or deputy chancellor. They carried red tape as a symbol of bureaucracy snarling progress; they also carried scissors—a sign of hope. As Moncrief explained, "After the deal dragged for three weeks, CC9 took some action, so they had parents deliver a white box, red tape, and a pair of scissors to the chancellor's office to cut the red tape, because at that point it really was just about red tape." After much negotiation between guards at the front desk and CC9 leaders, it was agreed that one parent would present the symbols of hope and delay to the chancellor's office. The message was heard. Shortly thereafter, on May 28, another meeting with the DOE and UFT was convened.

The May 28 meeting was a watershed moment for the lead teacher campaign. There were about ten participants from the DOE, UFT, and CC9. At the very outset, Cahill announced that "we think we have an agreement." The most significant items in the city and union agreement were a $10,000 salary increase and 50 percent release time for lead teachers. As Zachary noted, "A deal! We uncorked a bottle of champagne so that everybody could celebrate."

The final agreement was signed by principal decision makers on June 10. The following week, the *New York Times* reported that the lead teacher agreement had citywide implications. Zachary, reflecting on the complex reasons for this important step forward, emphasized the importance of historic opportunity, union–community partnership, relationships with key DOE decision makers, and the critical, independent role played by CC9:

> I think really this is a situation where change is a result of a complex
> set of factors. Clearly the relationship we built with the UFT is
> important. That the union had advocated for lead teachers in
> previous negotiations and got nowhere. . . . I would bet that that if
> we did this campaign in isolation from the union, we wouldn't have
> won. Second, it's relationships. The fact that Michelle Cahill, the

senior advisor to Klein, comes out of the CBO world, knows Norm well, knows me, respects our work. The Campaign for Fiscal Equity winning the lawsuit and the very strong likelihood of hundreds of millions of dollars coming down the pike in the next years to New York City schools got the department and Klein to think about how to use that money. All of that combined with good grassroots organizing on the part of CC9, politician support, petition support, persistence with all of the power players, created a gestalt that allowed this to come to be. And clearly if we were not spearheading this, without our persistence, without our listening, and giving respect to all parties, this would have fallen apart.

The achievement of CC9 was multilayered. It had succeeded as an "outsider" community agency in winning public education reform. Subsequently, CC9's focus shifted to the complex insider work of developing a public program. In the midst of maintaining and building its relationship with the DOE and UFT, CC9 was often caught in the cross fire of the intensifying enmity between management and workers. Even in those very difficult moments, however, CC9 managed to sustain a working relationship with the leadership of both the UFT and the DOE through negotiation, accumulated goodwill, and collaborative discipline.

Critically, the development of a lead teacher program converged with the interests of both the UFT and the DOE. As noted, the UFT wanted to create a career ladder for classroom teachers, while the DOE understood the need to create opportunities for professional development in order to retain and grow a cadre of effective instructors in the city's poorest schools. But even with this convergence of interests, the program was not primarily created out of the mutual needs of these powerful institutional actors. Importantly, the UFT had tried and failed in the past to independently advance a lead teacher proposal. The reform agenda was advanced by the organized, persistent efforts of a community group that understood and acted on a strategic opportunity. More to the point, the fuel for change came from outside the system, rather than from the inside.

The history of education community organizing is fraught with examples of exclusive reliance on confrontational tactics to promote needed change. Some of these campaigns were successful, and others failed to get the education establishment to bend. In general, however, none of those efforts was successful in changing the learning and instructional conditions within pubic schools and, consequently, did not have a substantial impact on student achievement.

CC9 learned from prior stages of organizing work. Its intention was to engage in the more complex practices of confronting power when necessary, while simultaneously struggling to maintain the language, process, and tactics of collaboration to build trust with critical sectors of the power structure. While stocks of trust were built and depleted depending on the demands of the campaign, the desire to work collaboratively remained constant. At times, this balance was tenuous, but in the end CC9 managed it successfully.

CC9 parents and organizers had allocated far more time, a precious resource, to finalizing the agreement than they had anticipated. Once CC9 concluded its outsider organizing campaign for lead teachers, it was welcomed to participate as an insider during the first stages of program implementation. The Region, UFT, and CC9 had to rapidly identify and interview a qualified cohort of lead teacher candidates to launch the program by September. This task was further complicated by the unprecedented involvement of the UFT and parents in the hiring process. It was agreed that representatives from the UFT, CC9, and the Region would review files and interview candidates during a first-stage screening of applicants. Final candidates would then be referred to a committee of teachers, parents, and the principal in each of the ten CC9 schools. Working out historic differences between participants in the midst of decision making, developing an infrastructure to carry out the work of the group, and achieving greater clarity about the professional qualities most critical to the work of lead teachers were just a few of the challenges facing the committee. These challenges further intensified the pressure-cooker environment as the September deadline drew nearer.

From Outside Organizer to Inside Implementer of School Reform

CC9's temporary transition from an outside initiator to an inside administrator of change was difficult but necessary. Both roles are essential to developing a fuller voice for citizens in any project designed to push large-scale public institutions to be more responsive to their needs. In this instance, such inclusion assigned value to the unique experience of parents, who daily wrestle with the failures and hopes of public education. CC9's groundbreaking role as a partner with the DOE and UFT in hiring professional staff or in the implementation phase of reform must be situated within the larger context of democratizing public-sector decision making through the creation of a more capable and powerful citizenry. Although CC9 derived a deep satisfaction in the short term from its lead teacher victory, that moment was short-lived. Quickly, it needed to turn its attention to the next challenge: hiring the first cohort of lead teachers in New York City.

Hiring Lead Teachers

Early in the hiring process it was determined that the $1.6 million from the DOE and the $350,000 from foundations could finance thirty-six lead teachers for the ten CC9 schools. Deliberations regarding the equitable distribution of resources resulted in a decision to allocate four lead teachers each to eight of the schools, and two each to the two remaining, smaller schools. The hiring process involved a two-step screening. In the first stage, a central committee composed of three CC9 members, three UFT representatives, and three regional administrators reviewed applicants and conducted an initial interview. Applicants were screened on the basis of a number of criteria, including teaching experience, advanced certification, commitment, and capacity. In the second stage, candidates went to each of the schools to be interviewed by a committee of teachers, parents, and the school's principal.

Part of the challenge from the beginning was enabling participants with different professional status and access to power to build effective working relationships. Different cultural assumptions embedded in organizations such as the DOE and CC9 about decision-making processes and professional prerogatives required constant attention. Zachary described the atmosphere thus:

What was interesting was when the teachers met with the principals, the whole tone changed. This whole sense of a hierarchy of different kinds of power being in the room, you could feel it. The teachers were less comfortable talking with principals. They were more defensive, it was more us versus them rather than trying to figure out how to put the program in place. Oh man, it was like night and day with principals in the room or outside. So that was a challenge. The school system is based upon this hierarchical kind of command-and-control structure. But CC9, we operate differently. By no means did we pussyfoot around, but we tried to listen to them. Our intent was that everything is not written in stone. We are going to try and construct this with you. Critically, though, the message that the principals got from the chancellor, the message that the principals got from Ms. Zardoya, was that this thing has to work.

As the hiring process moved into the second phase, it became evident that, as with every other aspect of the lead teacher program planning, the process would be hampered by a scarcity of time. The interviewing was initiated in early July, and hiring had to be completed by the beginning of August in order to implement the program in September. An initial ad for the position paid for by CC9 and costing $10,000 was placed in the *New York Times*. The position was also advertised on both UFT and DOE Web sites. The tight timetable would have consequences for the hiring process.

Hiring during the summer, particularly from mid-July through August, meant that principals and teachers were often not available because of vacation schedules. Additionally, the late advertisement of the position resulted in a much smaller than expected candidate pool. Consequently, the position was readvertised. Because the process was rushed, interviews were very brief, generally between twenty and thirty minutes. This affected both the depth and breadth of questioning. As Williams noted, "It has been chaotic. Sometimes you just have to close your eyes and go on faith." Of particular concern to organizers and parents was the unavailability of principals because of vacation schedules. The UFT assured CC9 that teacher representatives would participate in first- and second-stage screening. The nonparticipation of principals, however, would mean that critical leadership, essential to the success of the program, would be less inclined to support it. Some might feel left out of the process and resent the presence of a new professional cohort. Zachary noted, "The principals don't understand. . . . Number one, the Region didn't ask them, if you had a choice, where would you want to place them? Number two, you may not have a choice based on the applicant pool; be prepared. They haven't done that. We've done that preparation with CC9 parents."

Williams described the tension for CC9 parents: "Once again, the schools don't get much choice or play. You know, I guess that was always going to be a problem as we saw time running out. We kind of saw it in June, when it happened so late." The second-stage participation of local schools in decision making had to be weighed against the pressing need to get the program under way by September. It was in this second stage, however, that a broader cross section of parents could participate in both the interviews and hiring decisions. The parents understood this trade-off and were willing to subordinate their desire to participate in order to expedite implementation of a program that they believed was long overdue. More to the point, democratic participation was consciously traded off in favor of the more pressing concern for redistributive justice, or getting new critical supports and expertise into the schools as quickly as possible. Equally important, this committee work with the UFT and DOE enabled parents to more clearly understand the common ground they shared with teachers, principals, and regional administrators in wanting to improve the schools, and thus built increased trust.

Clearly, in the midst of the whirlwind of pressures and counterpressures, rapid accommodations were made to sustain the momentum for change. Moncrief expressed frustration with the committee's hiring criteria. She noted that early on in the process shared standards were quickly abandoned. She described her disappointment:

> I thought that CC9 rolled over on the lead teachers having to have
> five years experience. . . . Because one of the major issues with
> teachers is that they don't have that kind of experience. . . . I don't
> object to compromise, it's part of life. But I feel there are some areas
> where you just don't compromise. This was one of those areas for
> me that was the final straw. I left the committee.

Overall, however, very few differences emerged between parents, teachers, and administrators in the ranking of candidates. As Rivera remarked, "There was a general consensus. We worked very well together."

Throughout the process, CC9 was caught in the push-pull of responding to the mounting demands of hiring and neglecting pressing organizing work. Zachary noted that such a trade-off was necessary in the short run, but that a new balance between service implementation and organizing would have to be achieved in the longer run.

> This is a moment of implementation, and that is the bullet we've got
> to bite. . . . Come September, we've got to figure out how to do this
> in a way that doesn't sap our energy. This has a different rhythm.
> You know with interviews, it's time, there are real deadlines, there
> are thirty-six different people you know you are interviewing until
> you get to thirty-six. But if all we do this coming year is focus on
> ensuring that it's implemented, well, then in effect we become a
> service program and not an organizing one. Somehow we have to

figure out a way to consolidate our victory and presence in the ten schools while simultaneously broadening our political presence, our political power, and our range of influence within the region.

Historically, the dual role of organizing for change and implementing service programs has been straddled with various degrees of success by, for example, the battered women and housing/homelessness movements. In general, the intensifying, expansive demands of building programs have sucked resources from the less immediate but compelling need to invest in more organizing for a larger change movement. The urgency of meeting concrete needs at the door, whether for battered women, the homeless, or underachieving students, is often experienced as more compelling than the work of organizing. Critically, resistance to such a tendency requires a leadership with an internalized understanding of the concrete losses associated with abandoning organizing in favor of providing services.

At this particular moment, CC9 was carrying a disproportionate share of the responsibility for hiring lead teachers. The Region essentially turned hiring over to CC9. The DOE's limited participation was, in part, a statement of trust in the expertise and decision making of the UFT and CC9. As Rivera noted, "They trust us to schedule the interviews and do it professionally. They've totally turned it over to us. It's pretty remarkable."

The DOE's decision was also attributed to the fact that they were overwhelmed by other demands. CC9 refused to demonize the Region for its unwillingness or inability to more fully participate in this early stage of implementation. It remained steadfast in its desire and hope to build collaborative relationships over the long run. CC9 consistently posed the question: How do we take the collaboration with the Region to a next stage? This question was raised throughout the process of lead teacher hiring.

In a six-week period, committee members managed, despite obstacles of time, a small candidate pool, and the underinvestment by the DOE in the hiring process, to meet the objective of hiring thirty-six lead teachers before the beginning of the new school year. The sense of urgency was consistently evident in the pace of decision making. Equally important, the experience of interviewing candidates vividly highlighted the potential contribution of lead teachers to the ten CC9 schools. Williams noted,

> There were some lead teachers who seem really committed to the kids, real knowledgeable about education, and showed real

leadership possibility. There are a bunch of them who are really excited about becoming lead teachers. So you can see their enthusiasm. You put thirty-six of them together, give them some training, there is potential for them to change some things.

Zachary refined this observation when he noted that "there are differences between the people we hired. Some are outstanding, others are going to be good but will need a lot of support to get it done. But we never accepted anyone to just fill the role, to fill out the thirty-six, we held to our standards."

The next school year would escalate the external demands on CC9 organizers and parents. In the fall, CC9 with the UFT and DOE convened a series of trainings for the lead teachers. Both Klein and Weingarten addressed participants, signaling the importance of the project to both the community and the larger city. Some part of the next year's work would be constructed in the back and forth between consolidating the lead teacher victory, on the one hand, and organizing to expand the base of CC9, on the other. As in the past, the recomposition of roles would be calibrated to create a best-fit relationship to the demands of specific situations. The urgent need to change the conditions inside and outside the schools to better assure the academic achievement of students, however, would remain in the foreground.

III

The Future of Education Reform

7

Growing Community Power

Spheres of tension are part of any organizing landscape and require constant calibration and recalibration regarding next steps and best balance in any given moment of a campaign. The organizer must be flexible, cognizant of tensions, and capable of determining when and how to respond. The last point is especially critical. Organizing has a fragile ecology of stakeholders, opportunity, and power distribution. It is the organizer's role to determine when it is most critical or opportune to recalibrate the emphasis of the work. These strategic or tactical choices are often made in relationship to persistent dilemmas that require new responses. CC9 often chose to not address specific threads of a dilemma at a particular moment, consciously. This may seem like a contradiction. How can an organizer consciously neglect elemental tensions within the work? It is done as part of a larger assessment of the task at hand and available resources. For example, the need to move the lead teacher campaign forward was part of a larger calculation of opportunity, shifts in power, and CC9 legitimacy. It was always understood that by emphasizing lead teacher organizing districtwide, local school-based work would suffer.

Cost-benefit calculations were also made in relationship to individual CBOs' contributions to the collaborative effort. Critically, agency accountability was emphasized at the beginning and in the aftermath of campaigns, not during the hard push to change the schools. Such diversion of resources and attention was calculated as too costly to building momentum. Time and again, the strategic decision making of CC9 organizing was informed by assessing the benefits and costs of emphasizing one aspect of the work at the expense of another. These responses did not guarantee success. They were an informed gamble derived from the craft of making the best organizing judgments within the very complex, shifting terrain of change work.

Questions continuously emerged about the wisdom of the choices made. Does CC9 have the power to create a new type of classroom instructor, the lead teacher? Can the change be implemented by the beginning of the new school year? Do parents have enough commitment to the proposal to fight for it? Can the many power players who have a history of animus be brought together around a proposal for change? The questions were a reminder of both the daunting challenges faced by CC9 and the lack of certainty regarding outcome. As well, the search for the best practice in the midst of a complex campaign was part of CC9's conscious effort to organize itself as an intentional experiment in social change. And yet, despite these challenges and dilemmas, CC9 was able to create an effective, groundbreaking campaign for education reform. The decisions that were made had little purity, but they ultimately produced a power that leveraged a significant reform. The organizing was successful not in spite of the dilemmas, but rather because of the value they added when relocated from interior, individual struggles to collective dialogue about best practice choices. Eric Zachary describes the relationship between risk, the reinvention of organizing, and social change:

> We have accomplished what we have because we were willing to take risks to create change. I've seen ten years of organizing with all of their political purity not create much positive change for kids. CC9 was determined, I was personally determined, to produce something different. I knew there were political risks, trade-offs involved, and that we would have to make hard decisions to create important change. You don't create it by never deviating from traditional models. You have to be willing to risk if you want to create something new.

The work of organizing at CC9 was demanding. Oftentimes, the days were filled with pulls that required rapid responses. Yet within these daily, concrete demands of attempting to produce change from the "ground up," CC9 staff simultaneously struggled to consciously create an organizing framework for education reform.

The development of organizing campaigns and staff capacity, however, was frequently disrupted by the turnover of key personnel. Investments in specific organizers would be rapidly depleted by turnover, which in turn would nullify their anticipated longer-term contributions to the project of school reform. CC9's efforts to develop a more skilled cohort of organizers were, therefore, daunting, if not Sisyphean. The loss of organizers, although frustrating and disruptive, did not cause CC9 to disinvest in staff development. To the contrary, training, technical assistance, and more informal supports were increasingly perceived as a means of promoting greater staff identification with and commitment to CC9.

What remains remarkable is that in the midst of staff turnover and the uneven contributions of CBOs, CC9 was able to develop an effective campaign. The story of the lead teacher campaign and its successes were presented in the previous chapter. Missing from the narrative, however, were the critical, less visible contributions of organizing practices to campaign outcomes. CC9 built and strategically utilized the power of a group of parents to change the public schools. How was this accomplished? The lessons of CC9 are largely embedded in its practice framework and daily work. It is, therefore, critical that the structure and processes of CC9's practice be systematically explored and explained.

Organizing around Learning and Instruction Issues

Up to this point, parent organizing had been restricted to the most concrete manifestations of school breakdown, for example, nonfunctioning bathrooms, garbage inside and outside of the buildings, chaos in the cafeterias, and principals often perceived by parents as incompetent. Through the lead teacher campaign, CC9 moved parents from focusing on the symptoms of school dysfunction to addressing a core issue that undermined the achievement and learning of children. The transition, however, from the margins to the center of systemic failure was not easy for parents.

The visible breakdowns and dangers of school environments provoke great anger among community residents. The instructional issues, which the lead teacher campaign sought to address, are often far removed from parents' direct understandings of school failure. Parents are less immediately provoked by such abstract issues and more wary of engaging with them because they have less direct knowledge and experience with the internal workings of the school. As a result, many parents remained silent on these issues. Julia Allen described this self-imposed boundary and the difficulty that parents face in crossing it:

> We understand order and neatness, we understand kids acting out,
> we can relate to that. But getting into the instruction, to the very
> inside, it is stepping inside the system that for so long has made

parents feel unwanted and ignorant. That is a big leap in some ways, to even assume that you have an opinion about the quality of your child's education. For some, well, they are ready for it. They can see it. For others, though, they take it as their own problem or their kids' problem, and they're going to assume that the teacher knows best, that the teacher is educated.

For organizers, a fundamental challenge in the lead teacher campaign was helping parents cross this boundary. Some part of this "crossing" demanded that parents become more fluent with classroom instruction issues. To develop such fluency, CC9 convened a parent training. At first, the training focused on the low achievement of children in District 9 as compared to children in more affluent, suburban communities who had better-funded schools. As noted earlier, parents were powerfully confronted with and angered by the impact of race and class on the achievements of their children. Portes and Landolt have described how such emotional responses to injustice or exploitation can trigger political activism. Anjelica Otero, who helped to prepare the material for the meeting, illustrated this connection when she noted that

> the parents in the meeting, well, they saw in black and white how
> their kids were being cheated. They got upset. That helped us to talk
> about the lead teacher program as a way of investing in their kids, as
> a way of making up for what suburban kids were getting and their
> kids were not. It helped parents own the lead teacher proposal, and
> they began to get into the campaign in a different way. I guess they
> understood it after that as a part of their lives, as a part of their
> children's lives.

The challenge to consistently rethink the structure and direction of the organizing was consistently featured in CC9's practice. It was often stimulated by questions that framed many conversations among staff. What follows is a very short list of the questions raised during organizer meetings and trainings:

1. How do you balance the local work with districtwide organizing?
2. What techniques or approaches are most effective in engaging and involving parents?

3. What information is most critical in preparing parents for more public roles?
4. Who are the critical parent leaders in the community that need to be reached?
5. How can I anticipate obstacles that may impede the campaign?
6. How do differences of race and class influence the work?
7. What can be done to promote trust?

The number of questions grew, especially as organizers became increasingly sophisticated about the details of the work and the need to be critically reflective. The skill, knowledge, and capacity to make best judgments in the heat of a campaign underpin the craft of organizing, which, on the one hand, demands an openness and patience with the process necessary to draw people to the work while, on the other hand, requires strategic discipline to lock in on the most pressing demands of the moment. The orchestration of the many pieces of CC9 organizing was richly described by Allen:

> I think what became clear to me is that there's sort of a map of how to do this work. I think skillwise I have gotten better at understanding the balance between the various demands. That's always going to be there, having to achieve the balance. And there is something beautiful in it, something that I now appreciate about maintaining a clear connection to the big goals, while staying focused on specific school issues. Just the whole range of parts involved in this. There is a music to it. I have to give something to everything—just enough to everything to keep the music, the momentum going.

Dialogue, Critical Reflection, and the Development of Democratic Practice

CC9 provided organizational support to staff to help them develop a more holistic sense of the work and become more effective practitioners. Once a month, CC9 provided trainings that addressed particularly pressing aspects of the campaign, such as outreach and mobilization. Forms of technical assistance were also regularly scheduled. The meetings, phone calls, and e-mail exchanges between the organizers and coordinators, Zachary and Milli Bonilla, were especially important because of the uneven supervision and support provided by individual agencies to CC9 staff. Below, Allen and Otero describe the general contributions of these supports to the organizing:

ALLEN: I meet with Milli every two weeks, and we meet for a couple of weeks and we meet for two hours, and it really helps me hash stuff out. I think she has an amazing amount of experience with just this kind of population of people and kinds of issues. I find it is a wealth to loot as I can find stuff out. . . . It really helps me to gain confidence.

OTERO: Eric constantly gives me the opportunity to try new things and tells me to take on new projects. He challenges me and at the same time tells me not to only rely on him for answers. We talk on a regular basis. The more responsibility I take with CC9 the more it challenges me to grow as an organizer, in terms of leadership development, prepping a lot of leaders for different meetings, taking the lead with certain small groups in preparing for a meeting. When we did the lead teacher campaign, I helped prepare the agenda for what the campaign was going to look like. I also had the opportunity to present it to the larger CC9 and to develop my skills strategically and as a trainer.

Some part of what Allen and Otero are describing is a democratic dialogue with the coordinators. In this dialogue, questions emerge, and perhaps most critically, together they consider a range of possible solutions. As a result of these conversations, adjustments are also made in an ongoing effort to locate the best fit between the situation, available resources, and tactics.

Clearly, the most effective organizers have honed the craft and skill base necessary to make best judgments in highly fluid practice situations. To develop an effective organizing craft, organizers need a safe space for idea exchanges, learning, and innovation. This space is essential if staff are expected to risk presenting half-formulated ideas when they may fear presenting an idea only to have it rejected. This was precisely the kind of protected learning environment that CC9 coordinators attempted to create in their instructional encounters with organizers.

It is important to note that coordinators' willingness to admit to their own failures stimulated a number of organizers to openly discuss their failures and challenges. As Paulo Freire notes in *Pedagogy of the Oppressed*, acknowledging errors proved essential to establishing a process of critical reflection, dialogue, and capacity building. This point was underscored by Frances Calderon:

They are really good. Like I said, they bring their experience with them and share it. They are also not afraid for us to see their flaws, which help people to work with them, especially myself. So because they can admit their errors and if they can make a mistake, I can admit an error, and that gives me more confidence to say and do other things because it tells me anyone can fall, even a master organizer.

The conversation between organizers and coordinators is but one of the many forms of democratic practice nurtured by CC9. In the push between democratic process and the pull of meeting specific objectives, however, the aspiration to maximize inclusion can be easily washed away. Unless such practice commitment is deeply embedded in the organizing work and systematically attended to, it will be lost. The accounts of one after another failed organizing efforts attest to this trade-off. Collaborative culture that produces and reproduces democratic experience is unusual. CC9's effectiveness in developing and sustaining forms of democratic decision making is particularly noteworthy in light of Alejandro Portes and Patricia Landolt's depiction in *Social Capital* of the daunting challenges associated with key aspects of such project.

Much of the day-to-day work of creating a democratic organizing culture is done by CC9 staff. Critically, if organizers are not offered participatory experiences, it is less likely that they will involve parents in decision making. Michael Fabricant and Steve Burghardt in *The Welfare State Crisis and the Transformation of Social Service Work* note that organizers will often reproduce the practices that they have learned from supervisors. CC9 leadership's identification with and commitment to democratic decision making was clear. Less clear were the daily practices that promote identification with a collective project. CC9 experimented with dialogue, capacity development, critical reflection, and lowering barriers to participation for both staff and parents. This experimentation was intended to create a practice framework that generatively evolves some of the multiplying and overlapping threads that cohere into a fabric of democratic culture.

Especially important to nurturing democratic culture is facilitating dialogue between participants. As Freire has suggested in *Pedagogy of the Oppressed,* close listening, posing questions to deepen or challenge thinking, and strategic uses of affirmation to build confidence and facilitation are required. Moreover, dialogue requires that participants acknowledge failure and risk, sharing fear or vulnerability. Otero noted the dialectical relationship between expressing vulnerability and being perceived as strong:

> I think parents need to see us as vulnerable. . . . I think my fear in the beginning was that if people saw me as vulnerable, they wouldn't think I was qualified to do the work. But, I think interestingly enough, if people see you as vulnerable, they see strength in being able to do this work and seeing that you're confident to do it, so that it is OK to be vulnerable.

Similar to the organizing experience internationally that Arjun Appadurai describes in "Deep Democracy," CC9 was committed to highly participatory dialogue that held "steadfastly [to] the importance of slow learning and cumulative change" (30). Likewise other strategies and tactics were geared to long-term capacity building, the gradual gaining of knowledge and trust, and the sifting of more from less reliable partners. Importantly, such discussion was never an end in itself but rather joined to the concrete organizing work needed to build CC9's power and prospects for changing public education in the district. Conversely, part of the learning and socialization for organizers was in coming to understand that an enduring solidarity and power could only be built through dialogue.

Staff meetings and technical assistance work often focused on the complex demands of opening and sustaining such dialogue. How does an organizer know when to speak? When should an organizer remain silent? How do you balance the needs for democratic process against the often pressing demands to get various tasks completed? In such exchange what is the role of seasoned parent leaders? Alternatively, what is the role of parents who are more recent members of CC9? How can participation be dispersed through a group rather than located with a few vocal parents? How do you create an ethos within the group that values each member's voice, not simply one's own? How and when do you surrender some part of the control of expertise and professional prerogative to parents?

These questions enabled CC9 to achieve greater clarity about how to build a practice that joins democratic culture, collectivity, and grassroots power. Perhaps most concretely, these questions were critical practice reference points, helping to promote greater inclusion and reciprocal exchange between participants. This attention to creating a culture of democratic participation over time helped to determine the form, scope, and effectiveness of organizing work. Critically, a balanced attentiveness to both democratic forms of participation and the tactical demands of a change campaign is a cornerstone in building the organizing structure and power necessary to hold public institutions accountable to the communities they serve.

The Demobilizing Illusion of Ultrademocratic Practice

Although CC9 organizing practice elevates the voice of parents as a critical corrective to the historic silencing of community members in education decision making, it simultaneously values the involvement of organizers, the UFT, and the DOE. As noted earlier, CC9 learned from the limited victories of prior organizing efforts that parents alone could not change the learning environment of public schools. To improve student achievement, parents needed both to build an independent base of power and to collaborate with powerful institutions. The choice to collaborate opens the door to a number of contradictions and conflicts discussed in prior chapters. In the past, the community movements for education reform have had ideological commitments to paying almost exclusive attention to parent voice. Often, this resulted in intensely adversarial relationships with teachers' unions and the education establishment. The limitations of such ideological purity, or "ultrademocracy," when applied to organizing work is described by Zachary:

> I think the organizers are thinking most of the time about the right
> things. But they get caught up in ultrademocracy, all parents
> involved all of the time, and it can hurt the organizing work.
> Somebody has to provide the leadership here. It is your job to be
> constantly pushing people. There have to be a few key leaders that
> you are in constant dialogue with tactically. There comes a time
> when you have to make certain short-term decisions. You can't
> consult all of the time with everyone; at times you have to have a few
> key people to sort out tactics.

Ultrademocratic practice, Zachary indicates, can also trump effective organizing by disabling staff capacity to move forward with a campaign. Processing every decision with the full group or subordinating a potentially vital organizer perspective to parent voice at all times can be counterproductive to the larger project of education reform. Situational, rather than formulaic, responses, are required while remaining firmly committed to the practice principle of building parent voice and power. An organizing practice is built dynamically and thoughtfully as leaders and staff make critical decisions about when to push, inspire, point out obstacles, offer options, and recede to the background in order to encourage parent participation. Leaders or organizers make these decisions in the flow of an emergent campaign.

Competing demands between organizer participation and parent empowerment created a tension that, at times, was difficult for staff to sort out. This point is illustrated by the exchanges between Bonilla, Zachary, and Allen, the CAB organizer. Allen remarked:

> I see Milli, at the forefront of her organizing philosophy that parents or whoever you're working with do everything, steer the ship at all costs. . . . And I take that and try to live by it. I see it at meetings where she hardly says a word. . . . She doesn't lend her voice so much, she'll sit and listen to the whole thing without contributing more than a sentence or two. Eric, though, will often give me different advice that there are times I should step up and be that person. That there are times I have to be that person. I think it is a balance, but it is difficult to figure out. Sometimes, trying to know what to do can be frustrating.

Allen leans toward a purity of roles, meaning that she believes staff voices should be removed from campaign decision making. However, she has begun to question the appropriateness of such a stance. She struggles to determine which situations demand more than silence and attentiveness to the parents' voice.

The distinctive approaches to organizing presented by Bonilla and Zachary, combined with the complexity of the work, push CC9 staff to think more deeply about how to invent a democratic practice that is sufficiently dynamic and flexible. CC9 staff are frequently engaged in internal and external dialogues to create more robust relationships to the work, the parents, the community, as well as to the organizing goals. Critically, this feature of CC9 organizing is incubated by a learning culture that recognizes dilemma as the grist for developing a grounded and effective practice.

One such dilemma, living with permeable role boundaries, is often particularly daunting for young organizers searching for structures and certainty. More seasoned staff, on the other hand, are better able to rework strategically specific predispositions or boundaries. For example, Otero described the often fluid roles of parents and organizers: "There's a lot of energy and a lot of wanting to do this work and a sense that we are in this together. It's not like I'm the organizer and she's the leader. We're both in this together." Alternatively, Calderon eloquently described the often artful interplay between organizing practice and collective creation:

> I look at the platform, and I see my work in there. Bits and pieces because there are other people's ideas too—organizers and parents. But it's like you have a child, everything we do there's something in there. In other jobs, that didn't happen. I just did as I was told. And that makes it feel like it's a nine-to-five, and there's no being proud of anything, whether it succeeds or not. I've seen other things go down the tubes in my other jobs and not cared. But here, it actually affects me. If it doesn't work, it affects me, and if it works, I am very proud.

Crossing Professional Boundaries to Create a Dialogue of Solidarity

Parents' and organizers' cocreation of campaigns through exchanges of ideas and experiences can only be achieved through mutual trust. This trust cannot be rapidly manufactured. Rather, it evolves gradually as organizers find ways to build multidimensional relationships with parents. And essential to this objective is the understanding that the historic hardline stance of professionals regarding distance and the preeminence of technical expertise is counterproductive. In other words, the hierarchy of roles that has historically separated community members from professionals and, more specifically, organizers must be reassessed.

Organizers and parents usually have very different perspectives on how to build relationships. Professionals often assume a more objective, removed, and circumscribed stance. They frequently restrict conversations to matters of organizing technique, strategy, and tactic. The tactics necessary to strengthen community schools often animate the discussions. Alternatively, parents are more likely to emphasize the affective dimensions of relationships. They often wed the professional and the personal. For parents, trust and community can only be built when professionals are willing to take personal risks—they must share their history, dreams, fears, and failures with parents. In sum, community members frequently demand that professionals cross the boundary to the personal before extending the trust necessary to form a complete partnership.

At CC9, seasoned organizers like Bonilla, Zachary, and Otero have criss-crossed these boundaries and supported newer organizers, like Julia Allen, Frank Correa, and Theresa Anderson, to do the same. Calderon and Otero describe the ways in which organizers and parents have struggled to create multifaceted relationships threaded to the larger purpose of changing the public schools:

> CALDERON: X who was beaten and abused by her husband for years, didn't talk, was scared to. . . . Nobody knows, but as an organizer many times I have had to go to the hospital when she has called on my cell. I helped her get him out. So I was told by others as an organizer you shouldn't get so personally involved. And if I hadn't, she would have been killed. But that probably made her feel that these people at CC9 are her family, and she can count on us. So here she is rain, snow, sleet.

> OTERO: I think that the leaders with whom I have been able to share a private part of me and build a relationship with are most committed to the work. I guess they are the ones I felt closest to, and that we really are in this work together. So, my struggle recently has been, how do I begin to do that with some of the leaders I didn't do it with early on?

Allen describes relationships between herself and parents as "being there for each other." Parents and organizers have come to trust in each other's full presence. Presence is a multifaceted concept that extends beyond the physical. For Allen, it means that parents will show up for critical meetings of STOP, the local CAB parent group, and CC9 to improve the schools. They will be present despite the other demands in their lives. Job conflicts, fatigue, children's homework, or transportation problems will not keep them away. Allen understands that parent presence often comes with great sacrifice and struggle. She has made herself reciprocally available to parents with housing, job, and marital issues, which although far afield from the specific tasks of "traditional" organizing, helps to demonstrate her presence in their lives and cement personal relationships. Allen remarked:

> They show up. That's what separates them from other people who come to meetings, other people that I've encountered. They do what they say they'll do, I do what I say I'm going to do. You know

we show up for each other. I was thinking about Abigail. She
shows up at every meeting, and anything she can do to help she
offers it. We have a fondness between us because of that, but we
are not involved in other ways in each other's lives. Debbie is
completely different. I know the ins and outs of her. We talk about
her husband, her life experiences. We speak on the phone
multiple times a day. We show up for each other in a lot of
different ways.

Allen does not reciprocate the sharing of personal problems and stories. She
does not volunteer, nor do parents demand, details of her personal life. In a
sense, much of her private life is off-limits. Yet this boundary has not inhibited Allen's capacity to develop robust, reciprocal relationships with parents.
To the contrary, her relationships with parents are especially rich. There is no
simple formula for relationship building and reciprocity. No preconditions
exist regarding correct behavior. What remains inviolate, however, is that the
organizer and parent be attentive and responsive to the particular conditions
and needs of each other's lives. Only in this way can what is offered meet the
test of presence. Allen described these dynamics:

Often they will tell me everything about their relationships,
medical histories, kids. . . . They really want to be heard and seen so
desperately. Sometimes they will turn their gaze to you and ask you a
whole bunch of questions, but mostly it is about them and what
they want, what they need. It's about them growing and changing
and often me supporting them. I mean they love me, we love each
other, but it's not that I would talk to them about my family or my
problems in the same way they talk to me. For me, it is about the
organizing, their showing up and being ready to work to make a
difference in the schools.

For organizers who are already members of the community, the private
problems of parents can produce an echo of earlier difficulties in their own
lives. This convergence can contribute to identification with many parent
leaders. These understandings can create a bounded solidarity that Alejandro
Portes describes in "Embeddedness and Immigration" as "not arising out of
the introjection of established values or from individual reciprocity exchanges,
but out of the situational reaction of a class of people faced with common

adversity. If sufficiently strong it can lead to norms of mutual support appropriable . . . as a resource" for individual or collective benefit (1325). Theresa Anderson, an organizer from the Northwest Bronx, echoed these dynamics of an emergent, bounded solidarity:

> I see them as a mirror image of myself because I was in a very abusive relationship for over twenty years. I never spoke up, I was obedient. Finally, I said no more and ran screaming with my kids from the relationship. And finally it is like I have a voice, respect, and people listen. So when I work with these women, I see a lot of times they are in a similar relationship whether they see it or not. I try to help them see in very subtle ways—who they were before they got into these relationships. They kind of lost themselves. I work to see them get back some esteem, some self-worth. If you push somebody in the right way, that stuff comes back. And once it's back . . . you don't let it go. You get feisty and fight to come to these meetings. You're in it for the long haul, and you're willing to do what it takes. That's the way it was for me, and this is what I love to see in these women.

Otero described how relationships of solidarity are built out of a dynamic process of parallel experiences for staff and parents:

> I think a lot of the work is parallel. The same way I build a relationship with Eric, where we talk about our fears and challenges, I think I do a similar thing with parents, when I tell them what I struggle with. And being able to have sort of a parallel process where we are dialoguing back and forth. I think that makes people really trust you, and you build strong relationships. It's interesting because sometimes I tell parents that I am afraid to speak in public, and they would never have thought it. But then I explain where I come from and what I've done to move forward. I use that as a way to have a real dialogue with parents. Because it is not me as the expert, it's me saying I'm also afraid, I also have struggles, we're in this together.

Relationships of solidarity can also be traced to structural experiences that emphasize a safe space for risk taking, capacity building, sharing of vulnerabilities, and public collectivity. These features of CC9 practice were systematically built into encounters between staff and coordinators. In turn, these themes were reproduced in practice exchanges between organizers and parents in building the social network and power necessary to change the schools. A tension in building such relationships, however, is the risk of professionals getting too personal with community resident organizers and eliminating much of the distance necessary to assess performance, offer critical feedback, and maintain a consistent focus on the objectives of a campaign. These aspects of the work are not necessarily incompatible with the development of more personal–professional relationships, but they do represent points of potential tension that have to be negotiated by the community leader and organizer.

CC9 understands that the best hope for their work to improve the public schools rests with organizing parents who have deep personal investments in its successes and profound experiences with its failures. Two fundamental questions inform CC9's organizing work: (1) How can the power of parents be built and channeled to change the schools? (2) What factors are most likely to maximize parent identification with and investment in the work of CC9?

The first question is essential to the external work of social change; the second, to the internal work of building an activist community of parents. CC9 practitioners understood that the parent power necessary for school reform had to be built on a firm foundation of communal affiliation. As has been noted, what CC9 offered parents was an alternative to the hollow, or "window dressing," forms of participation that historically characterized their experiences as "citizens," both inside and outside of the schools. CC9 promised an alternative experience, which emphasized careful listening to parent perspectives and real roles as change agents. Ultimately, parents had to trust that their voices were not only being heard, but that they were inspiring action.

Organizing Practices That Grow Power and Build Campaigns

The day-to-day organizing tasks of the ambitious lead teacher campaign were varied and complex. At its best, the work was developmental and systematic. The following discussion identifies and explains its critical stages.

Outreach

At the beginning of any campaign, outreach efforts need to be initiated to both engage and involve a growing number of participants. For CC9, different kinds of approaches were used, including distributing flyers, house parties, petition drives, and door knocking. The objectives of outreach were three-fold. First, CC9 needed to spread the word about the campaign throughout the community. Second, parents had to be engaged and persuaded to partic-ipate. Finally, outreach through the petition work was a basis for demon-strating the breadth of support for CC9's lead teacher proposal to a larger world. Importantly, all of the outreach work promised to expand the active base of support for CC9, locally and districtwide.

For the staff of CC9, one-on-one outreach was labor intensive. There was a tension between the "inefficiencies" of meeting individually with members of the community and the press to generate large numbers of participants for the campaign. Yet it was also understood that an in-depth, intimate con-versation offered opportunities for engagement that were often unavailable through more sweeping outreach efforts. Frank, the organizer at Highbridge, described the one-on-ones as a technique for engaging parents on the periph-ery of CC9:

> I see parents who have the potential to be leaders but are on the
> edges of what we are doing. So that is when I started to do one-on-
> ones. It takes a lot of time but it's worth it. . . . A lot of times people
> are invited to a meeting but don't know what is going on, don't
> speak, and they never come back, and people wonder why. The one-
> on-one is the first time a lot of people ever have any understanding
> of what went on at a meeting or what CC9 is trying to get done.
> So that is what I am doing with some parents. These orientations
> are very important. Now a lot of these people are beginning to live
> and breathe CC9.

Similarly, Allen noted that "one-on-ones, like three hours in somebody's house, I can see the value in it. There is a value being established . . . because it feeds back to other relationships in CC9."

The lead teacher petition drive was experienced by organizers as an espe-cially daunting form of outreach. It required collecting ten thousand signa-tures in approximately six weeks. Parents and organizers targeted parts of the community where residents congregate, such as parks, churches, and commercial strips. They were required to coordinate schedules and develop a plan. Finally, a balance had to be achieved between the broader demands of the organizing work, for example, scheduling meetings with key policy makers, and the pressing short-term requirement to collect ten thousand signatures.

Organizers and parents were forced to shed an initial discomfort in reaching out to strangers to sign a petition for a complex reform that was initially incomprehensible to community members and, therefore, in need of a detailed explanation. And yet it was recognized that the petition drive, although extremely taxing, was critical to building parent power. Otero noted that because the petition drive forced parent leaders to explain the importance of lead teachers to strangers, parents increased their own understandings of the proposal and its benefits. In turn, as they achieved clarity, there was an increase in parent enthusiasm and energy for the petition campaign and lead teacher program. In effect, the petition campaign served the dual purpose of educating parents and building the external power of CC9. Organizers were sophisticated enough to anticipate this opportunity and create forums to capitalize on it. Otero remarked:

I think it was very exciting for parents and staff to be out in the community talking about the lead teacher proposal and for parents to begin to understand it and embrace it. Afterwards we had one meeting where parents had so many questions about the lead teachers. It was a good sign that parents were really beginning to understand the lead teacher proposal and wanting to learn more about it. In the meetings the feeling has grown that the idea is great. Things have built. Everybody is signing up to take petitions. Now there is a lot of commitment from community members to make this happen.

Allen added:

A turning point was the petition campaign. That required people to be more active. They had to answer their own questions as they were talking to people and trying to get their support on the streets. So, we had a few people who really bought in that way. And then they were able to transfer that enthusiasm to the rest of the group.

Outreach work is never completed at CC9. The need to increase community power requires constant attention. Repeatedly, CC9 coordinators emphasized and reemphasized the importance of outreach as the lifeblood of an organizing campaign. But outreach always competed with other compelling demands. The demands of organizing work were infinite, and the hours in a workday, although elastic, are finite. It was within the demanding whirlwind of CC9 organizing that outreach work occasionally disappeared. However, this was almost always part of a tactical decision to redeploy scarce resources rather than something that occurred accidentally.

CC9 organizing often required improvisation. Shifting situations produced new demands and responses. To remain rigidly or formulaically attached to a principle when the demands of a campaign require reallocating resources is tactically naive and ineffective. Therefore, the allocation of time devoted to a specific organizing task was recalibrated, and focus for staff and community leaders was shifted as circumstances changed, for example, from involving more parents to pressuring or persuading policy makers. CC9 organizing often required such recalibration. This was vividly highlighted when organizers were expected to shift their outreach focus from local school-based organizing to the districtwide lead teacher campaign. Allen remarked:

> We're all trying to reach out to parents to get them involved in organizing around local schools issues. But trying to develop local campaigns especially in addition to the lead teacher during the last three months seems pretty much impossible.

Added Otero:

> We are having a lot of difficulty pulling new leaders into the local work. It is hard to do both the lead teacher CC9 work and the local school organizing work. It is confusing for parents to understand both at the same time. So when we are doing the CC9 work, we work with our old leaders, and the work of bringing new leaders through the local work more or less stops.

Prep Work

For the collaborative to place parent voice at the center of dialogue, staff have to do preparatory work repeatedly and skillfully. It is often the case that parents simply do not have the confidence or capacity to effectively partici- pate without being systematically supported to perform specific roles. For organizers caught in the expansive web of concrete tasks and hard deadlines, locating the time for less immediately compelling, labor-intensive prepara- tory work is a challenge. However, the degree to which they attend to this work is a critical measure of a democratic organizing practice. CC9 organiz- ers perceive token or substandard parent participation as sloppy practice and a profound breach in their mission to develop community capacity to lead a change campaign. Both outcomes violate cultural norms of CC9. Yet in the midst of the many pressing, intense firefights of an organizing campaign, this critical leadership development work can disappear unnoticed. Zachary described the importance of avoiding such an outcome:

> Organizers need to prep and talk with parent leaders before the organizing. I send out the agenda on a Tuesday for a Friday meeting so that the organizers have the time to read through it and then get parents to talk with them so that people aren't coming in cold for discussions. That is one of the ways we are trying to build up participation. I'm under no illusions about how easy that is. It is very difficult because of the time demands on organizers. But that is the vision we've really got to work hard toward for organizers and parents to have conversations before the meetings.

Otero adds that PAC and CC9 bring both a special intensity and focus to their prep work:

> Leaders need the support of a lot of preparation. We have been suc- cessful because we prepare parents for meetings or rallies with a lot of intensity. The meeting with the chancellor—if we hadn't been so pre- pared, we wouldn't have been so successful. We have also gone into meetings where we haven't been as prepared, and we weren't as suc- cessful, like the meeting with Rivera. The prep work is so important.

For CC9, capacity development, as Steve Burghardt notes in *The Other Side of Organizing,* is a product of the "multiplicity of opportunities to exer- cise leadership." The intention is to involve a growing number of parents in as many facets of the work as possible. Roles such as agenda setting, facilitation of meetings, research, serving as spokespersons at public events, and strategic planning require that parents develop a repertoire of skills. Skills are not passed from organizer to parent through a hierarchical exchange that situates the organizer as repository of knowledge and the parent as receptacle. Rather, skill development occurs through dynamic, focused conversations that develop parents for new roles and responsibilities. By linking the preparatory work to specific needs of a campaign, these focused conversations contributed to new, practical skill sets such as articulating a clear public message, delivering a speech, or chairing a meeting for both the organizers and the parents. Zachary described the range of meetings that call for preparatory or capacity development work:

> People come to planning meetings and have designated presentations to make. Every two weeks we have organizing committee meetings at different CBOs. We make sure the people facilitating meetings are rotated. My job is to prepare the organizer to prepare the leader for those meetings. So for every meeting, leaders are prepped by the organizers. Also, for all of our large public events, we prep leaders. So a lot of it is kind of a one-on-one preparatory work.

For the organizer, preparing parents requires persistence and various kinds of substantive knowledge. These are qualities that are often in short supply, particularly among young organizers. Consequently, the work of empowering parents was paralleled by various forms of capacity development for organizers. Even the more seasoned organizers require refresher and advanced sessions provided by the IESP.

Systematic preparatory work did not contribute to an instantaneous upgrading of parent performance. Rather, as Appadurai notes in "Deep Democracy," capacity development demanded both rigorous reflection and a sustained patience, allowing parents to grow into new roles at an often slower than expected pace. For parents, lessons were not learned at a single point in time but rather over time through accumulated exposure to new ideas and skills. This learning rhythm is systematically structured into the preparatory work of CC9 through "reps or repetitions," as Calderon explained:

> One way to learn the multiplication table is through repetitions. After a while, for example, with the lead teacher proposal, when you keep repeating what the lead teacher campaign is, you know it. And you really begin to understand what a lead teacher is. So I think

that's genius. It is one way of getting our leaders to understand, to really understand.

Frank added that "just like the body builder, he gets better the more reps he does. And he does them religiously. And it is true to a degree, practice does make perfect."

Many forums, such as staff meetings, technical assistance sessions, and trainings, offer opportunities for organizers to assess their preparatory work. During these reflective discussions, organizers raise questions about the "how-tos" of the work and the barriers that limit their effectiveness. Commonly raised questions included:

- Often parents forget what they have learned when they are in a pressure-filled situation. How can I help them take what has been covered in a prep session into a meeting?
- How can I balance the efficiency of a lecture with the effectiveness of dialogue when prepping parents?
- What is my role during a prep session? How much do I do, and how much do parents do for each other?
- What can be done to maintain focus on preps during the heat of a campaign?
- When we put together preps, do we help determine which parents are best suited for particular roles?
- If parents volunteer for a role but aren't ready, what can or should an organizer do to influence decisions?
- In such instances, for example, do we sacrifice forward movement on a collective campaign in favor of individual development?
- How can parent leaders be prepared to anticipate the many break-downs that may occur during the course of a meeting?

Questions consistently stimulated conversations between participants and helped to evolve the critical thinking and mastery of expertise needed to take next steps. This dynamic is richly illustrated by Frank's explanation of the relationship between question posing and developing a parent's capacity to set a meeting agenda:

I found that he and other parents needed basic skills, so I taught him how to write an agenda. I had him and other parents come in, and we ran a workshop. But most important, we talked about why we needed an agenda. You know, think about a map. We start here and want to go there, how are we going to get there? I would raise specific questions to get parents to think about that map. What do we want accomplished by the end of the meeting? How are we going to get parents to do what needs to be done? The questions got a discussion going. Parents begin to know what an agenda means as opposed to looking at an agenda as a list and saying, "OK, the next thing we will talk about is . . ." They begin to see a structure for a meeting, they begin to see the purpose of the list and how the different parts of it come together to help move things along.

Enabling the group to understand options and trade-offs associated with specific decisions is also critical to preparatory work. For example, at CC9, taking on a leadership role is part of a developmental process, one in which members can assume more visible, public, and critical roles as they demonstrate both commitment and capacity. As members demonstrate commitment, CC9 is willing to take a major risk: the organization prepares leaders for roles in which they have yet to be tested during the heat of a campaign. Such calculated risk is essential if the leadership base of CC9 is to grow. In the calculus of growth, however, seasoned leaders must also be prepared to step aside and allow new parents to fill space that in the past they may have claimed as their own. A consistent critique of CC9's work was that it relied on too small a cohort of its leaders for large public events. The work of preparing and transitioning seasoned leaders to new or reconfigured roles is part of the complex, difficult work of capacity building. But it is especially critical in developing both individual and community capacity.

Anticipating dynamics of future meetings through "what-ifs" is another touchstone practice in prep sessions. During this exercise, which generally comes at the end of the preparatory work, questions are posed by the organizers and directed at parent leaders. These sessions often raise vexing questions that are not easily answered. Parents are expected to formulate best responses with the help of organizers. These exchanges are designed to enable parents to better manage otherwise abrupt, unpredictable shifts in the direction of a meeting. This exercise promotes a deeper fluency with material by projecting parents into future negotiations—like chess matches of move and countermove—with key public education policy makers. Equally important, parent leaders are projecting a future in which their expertise and power prevails. Zachary suggested that this improvisational fluency is essential if organizers are to recede and parents step forward during frequently spontaneous exchanges with official policy makers:

> We have to prepare parents so they are in a position where they can be effective negotiating with the school system. Parents have to be prepared. Getting them to the point where they can really work with our proposal in more of a back and forth with the power structure. When we do the "what-ifs," that certainly has helped. But at the same time, lately when there have been moments for spontaneous back and forth with the power structure, CC9 parents have not been as effective in doing that. So there have been moments where I have stepped in more than I would have liked, where organizers have. So clearly that is one of our challenges in the next year, getting parents better prepared for those situations.

Tactical Decision Making: The Exercise of Power to Leverage Change

Ultimately, relationship building, outreach, and preparatory work are about accumulating the power necessary to produce educational change. The practice of CC9 organizing was never linear. Rather, it was a constant spiraling circle of experiences and processes that, over time, yielded the network of relationships from which power can be derived and channeled. For the purposes of clarity, this complex practice has been described in stages that have a linear appearance.

Power is the currency of any organizing or change project. If a movement is successful in accumulating power, the effort is likely to prosper; if it stagnates or declines, the work will wither. Zachary richly described this stark reality:

> It is about showing . . . other interested people that your organization is growing, not stagnating. It's about showing the superintendent what you can do. It's about showing the UFT what you can do. It's about never being satisfied, because the struggle never ends. We are not on the inside; we are on the outside of a highly unequal society at its core. So as soon as you either begin to go back or stay the same, that inequality is only going to stay the

same or grow bigger. So what you are trying to do is shift that power imbalance. That's at the center of organizing. Of course you have to balance that against not overwhelming people.

Determining with parents which tactics are most likely to maximize pressure on key decision makers is especially important. For parents, involvement in such decision making is at least one measure of having moved from a selective participation in CC9 work to a fuller membership. Tactical choices may, at any given moment, focus on the structure or timing of a meeting, potential benefits of a press conference, or the kinds of confrontation necessary to pressure decision makers. Questions that often emerge are:

- What kind of reactions are particular tactics likely to produce?
- Have we given decision makers sufficient opportunity to work out differences with CC9 in private before more public, confrontational tactics are selected?
- Who are the people we need to have in a meeting? Which policy makers are being targeted?
- Do we have the resources or capacity at the moment to meet the demands of a particular tactic? If not, what work has to be done in the interim?

These and other questions are raised by both parents and organizers in working their way collectively through the maze of possible choices to a best decision. Again, posing questions is critical to this process of reflecting on tactical and strategic choices.

During the press of a campaign, rapid tactical decisions are often made in organizing committee and subcommittee meetings. Retreats have enabled parent leaders, organizers, and executive directors to participate in more extended, reflective conversations to map future tactics and strategies. During these discussions, Otero noted, "We are consistently working with parent leaders as sounding boards or as coworkers." Otero underscored that, at times, it is the organizers' job to enable parents to step back from their passionate attachments and to see the larger picture:

I think sometimes parents are really good about being passionate and very strong about pushing things forward. But when it comes to details, seeing the larger picture as we think about what we will do next, I think parents know them, but sometimes it doesn't come out as clearly. So sometimes that is where we have to step in and help.

Building CC9's power is contingent on promoting tactical, strategic dialogue to determine which choices promise the greatest yield. This dialogue, as Otero noted, also represents a threshold for parents as they pass from a narrow, circumscribed participatory role (for example, the role of facilitator) to the more demanding "coworker" dialogue on how to build the power of CC9.

Engineering Forums to Leverage Decision Makers

Earlier public education organizing efforts relied almost entirely on public confrontation to leverage decision makers. Conversely, strategic and tactical use of meetings was a hallmark of CC9 practice. For example, private meetings helped to engage key decision makers in early, serious conversations about the CC9 platform. This private conversation provided a foundation for later public dialogue. The practice of first encouraging private discourse to smooth the way for public conversation offered public sector decision makers an initial safety: to air differences, test counterproposals away from public scrutiny. These frank exchanges contributed to later decisions by many officials to champion the lead teacher proposal within their spheres of influence. Zachary described CC9's conscious use of private meetings during critical moments of a campaign:

> So here we are, a community organization, bringing to the table the union, the chancellor, and local elected officials. And we met with each of these players privately as well as publicly. . . . Part of our strategy was to have these public sessions but also quieter, private sessions where a staff person and a leader could meet with Michelle Cahill to feel each other out and prevent miscommunication. One of the guiding thoughts here is that we don't want to get locked into unnecessary confrontation. We want to understand some of the obstacles. We don't want to get to the obstacles in a public meeting where people's backs are up against the walls. We want to let them know what our priorities are and what our thinking is. We want to hear theirs, we want to hear what they think might be obstacles, so that when we get into public meetings, they can be more problem solving and not confrontational.

Officials unfamiliar with CC9 are often surprised by the thoughtfulness and effectiveness of parent leaders. As was noted in an earlier chapter, the efficiency with which CC9 conducts meetings has enhanced its reputation as a serious, important force for parent-led public education reform. Such respect is generally not accorded to community-based, grassroots groups, which are often dismissed or condescended to by public education decision makers as too marginal or unfocused to be taken seriously. For CC9, skillful leadership and well-run meetings are sources of legitimacy and power. Zachary noted:

I think CC9 runs these meetings incredibly well. We get a lot of positive feedback for being as organized and efficient as we are so people don't waste their time. That's important in establishing a sense of legitimacy that is not just based on turning out five hundred people or having a petition or phone drive. It's also a recognition of our capacity to provide leadership. That is a very important message that we get across. If we expect the system to take our demands seriously, we have to act that way. And part of the way you act that way is to give them respect by getting people out on time, by listening to them at meetings, by providing food, by being respectful, and having effective facilitation and getting the agendas out in advance. So they can't put a parent group in the stereotypical box that they're well meaning but not very effective. . . . We were well meaning and effective.

The power of CC9, however, is most palpably demonstrated through the number of parents that it can mobilize for public events like a rally. These numeric measures are especially important to public officials, who frequently assess power on the basis of the visible and quantifiable. This part of CC9's organizing practice has been particularly effective, as it has been able to increase its rally numbers from about one hundred parents in 2001 to five hundred in 2004. Each CBO has a turnout goal that is collectively agreed on, and the coordinator's role is to hold each agency accountable for hitting its mark. The practice of producing turnout for rallies can be daunting when parents' promises to appear often do not materialize into presence. Consequently, CC9 organizers' rule of thumb is that only half of those who commit to an event will in fact show up. The dramatic discounting of verbal commitment is both a practice necessity and source of substantial frustration, as the following anecdote from Calderon illustrates:

Parents can be frustrating, too. I am going to be honest with you. They tell you they are going to be at a meeting, and they don't come. So you got to get twice as many people to say yes as you need to have there. At the last rally, we committed to getting 150 parents there, but my goal was to get about 250 parents at least to commit to coming. That is especially hard.

Otero describes the specific relationship between turnout at rallies and perception of CC9 power:

We sit at the table with Klein and DOE in part because we can get five hundred people to a rally. I don't think we would have the power to get that meeting without that kind of turnout.

Theresa Anderson puts it differently:

Part of the process of creating power is about creating numbers. It's about having a big number of people with you. . . . Having a lot of parents at rallies, for example.

And as Zachary suggests, if a rally has little energy or is unfocused, its effectiveness is diminished. The tone of a rally can also affect perception regarding power:

A couple of times they have talked about the size of the CC9 rallies at our meetings, and they don't want three hundred people coming down to Tweed. Michelle has been to our rallies. Irma has. You know three hundred to five hundred people screaming, that leaves an impression. That's the reason you do these rallies, it's exactly the purpose.

CC9 preparatory work is designed to produce a tightly orchestrated, high-energy event. Organizers prepare parent facilitators to engage the crowd. Their job is not simply to move mechanistically from one agenda item to another but to involve the audience through call-and-response chants. Facilitators understand that they must watch the clock. Parent speakers are expected to inflame the passions of the audience. Their speeches are laced with personal stories of communal neglect and calls for action. A spirit of transgression and urgency fills the room. As the crowd's level of energy mounts and its voice is heard, the experience of CC9's power is felt throughout even the largest auditoriums.

What was interesting about the rally, Zachary stated, was that the people really seemed to be following the speakers:

> They clapped at the appropriate times, their body language, their
> verbal responses, they really seemed to be engaged. When we had the
> chanting, it really seemed genuine, it felt robust. It was one of those
> remarkable moments. The point of the rally is to make all of the
> work public. Getting people revved up, well, it gets everybody in the
> room resonating, jazzed up and excited. Our guests, everybody.

Based on strategic considerations, organizers will at times prepare parent leaders to avoid harsh confrontational language during rallies. Their presentations consistently call on public officials inside and outside of the room to join CC9's campaign to improve public education. The organizing intention is to demonstrate that CC9 has the power to wage a public fight for better schools, but that its desire is to collaborate and avoid conflict, if possible. The final point is critical. CC9 understands that collaboration is the most effective and perhaps only way to change the public schools. However, if public officials fail to genuinely respect and respond to its commitment to collaboration, CC9 is prepared to consider a more confrontational approach. The effectiveness of CC9's veiled threat of confrontation and direct call for partnership is derived from its independent power. Without substantial public parent support for CC9's agenda, there can be no expectation of collaboration. The organizing tactic of using rallies to publicly flex political muscle and deepen collaborative relationships with power brokers is described by Zachary:

> Demonstrating your power on the basis of hopefulness, collabo-
> ration at the rallies, not on the basis of confronting someone. So,
> for instance, we let the power structure know we were going to ask
> them to sign the pledge without blindsiding them. And the spirit of
> the rally when parents could speak about how their children had
> been denied too long, that they would not allow that to happen any
> longer, that resonated powerfully with people. But what resonated
> with Irma was that when she was introduced, people were excited

to see her. When Herb Katz spoke and said we will not break this collaboration, people were excited. So we've managed to use these rallies to demonstrate real power and partnership without offending anyone.

Rallies are just one mobilizing tactic to pressure public decision makers to join with CC9's platform. In addition to rallies, CC9 flooded DOE officials with parent phone calls during the lead teacher campaign. Press conferences have also been used to rally members to reach a larger public. These actions have had multiple benefits. As CC9 has created ever larger rallies attended by influential officials, the reputation of CC9 has grown. For organizers, the practice lesson is reasonably clear. Parental affiliation with CC9 is, in part, propelled by a perception of power and effectiveness. Such outcomes, however, are not simply traced to changes within the public school system. Importantly, public events that demonstrate CC9's power have the dual purpose of pressuring public officials and inspiring new parents to affiliate. As Allen put it,

You hope that the kind of legitimacy that comes, for example, with strong rallies lifts your base building. The more your reputation is out there, and the more legitimacy you have, and the more you are able to show you are creating change, the more likely it is that parents will want to join forces with you. So I think it is a back and forth between those pieces.

The Daily Discipline of Hope as a Tactic for Renewal

When describing the organizing practice of CC9, Zachary referred to the "discipline of hope." He noted that discipline and hope are often thought of as "mutually exclusive terms." CC9's practice, he suggested, is in large part about the discipline of building a critically conscious, effective hope. Oftentimes, practitioners want to adhere to formulaic responses, even in complex situations, to produce needed outcomes predictably and repeatedly. In successful organizing, however, no single prescription can achieve prominence given the complexity and volatility of most social environments. Disciplined organizing demands tactical and strategic flexibility. Yet in this often volatile work, certain constants must exist, for example, a vision of change. The core questions and principles that frame the work are a touchstone and source of renewal for organizers. Part of the discipline in organizing is returning to those questions and principles during difficult moments. Zachary elaborated:

> At first you think that hope is this amorphous thing that you have or don't have. Whereas hope is something achieved and built in part through disciplined activity. So people may say, Eric has so much passion and energy, as if that is just my roots or my personality. But it's there because of the discipline of doing this work. You can allow yourself to be distracted by a hundred and one things. There have to be some core questions and core values that you return to when things get muddled or confusing, when you do lack hope. We're not in this for some abstract reason. We're in this so kids get a better education. Will these lead teachers do that? I wake up every day asking that question. Are we on the road? Are we building something that can contribute to that? You have to have a question or two that you return to like a compass. Unless you can return to home base, then you can lose your way. Also, organizers have to be able to incorporate new thinking if they are going to be effective; we can't get stuck in one approach. I think it's about the questions. . . . So focus and motivation and inspiration are not abstract amorphous qualities. You develop them through the exercise of disciplined activity and thinking all of the time.

For Zachary and the other CC9 staff, the bottom line is the change that "bottom-up" organizing creates. In this case, then, the hope of a disciplined practice is its potential to improve the public schools and increase student achievement. CC9 hopes that as its work proves effective, it can revitalize interest in organizing as a primary change strategy for public education. Finally, CC9's hope is that it will build a base of parent power outside the school system that is capable of successfully pressing an ever more ambitious movement agenda for change. According to Zachary, these dimensions of visionary aspiration and hope are embedded in CC9's organizing practice:

> At a certain point, a field of work like organizing for education reform is not going to be able to sustain itself without being able to point to the positive change it helps to create. We just don't have

too much in New York City, so this is an opportunity to inspire the foundation world, but as well to inspire parents. I see this lead teacher victory as a victory of course primarily for parents, CC9 parents, but we also hope to trumpet it as a victory for parents fighting for educational justice throughout New York City. . . . That is what we hope to create, a third stream that is really a vehicle for parents in poor communities to try to create change.

The Challenge of Building Collaborative Relationships

The work of CC9 is largely about building solidarity with allies to dramatically change District 9 public schools. The project of creating solidarity across agencies, among organizers, and over racial barriers that often divide parents is extraordinarily difficult. Yet despite these obstacles, CC9 has had great success in creating partnerships with the UFT and parts of the DOE. Just as clearly, solidarity has been built among parents. These partnerships largely explain CC9's successes. However, CC9's limited number of organizers and ambitious agenda to organize at both district and local school levels have been very difficult to balance.

In fall 2003, CC9's undivided attention was directed toward school-based organizing, and this work produced uneven results. As more of CC9's resources were reallocated to the larger district campaign, however, school-based organizing was neglected. This push-pull was a natural by-product of choices and trade-offs that organizers always make. The choice to invest almost all of CC9's resources in the lead teacher campaign during spring 2004 ultimately meant that base building, that is, the work of pulling new parents into CC9, came to a standstill. There simply was not enough time to organize both locally and districtwide. More specifically, the push-pull was between campaigns that emphasized school-based change in learning culture and systemic policy change. Organizers felt that CC9's strategic choice was both necessary and frustrating. Allen described the tension:

I'm just thinking about the difference of when we focus on lead teachers and principal mentors versus speed humps and local school conditions. Eric and I would argue about the importance of working on both. I am trying to figure out how to do both. There is just not enough time. And when we give up so much of the local organizing, well, we stop bringing in new parents.

And as Otero stated,

> If we don't make the local school work a priority in the same way, we will not have a sense of how to really change the schools and also may not be as effective in bringing in new parents. It's a worry. So I think at some point we're going to have to think about a trade-off in our work in favor of the Family School Partnerships.

Efforts to combine local work and the larger lead teacher campaign were also affected by the uneven contributions of CBOs. Collaboration between agencies or organizations is often difficult and frustrating. CC9's experience was no exception. CC9's emphasis on local and district organizing and the platform was often in tension with the practice approaches of some agencies. Consequently, it was a challenge for them to find ways to integrate the work of CC9 into their day-to-day practice. "Some of the groups do their organizing work in a certain way, and part of the struggle from the beginning was that we expected them to do it our way," explained Otero. "And it's been clear that it is going to be hard for us to make them change the way they have been doing organizing when they have been around for twenty-five years. Because for them it is very defined. Organizers are trained with a very specific methodology which they use."

Also, in a number of CBOs the supervision of organizers was deficient. CC9 attempted to fill a part of this gap by having Bonilla and Zachary provide technical assistance to individual organizers. However, technical assistance was not seen as a substitute for a more multifaceted organizing supervision. In addition, as the lead teacher campaign gained momentum and demanded a vigilant attention, Bonilla and Zachary were less available for these labor-intensive, one-on-one sessions with organizers.

These breakdowns often produced resentment and tested internal solidarity. A number of organizers felt that specific agencies were not shouldering their fair share of the work. At times, this caused some staff to question the contributions of these agencies to the organizing work. These low-temperature grievances never deflected the most committed and able organizers from the work of CC9. However, these staff members were increasingly estranged from member agencies considered to be less involved or committed to the work of CC9. In turn, their relationships of solidarity with the larger collaborative were more fragile. Especially critical, however, was the lack of supervisory and collegial support for organizers who were affiliated with certain agencies. In agencies that lacked a strong organizing culture, organizers attributed their sense of isolation to the frequent disconnect between the primary work of the CBO and CC9. This gulf was, at least to some extent, a natural product of member agencies having multiple projects and CC9 occupying a small niche in their work. This isolation was also a consequence of a collaborative structure that "out-stationed," or located organizers in often alien agency environments.

The dilemma of aspiring to create interorganizational collaboration when staff were feeling alienated from their "home" organization was especially thorny for CC9. Time and again, the very thin relationship between an organizer and her "home" agency contributed to a choice to leave CC9. This was an underside of interorganizational collaboration that affected the momentum and continuity of the organizing work. Moreover, the often intense work demands of both CC9 and the home agency frequently caused organizers to pull away. New cohorts of organizers required CC9 to reinvest in basic forms of training and acculturation, thus diverting focus and scarce resources. Although the organizing staff of CC9 remained relatively stable during the lead teacher campaign, immediately afterward there was a wave of turnover. During spring and summer 2004, five of the six agencies were searching for new organizers. And this was only the most recent instance of staff out-migration. This instability was a hindrance to deep relationship building, and it therefore stunted the development of CC9's practice. This was an especially important dilemma because the complexity of education organizing requires sophisticated and experienced organizers. Departure represented a lost opportunity to deepen the expertise and effectiveness of CC9's organizing staff. The context and consequence of organizer turnover are described below:

THERESA ANDERSON: Part of our problem right now is how do we create a support system where we're not just burning ourselves out to the point where we just walk away? It has happened a number of times.

ALLEN: I'm the third organizer here in less than three years. They were both here for nine months. And I've made no commitment to stay really. I feel like what I am doing here at my agency is different, entirely different from what other people do, in that it's not social service but organizing. I'm totally on my own. I mean, because of this, people leave all of the time.

OTERO: The organizers are also part of the community. We're trying to build community. The problem though is that Eric, Frances, and I are the only consistent members of the community. I think for the other organizers, because there is the turnover, there isn't as big an investment in CC9 as there is for me, because I have been here for the three years that CC9 has been around. I think that the longer that an organizer is around, the more invested they will become, the better they will become, and the more responsibilities they will take on.

The Struggle to Bridge Racial and Ethnic Difference

The difficulty of building a collaborative solidarity extends to parents. Racial and ethnic differences have long been a source of tension between Latinos and African Americans, for example, and more recently between Caribbean residents and African Americans. The distrust expresses itself in many ways. Some parents are disturbed by "newcomers" or recent immigrants, especially those who do not speak English, becoming increasingly visible and vocal in local political struggles. These new groups are often viewed as threats to the established order of doing business in a community. More to the point, residents with a longer history in the community are fearful that they will be rendered less visible or powerful as new groups try to "take over." Equally important, simmering racial distrust can boil over into overt animus when, for example, African Americans believe that professionals or parent leaders from their group are being relegated to diminished roles. The reasons for leadership transitions are often less important than the perception that the hard-won gains of historic struggles are being lost. This is seen by African Americans, for example, as one more example of recently arrived "whiter" populations displacing and oppressing people of color.

Experiences based on racial and ethnic differences can be powerful counter pulls as well as complementary to intergroup solidarity. CC9 has been quite successful in creating a culture of communal solidarity that joins many groups, including Latinos, African Americans, Caribbeans, and West Africans in a common struggle. However, it is also clear that such solidarity is fragile and can unravel at any time. During the 2003–4 school year, CC9 had put out many brushfires that erupted between parent groups. These isolated incidents produced a rapid response from organizers. They understood that if these tensions were left to burn slowly, a much more dangerous and damaging prairie fire might be ignited. As Allen explained,

> People would sit with their own kind. African Americans with West African and Spanish speakers all together. I hear it more in a meeting, this person does this, that person does that. I think around West Africans, especially, there is a lot of tension in the neighborhood because there's an influx of people and because they are owning businesses and raising themselves up. I see it when I'm door knocking, graffiti on doors saying, "Go back to Africa."

Theresa added,

> There is a big division between the cultures, Africans, Latinos, Albanians. It is very hard to work with all of these groups together. So bringing these groups together as one group and not six different groups, that is the challenge. I have tried many different approaches to create a common ground, but I can't figure out how to find one yet. I thought that maybe if I took a strong leader from the African group and strong leader from the Hispanic group, it would work, but all that happened was that they clashed. They just refused to work with each other.

Reflecting on Future Campaigns

As the school year drew to a close, CC9 was thinking deeply about building on its recent victory. Some part of its thinking was informed by a staff retreat. The central question of the retreat was, What had CC9 learned in the last year and how could it correct for missteps and breakdowns? In the discussion, participants emphasized the uneven contributions of organizers and CBOs to the work of CC9. Some part of the proposed remedy was to structure mutual accountability into staff meetings. Staff members were expected to challenge each other and engage in more collective problem solving.

In this moment, the focus of CC9's broader work also shifted to matters of school safety. CC9 leaders and organizers considered breakdowns in school safety a broadly galvanizing issue, unlike the lead teacher initiative. Many parents passionately described unsafe conditions in and around the schools and the consequent risks to their children. In response to this, CC9 incorporated safety as a fourth goal of the CC9 platform. CC9 leadership believed that an independent and growing parent engagement with issues of school safety offered greater opportunity to expand beyond the district to regional or Bronx-wide organizing.

Expanding CC9 beyond District 9 was an emerging priority because of the interest in having greater influence. Yet the trip wire of labor-intensive, school-based organizing threatened such growth. The difficulty of distributing scarce resources to both local and boroughwide organizing in the next campaign inspired a rethinking of CC9 structure. New roles were being formulated for the CBOs based on their strengths.

To drive their work forward, organizers had to remain sufficiently nimble and alert, inventing new approaches out of the materials available. The ability to risk and reinvent within a context of frequently frustrating imperfection and shifting contradiction is elemental to effective organizing. This is a dynamic process that demands constant vigilance, a disposition to change course, the hardiness to work through disappointment, and the strategic fortitude to make best choices even as the horizon is less and less perceptible. Zachary described how these qualities helped to fuel CC9's reconfiguration:

> We have a model that has brought us this far with lots of voices. At some point even if the model is generally working, it doesn't mean you stay with it. You have to anticipate a little bit. I think it's an interesting moment to really think about shifting the model and thinking more deeply about the strengths and challenges each organization brings. And what is the fit between the new direction and these strengths and challenges? That is how you develop a new model. That is exciting to me, that willingness not to stay stuck. My commitment is to not let CC9 get stuck trying to repeat what has worked in the past but won't work in the future. I'm always pushing challenges. The older I get, the more willing I am to be open to challenge personally, and that is what I am trying this year to bring to CC9. So it will be interesting to see where it ends up this year. What will the new model finally look like? What will the new organizing strategy be? We have the questions. In the next year some of the answers will also begin to emerge.

By differentiating CBO responsibility, CC9 expected to be better able to sustain its local work while simultaneously expanding the geographic reach of its organizing. This new structure would be tested in the next school year. Again, the first half of the year would be devoted to local organizing or building Family School Partnership Committees in each of the ten schools, in part to support the implementation of the lead teacher program. During the second half of the year, a boroughwide campaign to improve school safety would be organized.

8

Grassroots Democracy and Parent Organizing

The story of CC9 unfolded within a turbulent political and economic context that significantly influenced both the fiscal health and performance of public schools in New York City. The institutions and social forces that produce social problems such as under performing public school systems are so complex and obscured that they are often invisible to the very communities most affected. At that same time, public officials often distance themselves from unsatisfactory academic outcomes of public schools in the poorest communities by ascribing poor performance to large, intractable forces beyond their control. Charles Payne notes in *I've Got the Light of Freedom* that "a black child born into poverty is pushed into the ranks of the structurally unemployed by the schooling process he undergoes. What is remarkable is that no one involved perceives himself or herself as having anything to do with this outcome. This denial of responsibility is the rationalization of inequality made possible by the fragmentation of responsibility" (18).

The failure of public education was powerfully evident in District 9. Year after year, parents witnessed the low levels of academic performance of their children. As these outcomes became increasingly intolerable, parents chose to act to change the conditions of neighborhood schools. What is striking about this South Bronx community is not simply that parents acted, but that the systematic methods they employed stimulated reform. Previously, parents had routinely met with principals or teachers to register complaints, but with little effect. What is remarkable about CC9 is that parents began to understand that change would not occur without a proactive plan, independent power, and an infusion of targeted public resources directed to improve learning and instruction conditions. What distinguished CC9 was its effectiveness in building community power and a reform plan that broke through the institutional gridlock of neglect. This required patience in the midst of an urgent need for change, innovative, risk-taking practices, and individuals willing to channel their hopes into a collective project. The parents of CC9 created a form of citizen activism and established a sphere of public space. By injecting themselves into the public sphere as activist citizens, they challenged the prevailing discourse that parents in working-class communities could not bring about public education reform.

For decades, poor communities have battled to change public schools with little or no success. Local groups frequently demanded an increase in the allocation of public resources for their schools, a strategy that public officials often met with firm resistance. Time and again, school administrators and government officials employed neoliberal logic and its discourse of scarcity as justification for denying parents' requests for change. Over the past three decades, the language and policies of scarcity have dominated reform discourse.

It is important to recognize that many public institutions are failing for a number of reasons, some subtle and others more apparent. Bureaucratic control, inefficiencies, and resistance to fundamental reform certainly explain part of the breakdown of public education. However, differing levels of investment in public schools, which create inequalities along race and class lines, explain the largest part of the dysfunction of inner-city schools. Substantial new investments in programs that have proven, successful track records are essential. Until that occurs, inner-city schools will continue to decline, even as the needs of an ever poorer and increasingly immigrant urban population grow. The combination of a growing student census and diminished public funding perpetuates disappointing student achievement. In the absence of new resources, poor communities cannot test alternate approaches to educating their children.

Few educational alternatives besides public schools exist for the overwhelming majority of poor and working-class people in the United States. The evisceration of the public sector in favor of expanding privatization raises troubling questions about access, democracy, and new forms of inequity. The persistent, historic hope for many poor adults is that their sacrifices today will be repaid through the accomplishments of their children tomorrow. That hope is linked to the imagined benefits of a quality public education.

However, the link between hope and education has had little strength in the poorest urban communities of color. Recent policies have exacerbated the tension between school performance and income and race. In this landscape, poor parents are left with few alternatives. They can move to find better schools elsewhere or locate educational options outside the public school system. But the choice of flight only exists for the most resourceful or advantaged residents of poor neighborhoods. For the overwhelming majority of parents caught in the crosshairs of such scarcity, the choices are difficult. They can accept conditions, impotently complain, or find a way to change the financing and program discourse regarding public education. Most parents gravitate to the first two options, even though they are the most self-defeating. The third option offers hope but demands enormous commitment, endurance, and support from third parties, such as community organizations, if present policy and discourse are to be changed. As Jeannie Oakes, John Rogers, and Martin Lipton suggest in *Learning Power,* "the project of revitalizing public life and more specifically schools is bound up with the struggle to overturn the logic of deficit and scarcity" (163). Michael Apple amplifies this point in *The State and the Politics of Knowledge* when he describes the case of Porto Alegre, Brazil:

> In the dominant discourse, an emphasis on education is related to a consistent attempt to colonize the space of "legitimate" discussions of educational policy and practice . . . to produce an educational environment more in tune with the economic needs of the market. But when this global process enters [the local circumstance], contradictions are created and a hybrid product is formed. This is the case because even though the hegemonic discourse tries to colonize the educational sphere, once it meets the realities of the [local] context it creates unintended spaces for alternative experiences.

This is precisely what occurred in the South Bronx. The DOE promised improvements, but the results were nothing more than flat levels of real dollar public investment and persistent educational failure. In the wake of this disappointment, parents began to rethink their role in relationship to local public schools.

CC9 parents became increasingly disenchanted with neighborhood public schools, and they were skeptical about the capacity of central leadership to fix them. Historically, parents were comforted by the idea that the right school administrator or political leader could remedy this state of affairs. But the likelihood that regional or central administrators and local politicians can override more powerful political and economic interests on matters of public education investment is a long shot at best. In addition, these officials are often unwilling to risk their professional and/or political standing by pressing to fundamentally alter the conditions of schools. Finally, public education managers are generally not considered sufficiently wise, stable, or prudent to initiate such reform. This last point has substantial implications regarding the prospect for improving public schools. If community groups cannot count on local or central educational leadership and politicians to improve the conditions of neighborhood schools, they have to find an alternative route to meaningful reform. It is against this backdrop that District 9 parents, acting as a united third party, entered the contested landscape of public education.

New Forms of Accountability and Public Space

A central challenge for poor communities is to create new structures of accountability for public education officials. To whom are public officials accountable for the continuing failure of inner-city schools? In what ways are parents and community groups integrated into a structure of accountability? How can parents maximize their influence in holding schools accountable? Recent discussions regarding accountability and public education have focused on the relationships between funding and public education managers. For example, the No Child Left Behind legislation, which holds states and schools accountable for closing the achievement gap by wedding performance to budget, is a technical, rational system that blames teachers in highly underfunded schools for failure. Teachers are a critical determinant of success and failure within the classroom. However, implementing tougher forms of teacher or principal accountability within schools that are resource starved simply creates new political targets and cover for broader failures.

Instead, the question of accountability must be linked to the systematic underfunding of public education and the isolation of poor schools and their staff. It is within this context that Anthony Alvarado remarked in the volume *Rethinking the Urban Agenda*, edited by John Mollenkopf and Ken Emerson:

> We should try high standards, yes bureaucratically mandated. We
> should try new assessments and hold schools accountable. . . .
> However, all of us know that there are thirty schools in New York
> City that are unfit for habitation no less education. . . . If you're
> in those schools and you're a teacher you are dying to get out.
> Everybody knows which schools fail. You stick your nose in it. But
> then you have to do something about it. Where is the accountability?

Clearly, the system cannot and will not hold itself accountable for persistent failures, particularly if they fall outside of relatively narrow and relatively inexpensive definitions of problem and remedy, for example, professional incompetence or technical, performance-based problem solving. This policy frame is myopic and self-defeating. However, without new structures of accountability, it will continue to shape public education. More generally, as Michael Williams notes in *Neighborhood Organizing for Urban School Reform,* "internal institutional reform is largely a myth. Institutions demonstrate a remarkable capacity for absorption of reform plans and ritualized adaptation to them while maintaining their former patterns of behavior. In other words, reforms instituted from within the system probably will not change the modal regularities within them" (58).

Only by creating other mechanisms for accountability can we reframe and expand the discussion of public education failure. As an outside force, a community of parents is one key group that can work to hold policy makers accountable. This is not a new idea; it is as old as the earliest conceptions of public education. This reconfigured structure of accountability promises to invigorate the relationship between citizenship, democracy, and public education. These outcomes are evident in the experience of CC9. The structures that governed their experience form the very bedrock of democratic practice.

Some have called for new governance structures of reciprocal accountability relationships in which all stakeholders are responsible for the intellectual growth of students and the success of public schooling. On this premise Kavitha Mediratta, Norm Fruchter, and A.C. Lewis in *Organizing for School Reform* have advocated for a more "bottom up accountability" (5). They characterize this process as the development of structured relationships between parents/communities and school people based on mechanisms of transparency, representation, power, and oversight. Such "bottom-up" accountability, however, requires an independent activist citizenry with sufficient power to press its authority and agenda. Mark Warren, in "Communities and Schools," underscores this point, noting that urban schools will continue to fail when communities lack the power to demand accountability. Equally important, and especially salient to the practice of CC9, Warren notes, "as powerful as building social capital can be for individual school and neighborhood improvement, a broader solution requires creating the political capital to address the structural inequality like the pernicious under funding of urban schools." Bottom-up forms of accountability do not exist simply because of benevolent public decision makers. Ultimately, the degree to which public institutions hold themselves accountable to community groups is commensurate with the degree of political power exercised from the bottom up. CC9 confronted the question of how to accumulate the power necessary to influence public decision making. The answer to that question, at least in part, was that CC9 created a new public space in which to contest the record and reform agenda of public education in District 9.

Increasingly boardrooms and principals' offices, the locus of official power and decision making, exclude community leaders. The struggle to create new forms of democratic space must challenge both state decision making and the very definition of a larger public interest. By re-creating public space, public education activists challenge the status quo. Critically, these new public spaces nurture democratic discourse and resistance to policies that wound the poorest communities. This model stands in marked contrast to understandings of public space as a synonym for the state. As community leaders challenge both the efficacy and effectiveness of current education policies, they create a space that is overtly political. Clearly, CC9's vision, most vividly captured through both its platform and culture of strong democracy, offered a new public space for democracy, hope, and resistance to the present failures of public education.

It is precisely this space for discourse regarding the state of public education and alternate approaches to improve student performance that local nonprofit agencies provided CC9. Neighborhood organizations are often mediating institutions between communities and public schools, and, therefore, they are critical to the development of a new public space. As Williams notes, "A mediating institution is a group structure that stands between the private life of the individual and the giant mega structures of modern society, . . . such as government. Standing between implies a dual role: advocacy for the needs of the individual and education of the individual in coping with the outside world. Thus the mediating institution is both instrument and instructor" (110). These roles produce a fundamental tension. As advocates for its neighborhood, it makes demands on the mega structures to recapture, retain or improve scarce goods and services. Such actions create strained relations with these outside agencies. As internal educator, the neighborhood organization must attempt to unify diverse interests within the neighborhood.

Critically, this mediating role, as described by Williams, involves a political perspective and an educational component that builds indigenous collectivity and capacity. In a fiscal environment that increasingly weds nonprofit budgets to government grants, such initiatives are fraught with potential risks. For example, nonprofits that engage in overt political advocacy that challenges state policies may be in greater danger of losing parts of their funding base. Agencies prepared to take such risks generally have greater commitment to political action and a willingness to engage in conflict. Clearly, a number of CC9 agencies shared such commitment and disposition. The alternate public space created by CC9 was not located in a single existent neighborhood institution but rather in a collaborative. This new formation provided individual agencies with the necessary "collective cover" to challenge government institutions and not fear immediate reprisal.

Importantly, CC9's understanding that democratic practice and parent power are essential ingredients in affecting both civic engagement and a revitalization of public institutions challenges the dominant communitarian discourse on rebuilding communal life. In general, communitarians view public disinvestment in the poorest communities and the drift toward privatized initiatives as outgrowths of a fixed and naturalized, rather than dynamic and alterable, political landscape. Consequently, they tend to view the crisis of collective affiliation and citizenship as a depoliticized phenomenon that can be resolved through status quo relationships of power. The alternate public space, civic dialogue, and citizenship role created by CC9, however, offer a different model; it is embedded in a practice and vision that understands that only by redressing power differentials can poor people effectively participate in the process of remaking public institutions.

As they were constructing alternate forms of democratic public space, CC9 leaders understood that the task of changing present policy was both complex and daunting. Exclusive or rigid reliance on tactics of confrontation or single agency initiatives were simply inadequate, if not counterproductive. Instead, what was required was a politics of base building and alliance tethered to patience. Arjun Appadurai notes in "Deep Democracy" that "the politics of alliance is a politics of accommodation, negotiation and long-term pressure rather than of confrontation or threats of political reprisal" (29). Clearly, significant and powerful allies are indispensable to creating the pressure necessary to alter public policy and practice.

As CC9 created an alternative public space, the group incorporated collaboration as a basic practice theme and searched for opportunities to "scale up" their power through new forms of alliance. Mustafa Emirbayer and Ann Mische note in their article "What Is Agency?" that the logic of promoting innovative change through collaboration is also necessary when actors such as parents are

> located in complex relational settings and therefore must learn to take a wider variety of factors into account, to reflect upon alternate paths of action, and to communicate, to negotiate and to compromise with people of diverse positions and perspectives. . . . It is precisely at the interorganizational level that the need for a purposeful search for alternatives, critical discourse and formal equality in contrast to the routine, scripted forms of rationality and hierarchy which predominate inside organizations is especially necessary. (1007)

The interorganizational sphere can, therefore, simultaneously offer a pathway for accumulating power and forcing more democratic, critically reflective dialogue. Each of these practice features is especially salient to the work of CC9. For CC9, the work of a public sphere is to build community power through organizing. Oakes and Lipton make a similar point, in "Struggling for Educational Equity in Diverse Communities," when they suggest that the purpose of organizing proposals is "to redistribute schooling resources, opportunities and outcomes on behalf of low-income students of color" (383). Such proposals, as Oakes and Lipton point out, face steeper obstacles than do nonredistributional initiatives. The public space developed by CC9 was organized to force a reinvestment in public education, or to push back against recent policy trends.

The Recent Record of Parent Organizing for Improved Schools

Mediratta, in her monograph *Constituents of Change,* suggests that the impact of parent organizing on school performance has a mixed record. A growing literature suggests that community organizing for school reform is changing public schools and districts in important ways. Notable examples of effective organizing include the work of the Education Justice Collaborative in California, the Logan Square Neighborhood Association in Chicago, and the Industrial Areas Foundation (IAF) in Texas. Each of these groups, like CC9, created a strong parent base and external alliance to change the conditions of public schools. A number of recent studies of parent organizing in low-income areas underscores the rapid increase in their number and influence since the 1990s. As Jean Anyon notes in *Radical Possibilities,* organizing for school reform is about an "intentional building of power." The presumption is that the power of collective action in poor communities can change the condition and performance of public schools. This belief has been confirmed by the findings of a recent study, *Organized Communities, Stronger Schools* by Mediratta, Seema Shah, and Sara McAllister, which suggests a strong association between improved achievement of poor students of color and parent-led organizing campaigns. The hope of democratic experiences of meaningful participation is expected in turn to promote enfranchisement and civic engagement in places that have long been considered part of an invisible political netherworld.

What CC9 offers readers and organizers interested in school reform is an exemplar. Organizing initiatives in other parts of the country have tested many of the same ideas advanced by CC9. In the difficult work of social change, and more specifically school reform, there are no templates or one-size-fits-all approaches that will guarantee a positive outcome. That said, what the CC9 experience provides is a way of rethinking parent organizing in this historic moment. The hope is that there are universals, some clues and bits of advice that can be culled from the CC9 experience and recommended to others striving to improve opportunities for inner-city citizens.

CC9 organizing is especially instructive in thinking about the convergence of strong democratic practice and the creation of collective power. Equally important, the "scaling up" of power through alliances with critical institutions, an essential element of CC9 organizing, offers otherwise isolated communities an alternate pathway for advancing a local change agenda. The challenges of building such alliances are richly illustrated through CC9's groundbreaking work with the UFT, community agencies, and the DOE. CC9's specific practices of building parent solidarity, capacity, and hope were foundational to its later success. Additionally, these practices offer us signposts for assembling a practice framework for building parent solidarity.

Finally, the development of new spheres of public space to practice democracy and social change is an essential aspect of CC9 organizing during this historic period. This is an important response to neoliberal policy regarding public institutions. As noted, the dominant discourse and practice of neoliberalism, which starves the state through policies that increasingly diminish resources, must in large part be challenged from the outside. Internal decision makers have less and less room to maneuver around or directly challenge neoliberal policy. Equally important, public sector decision makers are increasingly drawn from the business sector and are, therefore, often predisposed to certain aspects of neoliberal reform: corporatizing public sector culture and reducing funding. The work of forcing public institutions to change course increasingly rests with community groups such as CC9.

The Hope of Organizing

Mike Gecan, a seasoned organizer with IAF, noted a number of years ago in "The Discovery of Power," that "it is easy to talk yourself into despair. Hope is physical and visceral. I don't think you can talk yourself into it. I think you have to do yourself into it. The more people try things, work at things, test things, push boundaries, experiment, the less we just angst about it the better" (242). This aspiration is part of the organizing DNA of CC9. Eric Zachary, Ocynthia Williams, Denise Moncrief, and other CC9 architects returned, time and again, to the hope that CC9 offered. Hope as a resource and touchstone sustained parents by stimulating them to reflect, for example, on their present struggle in relationship to similar challenges faced by leadership in the civil rights movement. Their links to earlier leadership and enduring hardship to promote just change were a rich source of hope even during the most difficult moments of the campaign. For organizers like Zachary, hope was associated with always returning to the reasons for the campaign and clearing away the underbrush of present difficulty or disappointment. The abject failure of public education and the need to revive schools for their children enabled leaders and organizers to keep their heads and hearts in the struggle, even during especially trying moments. This "discipline of hope," articulated by Zachary, was embedded in the day-to-day struggle of building both the capacity and power of parents.

Flexible problem solving was one of CC9's most important capabilities, and it was evident at a number of critical junctures in the organizing. Such responses were part of the consistent practice and commitment of CC9 to navigate through difference strategically. Why? Because leadership never lost sight of the importance and delicacy of interorganizational collaboration. To harshly confront stakeholders and incinerate relationships at critical moments, although perhaps viscerally satisfying, were counterproductive to the larger purposes of CC9. This is easy to say and very difficult to accomplish in the heat of a campaign. Yet it was leadership's capacity to keep their "eyes on the prize" in the many moments when the campaign was stalled or tested by "stakeholders" that offers the most vivid examples of a disciplined, flexible practice of hope.

Importantly, CC9's commitment to collaboration never caused leaders to forgo the option of confrontation when it was perceived as necessary. Again, this choice was made not in the heat of battle but rather through dialogue that determined the campaign could not move forward without confronting, for example, a lack of urgency or resistance on the part of decision makers. Tactics were selected on the basis of best fit to the organizing moment and need. Confrontation was used only as a last resort or in the most dire circumstances. However, the threat of confrontation was constant as, for example, CC9 flexed its growing political muscle at public rallies. Sustaining the hope and discipline necessary to change the public schools required the power of both collaboration and an independent base of parents. At times, parents needed to exercise their independent power to remind decision makers of the seriousness and authority of their grassroots agenda. These moments reminded parents that they were not an appendage of larger institutions but rather a unique, independent power and a source of hope for changing public schools.

From the Hope to the Power of Organizing

To translate hope into an effective change campaign, power must be built. There is, of course, no single answer as to how to organize the community power necessary to change the institutions, policy, and social structures that oppress. Saul Alinsky, for example, emphasized self-interest as the fundamental impetus for organizing. For Alinsky, self-interest was a synonym for class interest. Relationships were formed on the basis of strategic necessity. Oakes, Rogers, and Lipton indicate in their book *Learning Power* that Alinsky believed groups must have no "permanent friends and no permanent enemies" (103). Alinsky emphasized confrontational tactics and the exercise of collective power. He is cited by Oakes, Rogers, and Lipton as suggesting that only in this way "could poor people wrest concessions from rich people, who skillfully used the power of wealth and political position to maintain social and economic advantages." For Alinsky, what remained inviolate was the building of strategic, collaborative relationships, an independent community power, and the consistent use of confrontational tactics to produce change.

As an organizer, Ella Baker emphasized building relationships, promoting respect for collective leadership, evolving an expansive sense of democracy in everyday practices, addressing local issues, and structuring community groups for the long haul. Oakes, Rogers, and Lipton note that she attended to issues that cut across the black community, even as she brought special sensitivity to the issues of the poor. Building relationships of solidarity was at the core of Baker's organizing work. Robert Moses describes Baker's organizing approach in Payne's *I've Got the Light of Freedom:* "whenever you really want to do something with somebody else then the first thing you have to do is make the personal connection, you have to find out who you are really working with. You have to be really interested in the person you are working with. You saw that in her organizing work all across the South in the grassroots work and with rural people" (98).

CC9's organizing framework borrowed from both Alinsky and Baker. On one hand, it was committed to building strategic relationships and local community power. On the other hand, it was deeply committed to practices that emphasized relationship building, democratic decision making, and leadership capacity. These practices cohered over time into a CC9 culture of solidarity. For CC9 leadership, the challenge was not to embrace one or the other of these approaches but rather to find a way to integrate them— to develop a more muscular organizing that combined independent parent power and an interorganizational alliance. What remained inviolate was that both sources of power were joined to parent-led campaigns to improve public education. The more specific organizing lessons of these campaigns will be elaborated in subsequent sections.

Building a Change Platform

From the outset, CC9 understood that to be an effective change agent it would have to develop a proposal for structural reform, not simply react to breakdowns in learning and instruction. For parents to make an informed judgment about the utility of various change proposals, they would need to more fully understand the systemic failures of the local public schools and master the discourses of public education reform. To achieve this, a number of parent leaders attended conferences and read materials on reforms being tested in poor urban school districts across the country. This exposure to reform discourse and materials led to extended conversations between parents and CC9 staff about developing a CC9 platform or proposal for change. Ultimately, this process helped to chart a direction for reform.

Part of what CC9 was engaged in was a discourse regarding vision of a future for public education. The proposal that grew out of these discussions served an important social and political purpose. To begin with, it offered parents a vision of change that provided hope and a locus for struggle. Additionally, it utilized a language and logic that was familiar to education decision makers. Officials such as Michelle Bodden and Michelle Cahill described the CC9 platform as having a powerful legitimacy because it offered an especially compelling logic or theory of change. In turn the legitimacy of the platform was transferred to the parents and staff of CC9.

Embedded in the platform is a logic that is indisputable for many regarding the failure of public schools. Increasingly, staff are being asked to spend their time on the crisis of the moment. As they are faced with more complex problems and intensified resource scarcity, they are increasingly on the firing line. Importantly, their capacity to improve learning and instruction is compromised by conditions over which they have less and less control. Perhaps most critically, they experience a chronic lack of support in their often Herculean efforts to offer a quality education to students. These conditions and outcomes have produced a significant churning of classroom teachers and principals in New York City. The most recent estimates indicate that every five years, 50 percent of the teachers leave the public school system. This is an especially revealing statistic that has enormous implications. While these dynamics do propel many underequipped teachers out of the system, the forces producing these outcomes do not necessarily discriminate between the competent and incompetent, the committed and detached, the innovative and the mechanistic. Instead, they simply promote profound estrangement. This sorting has served to further impoverish the instruction and leadership capacity of the poorest public schools. The question is, What do we do about it?

It is precisely this question that CC9 has tried to answer through its platform. Its proposal is unequivocal in its call for new targeted investments in District 9 schools. As well, the platform does not blame professionals for the failure of public schools. Instead it acknowledges the systemic failure to provide teachers and principals with the support necessary to improve education outcomes. The CC9 platform focuses on breaking the cycle of blame that has separated schools from the communities they serve by proposing that investments in staff development and support are a critical ingredient necessary to improve public education. Lead teachers, mentors for principals, and community–school partnerships are expected to provide professionals with some of the supports necessary to improve the learning instruction environment of public schools.

Staff development, as C. Payne and M. Kaba notes in the article "So Much Reform, So Little Change: Building-Level Obstacles to Urban School Reform," "is the universal answer to all problems of instruction. . . . It should be responsive to teacher identified needs, built into school operations . . . and be content rich." This is precisely what CC9 proposed through the lead teacher and mentoring proposals as planks of its platform. Provision of such support was expected to produce many forms of benefit or value to the schools. To begin with, it offered a space to problem solve and test the often underexercised muscle of staff expertise. It provided a venue for building a relationship between seasoned professionals and the frequently inexperienced staff of public schools. The proposals also produced a new hierarchy of classroom teachers and provided necessary incentives to attract more expert teachers to the poorest districts. Finally, the creators of the platform understood the importance of community–school partnerships in relieving the isolation and increasing sense of powerlessness of professional staff.

The platform broke with recent paradigms for school reform. First, it resisted simplistic change initiatives of blame and confrontation. Instead, CC9 used the platform to signal to both parents and school officials that it understood the importance of stakeholder collaboration and staff development in fixing the problems of the schools. It also announced that the failure of public schools could not be fixed without new investment. Finally, the platform's reform agenda was focused on improving neighborhood public education, not on creating an alternative sphere of education in charter or private schools. Critically, this vision also promised parents greater opportunity to share their experience with professional staff. This exchange was expected to promote greater parent participation and influence in school decision making. The platform publicly announced both the concrete objectives and strategic emphasis of CC9. The importance of building internal capacity and external support is one of its central propositions. In turn, it has helped to frame the organizing practices of CC9.

Practicing Citizenship by Incubating an Activist Community

Central to any grassroots organizing work is the development of relationships, common understandings, and action. Oakes, Rogers, and Lipton cite Marshall Ganz as asserting that the goals of this work "are to create networks that can sustain activist communities, to frame a story about the networks, identify a purpose and develop a program of action that mobilizes and expends resources to advance community interests." Of particular importance to this discussion is determining how CC9's collective identity and activist network were created through specific practices. Each thread of CC9 organizing shares a dynamic, interdependent relationship. For the purposes of analytic clarity, however, the practices of CC9 will be presented as discrete items.

Benjamin Barber in *Strong Democracy* suggests that in building an activist community, organizers must facilitate the development of local leadership. Within CC9, parents had to internalize a relationship to the ideas, tasks, and actions of changing neighborhood schools. Individual ownership of a change project, however, does not occur simply through a relationship to ideas and action. Rather, it also requires engagement with other activists equally committed to the change project. Over time, relationships of solidarity may be incubated through shared struggle, for example, to improve public schools. Such relationships can only occur, however, if the practices of the agency actively promote them. For CC9, the tasks of creating collective identity and individual ownership were linked to the collaborative's systematic development of strong democratic practices.

CC9's work in building an organizational culture of strong democracy is perhaps the most essential and complex part of its practice. Like the citizen schools developed by Highlander organizers in an earlier era, this work was largely about transforming the community's everyday concerns into broad, significant, political issues through participatory practices. The theory of strong democracy, Barber argues, "envisions politics not as a way of life but as a way of living . . . so that human beings with variable natures . . . and malleable but overlapping interests can contrive to live together communally" (117). He continues, noting that through strong democracy, "politics is given the power of human promise. For the first time possibilities of transforming private into public, dependency into interdependency, conflict into cooperation, license into self-legislation, need into love, and bondage into citizenship are placed in a context of participation" (120). Participation is not a hollow gesture but a substantive experience of an enfranchised citizenship.

A presumption of Ella Baker, Highlanders, and CC9 was that such participation promotes affiliation between individuals and a collective. When linked to a political agenda for change, it also offers a trajectory to solidarity and activism. What is demanded of a deep democratic culture, however, is to practice what John Dewey described as egalitarian social relationships. CC9 offers a window into understanding how a practice can be organized to build such deep democratic experience and, over time, yield relationships of solidarity. As well, it provides a glimpse into the transformative possibility of democratic experiences. For CC9, democratic practice had to assure the development of expertise (which is linked to the capacity to participate effectively), the trust necessary for parents to participate without fear of reprisal or ridicule, respect for the different voices of parents, access to important events, and accountability regarding tasks undertaken by parents as well as staff. Democratic practice, then, is not simply about a generic language of participation, but rather about the work that must be done to sustain, widen, and deepen relationships to a larger world. Importantly, CC9's strong democratic practice should be viewed through a teaching lens. It is within this context that Oakes, Rogers, and Lipton reference Dewey's remark that teaching is a visionary work that has a moral purpose that ultimately helps to develop a citizenry. This description of teaching captures part of the essence and aspiration of CC9 practice.

Democratic Dialogue and Citizen Empowerment

The practice question that vexes every organizer is how to facilitate dynamic conversations—not simply in the moment but over time. As Barber notes in *Strong Democracy,* "'voices which speak in such conversation do not compose a hierarchy.' So it is with democratic talk, where no voice is privileged, no position advantaged. . . . Every expression is both legitimate and provisional, a proximate and temporary position of a consciousness in evolution" (183). This is easily said and very difficult to accomplish.

When effectively practiced, democratic dialogue can change consciousness. As Barber notes, "This consciousness alters attitudes and lends to participation that sense of the *we* . . . associated with community. . . . Indeed, from the perspective of strong democracy, the two terms *participation* and *community* are aspects of one single mode of social being: citizenship" (155). An empowered citizenry that joins dialogue and community is precisely what CC9 struggled to create. Over time CC9 joined this sense of collectivity to parent inquiry about the complex problems of neighborhood schools.

Dialogue and instruction dedicated to citizenship empowerment, although necessary tools for creating an alternative public space, were not enough to compel parents to action on their own. The parents' political and personal aspirations were also to emotionally claim a dignity or respect long denied to poor people of color. Only through the concrete, often affective charge of mutual respect could an alternate, more politically activist citizenship experience be lit. James Jasper, for example, notes in *The Emotions of Protest* that "trust and respect are examples of affects with enormous impacts on political action" (402). The parents of CC9 affirmed this point when they characterized the respect accorded by professionals as both jarring and essential. They were initially distrustful of CC9 staff because of their warmth, welcoming, and attentiveness. Jamilla Anderson remarked, "I couldn't handle it. It was so different than anything I had experienced in other nonprofits. They really wanted to hear what we had to say. And maybe most important, they didn't just listen, they used what we said." Another parent, Veronica Rivera, indicated,

> You get a feeling you know whether they are real or just full of it. They can say we count, they're listening, but you got to feel it, not only say it. For me, that was the thing about CC9, the organizers, the other parents, they felt it, in their gut. It was there when we were in meetings, helping us get ready for a rally or just talking. You could feel that what we said and thought really mattered. That is why I have hung in there.

Repeatedly, organizers affirmed parents' critical contributions to a particular task or a larger campaign. As well, when parents failed to complete assigned tasks, they were held accountable. Affirmation and accountability were powerful signifiers that respect was not offered to leaders for simply showing up, but they also had to deliver on their promises. This dynamic experimentation in leadership and capacity development could not have occurred unless CC9 offered parents the kinds of respect, trust, and reciprocal exchange missing in most every other part of their public lives. Learning in a public space demanded an alternate reality to the cold indifference and invisibility parents experienced as they entered spaces like neighborhood schools.

Many CC9 parents are either first-generation immigrants or African Americans who have resided in New York City for generations. In both instances, there is a shared experience of being an outsider. This outsider status has manifested itself in many different ways. Important to this discussion is the frequent lack of respect that mainstream institutions accord to immigrants and African Americans. Their personal, experiential knowledge is often disparaged by professionals as being technically or institutionally uninformed. In addition, they are often granted very limited individual access to school principals or teachers to advocate for their children. Finally, language and other cultural differences often impede conversations between schools' professional staff and parents. These differences generally are unacknowledged by school professionals. The consequence is that parents experience local schools as both unfamiliar and unwelcoming. More to the point, CC9 parents consistently describe local schools, and more generally public institutions, as foreign and hostile.

It was within this context that the parents of CC9 were both hungry for and sensitive to signs of respect from professional workers. Matters of respect, as Apple points out in *The State and the Politics of Knowledge,* are highly associated with the development of citizenship schools and participatory thick democracy. In this process, he remarks, "a new respect for diversity of cultures is generated" (211). For many CC9 parents, the fight for improved public schools was also a search for dignity. Jasper notes, in *The Emotions of Protest,* that "many black civil rights protestors participated to gain dignity in their own lives through struggle and moral expression" (417).

As noted earlier, norms of respect and trust were incorporated into every aspect of CC9's practice. Access was provided to parents through translation services, child care, and meals provided at meetings, showing respect for parents' needs and lived realities. The respect for indigenous expertise was conveyed through providing leadership development programming, encouraging broad participation, and utilizing parent ideas when developing action plans. Trust in parents' decision making was encoded through democratic process. Trust was also extended to parents as they delivered speeches at large public events, discussed the lead teacher proposal with powerful public officials, and facilitated important strategic and tactical discussions.

The vigilant attention paid by CC9 to norms of respect and trust in turn provided the basis for reciprocal exchange between professionals and parents. As their leadership capacity grew, so too did parents' confidence that they could function as equal partners in the work of changing the public schools. As Jane Mansbridge notes in *Beyond Adversary Democracy,* "many individuals want the exhilaration, mutual trust, and reciprocity of working with equals. They want colleagues, not minions or bosses" (29).

Despite CC9's aspiration to break down hierarchical barriers to participation, the tendency of neophyte members to look to the more experienced parent leaders for cues was consistently evident. As well, parent leaders often looked to expert professional organizers to provide strategic direction in critical moments. What CC9 struggled with was predictable: the natural pull to reproduce hierarchies of expertise and status, and the push back of deeply democratic norms of dialogue that valued the voices of all participants in the room. This push-pull was a healthy hallmark of CC9 conversation. It marked maturity by recognizing the lack of purity in the process and the need to be vigilant in including and hearing the different voices struggling for recognition.

Narratives of Oppression and Bounded Solidarity

Mansbridge suggests that some part of the genesis of social relationships and social capital depends on the development of a "vivid sense of underlying identity" (29). Shared identity does not occur in an emotional void. To the contrary, it is highly intertwined with a sharing of narrative, feeling, and common fate. For example, Mansbridge notes, "as women discovered their common history, those in the movement felt a tremendous sense of sisterhood. To feel that all women were sisters meant that other differences faded into insignificance besides the overwhelming understanding . . . that they had shared the same fears, troubles, ways of coping, humiliations and joys. In the era of sisterhood, institutional reminders of the distinctions of the larger society became intolerable. Women found too much in each other to respect" (30).

Emotion often binds people in relationships, be they political or apolitical. Jasper suggests in *The Emotions of Protest* that "emotions give ideas, ideologies, identities, and even interests their power to motivate. . . . Emotions help explain the networks and communities through which movements survive" (420).

Although members and leaders may share emotions during a meeting about a particular point of frustration, for example, these moments are often fragmented and decontextualized. They are not presented in relationship to a history or narrative that draws people to a common fight, for example, to public education. Consequently, such affect is only perceived by others as a reaction during a heated exchange rather than as part of a common story with emotional resonance.

As CC9 leaders and organizers developed their practice work, they understood the importance of retreats in surfacing the otherwise hidden stories that members brought to the social change work. CC9 leadership convened a number of retreats where parents and organizers shared the pain, humiliation, and hope of public education. During these exchanges, many members talked about the sacrifices of their parents to educate them. They also related the choice to immigrate and the promise of greater educational opportunities for their own children. Finally, they recounted the often humiliating attempts to discuss their children's difficulties with often overwhelmed, indifferent, or hostile public school staff. Alternatively, organizers frequently shared their frustrations growing up in decaying communities and watching friends or family members drop out of schools and lead dead-end lives. The nexus between degraded schools, declining communities, and shame, as well as pain, was threaded through many of these conversations.

These formal and informal conversations enabled participants to see each other as more complex, vulnerable, and engaging. The sharing of stories created a bridge to more intimate relationships, and crossing that bridge had substantial implications. To begin with, it frequently promoted greater trust, identification, and respect. As well, it further cemented the development of more reciprocal, equal relationships that resulted in stronger bonds. These bonds of emerging friendship based on empathy helped CC9 withstand many trying moments when individuals, frustrated with the pace of the lead teacher campaign or the number of meetings, considered withdrawing. Their empathy with other members and organizers was often the glue that kept them in the struggle despite mounting doubt and tension. The social capital of any activist community must be assessed on the basis of not only the quantity but also the quality of the relationships that are being formed.

As Barber notes in *Strong Democracy,* empathy has a "politically miraculous power to enlarge perspective and expand consciousness in a fashion that not so much accommodates as transcends private interests and the antagonisms they breed" (189). By sharing stories of oppression and discussing their choice to fight, CC9 parents, like earlier activists in the women's and civil rights movements, formed relationships of bounded solidarity. Bob Moses richly conveys the meaning and experience of solidarity for SNCC students during the civil rights movement in Payne's *I've Got the Light of Freedom:*

> What happens with the students in our movement is that they are
> identifying with these people—people who come off of the land. . . .
> they simply voice time and again, the simple truths you cannot
> ignore because they speak from their own lives. It's this the students
> are rooted in and this is what keeps them from going off at some
> tangent . . . and as long as the students are tied in with this, their
> revolt is well based. (200)

Foundational to the solidarity experienced by SNCC workers and CC9 parents was their empathic connection to these shared stories and truths.

Solidarity, however, demands that empathic identification be joined to a deepened understanding of shared oppression. Critically, the personal must shift to the political, as it did in the civil rights and women's movements, as well as for CC9 parents. Once people explore and feel this part of individual and collective narratives, social capital begins to be converted into a political capital.

As citizens articulate narratives of shared exploitation and reveal common problems, they begin to shift the blame for specific difficulty from the individual to a larger world or context. Importantly, such a dynamic often sparks the necessary agency to solve festering resentment with public institutions. The conversations among parents and leaders during CC9's retreats consistently emphasized themes of parent/child oppression in relationship to public schools, the historic institutional failures of schools in the poorest communities, and ways to begin to fix these breakdowns. As the discussions wended their way through a thicket of shared pain emerging from poverty, immigration, racism, and self-blame for the performance of their children in degraded public schools, the participants were able to more sharply identify external forces contributing to their difficulties as well as develop more vibrant relational connections.

As the individual consciousness and collective power of parents was altered, so too were their senses of self. Repeatedly, members remarked that CC9 had increased their esteem, willingness to take risks, sense of safety, and hope. As their capacity and esteem began to grow, parents were willing to take the risks necessary to speak at a public rally, facilitate a meeting, and, perhaps most fundamentally, help lead a change campaign. These dynamics of individual empowerment were consistently threaded through organizing work that promoted collective identity and power. It is in this nexus between individual development and collective identification that relationships of solidarity and the power of CC9 were built.

Power, Effective Organizing, and the Deepening of Collective Identity

The emergence of collective identity for CC9 parents was, of course, a dynamic and nonlinear process. A number of critical features can be discerned from the experience. Parents had an opportunity to reveal experiences of oppression and deep frustration with a failed public school system. Consistent with Aldon Morris and Carol Mueller's suggestion in *Frontiers in Social Movement Theory,* parent leaders understood that cumulative experience of dialogue, shared decision making, capacity development, exploration of

the root causes of public education failure, and creation of a change platform would eventually help to alter the consciousness of members. Each of
these features of CC9 practice was essential to creating an internal solidarity
among members. Over time, these practice elements were woven into many
meetings and conversations. From the beginning, however, this internal process had a purpose of improving neighborhood schools. For that to occur,
the growing internal solidarity or collective identity of parents had to be
joined to the external work of organizing for change.

CC9 organizing, although frequently collaborative, always implied a direct
opposition to the dominant order. During every organizing drive, CC9 challenged the presumptions of the educational establishment. For example, at
an early stage, parents were insistent on having a role in the hiring of a new
district superintendent. At every turn, the board resisted by excluding parents from critical moments in the deliberative process. Ultimately, a new
superintendent was hired with little parent input. However, the organizing
served a number of purposes. First, the board was made to understand that
business as usual would no longer be tolerated. Second, the organizing helped
to solidify collective identity among CC9 parents. Many parents developed
strong relationships with each other during the campaign, working together
to change the fundamental dynamics of board decision making. Despite the
outcome, many indicated that for the first time they felt the power and voice
necessary to hope that they could improve the schools. This organizing work
challenged the basic presumption of educational decision makers that despite their record of dismal failure, the community would continue to hold
them unaccountable. The campaign was an early signal that a growing number of parents were no longer willing to cede neighborhood schools to professional decision makers.

Over time, the CC9 organizing focused on the lead teacher proposal. This
decision was made on the basis of pragmatic public education politics. Both
the teachers' union and DOE signaled early support for the concept of lead
teachers. Step by step, rallies, private meetings with administrators, e-mails,
and petitions were organized to pressure public school administrators to
move from an early conceptual interest to a policy initiative. The combination of organizing pressure and joint interest resulted in a major policy initiative being developed over a four-month period.

The incremental successes of the campaign were a source of great pride
for many members. Unprecedented turnout at rallies, access to powerful education decision makers, newspaper reports about the campaign, and the

effective public performances of members combined to create the sense among many parent leaders that CC9 was engaged in historically significant work. On this basis parents associated CC9 with the civil rights movement of an earlier era. The experience of sustained success and the perception of historic importance deepened parents' identification with CC9. As these successes accumulated, CC9 leaders became increasingly recognized in their communities. The organizing stimulated a recomposition of their identity as part of a successful and powerful change project.

It is important to step back for a moment and remind ourselves that this shifting sense of identification is also a consequence of many parents' new relationships to power. The women who joined CC9 often felt powerless in their personal and public relationships. They were frequently oppressed in violent domestic relationships, very low-paying jobs, racist encounters, and as undocumented immigrants. These specific experiences were wrapped in a perhaps more generic sense of powerlessness associated with poverty, modest formal education, and outsider status. CC9 consciously attempted to shift these dynamics of power, first by constructing an alternate public space of deep democratic practice, and later by organizing to challenge the injustice of failed education policy and schools. CC9 did this by creating the democratic praxis necessary for moving outsiders to insider status, displacing the deep sense of inadequacy of modest educational credentials with capacity development, working to foster a broader understanding of the relationship between impoverished conditions and unjust policies, and building a campaign for educational justice.

This internal accumulation of social capital through the development of an activist community of parents remains a latent political resource until it is deployed in public organizing campaigns. Eva Gold and colleagues recently argued, in "Bringing Community Organizing into the School Reform Picture," that "there has been a confluence of interest in social capital, and widespread agreement about the importance of relational networks, shared norms and social trust." They further suggest that "the mere existence of social capital does not guarantee its activation" (59). This conversion was elemental to CC9 praxis. Its primary intention was not to build social capital as an end in itself but to politically contest the failure of neighborhood schools.

How to develop and strategically deploy an activist community of parents to leverage change is a primary and vital practice lesson of CC9. Importantly, CC9 does not offer a cookie-cutter approach to parent organizing. What it does provide, however, are the clear practice themes sketched throughout this chapter that cohere into an overarching framework that can be applied elsewhere.

CC9 leadership understood very early on that parents could not expect to unilaterally win a campaign or implement its proposals. Change, particularly in this historic moment, would require the support of other stakeholders. In effect, CC9 would have to "scale up" or expand the power of parents by developing alliances with other groups. It was on this basis that CC9 systematically initiated meetings before and during its lead teacher campaign with the UFT and key DOE officials. This effort to scale up parent power through alliance is an especially important practice lesson of CC9.

Scaling Up Power: Alliance and Reform Aspirations

CC9's lead teacher campaign challenged basic learning and instruction dynamics in neighborhood classrooms. An initiative of this magnitude had implications for public schools throughout New York City and exceeded CC9's capacity to leverage reform independently. CC9 managed to draw attention to its campaign by setting the reform bar high. Conversely, the ambition of its agenda also raised the specter of Ocean Hill–Brownsville and a politics of confrontation over school control.

From the very beginning, CC9 worked to defuse the potential resistance of regional and citywide public education officials. It convened meetings to explain its proposals to key administrators, like Michelle Cahill and Irma Zardoya. CC9 also worked to build common ground with the UFT and its proposal for a career ladder to reward expert teachers for remaining in the classroom. CC9 met with leaders of DOE and UFT before rallies and other public events to solicit support and solidify working relationships. Parents and organizers understood the importance of building trust, first through private conversations with DOE administrators and UFT officials. In these discussions, participants aired their differences, identified their expectations, and floated proposals. These discussions also previewed public events being organized by CC9, which required these officials' attendance. At the public rallies, officials were expected to sign a statement of commitment to the lead teacher proposal.

Critically, in a highly charged political environment, decision makers never felt "blindsided" by CC9 leaders. This is not a small point. Building trust between frequently estranged political actors demands a foundational commitment to at least trying to work through differences privately before going public. This is especially important to powerful decision makers, who are quite reactive to being publicly embarrassed. Such trust was an important lubricant in enabling public officials to move from private to public statements of support for the platform, which in turn added momentum and legitimacy to the lead teacher campaign. Importantly, the strength of CC9's relationships with the UFT, the DOE, and the IESP varied substantially. On the basis of its shared commitments and history, parents perceived the IESP as an especially trustworthy partner.

Through Eric Zachary and, later, Milli Bonilla, the IESP helped to found, fund, and coordinate the work of CC9. The working relationship between the IESP and CC9 is a model for university–community collaboration. The IESP brought critical resources to this community project including the organizing expertise of its coordinator, technical skills to develop and disseminate reports, training experience, access to key decision makers, and a fund-raising capacity that solidified and enlarged the work of the collaborative. Time and again, the IESP helped to provide parents with the supports critical to developing an effective campaign. Simultaneously, Zachary and Bonilla helped to promote the deep democratic experience and parent leadership that were hallmarks of CC9 practice.

The UFT provoked much early suspicion among parents. CC9 parents saw UFT members as uncommitted to the children and the community. Parents blamed public school teachers for the failure of the schools; they described teachers as in it for the paycheck and out of there as soon as the "bell started ringing at 3:00." Conversely, teachers often viewed parent activists as irresponsible, lacking basic knowledge about the complex demands of classroom instruction, and confrontational. This wall of mutual suspicion and blame was very difficult to overcome. As a result of a series of meetings between regional officials, such as Herb Katz, and parent leaders, attitudes began to shift. At the same time, many UFT officials indicated that the necessary transformation of public schools could only occur if teachers began working with parents and communities to create a broader social movement for educational change. The dinner sponsored by the UFT to honor the parents of CC9 broadened and deepened an emergent sense of partnership. Subsequent meetings convened during the heat of the lead teacher campaign tested and solidified the alliance.

It is important to note that this alliance was in part a marriage of mutual interest. The UFT was the target of an intensifying attack, in which management blamed the union for the failures of the public school system. The UFT was described by managers and politicians as an impediment blocking a series of necessary reforms. This public campaign was intended to win the support of parents throughout New York City, especially in the poorest communities. To repel this aggressive antilabor message, the UFT needed grassroots allies. The alliance that the UFT formed with CC9 offered immediate benefits, as parents countered "official" testimony at a city council hearing that was often vitriolic in its condemnation of the UFT. As well, the lead teacher proposal benefited UFT members by rewarding a cohort of teachers for their expertise and developing a career ladder for instructors. The longer-term potential benefits of working with CC9 to build a community–labor alliance for education reform was also part of the UFT leadership's thinking. For its part, CC9 understood that to move the lead teacher proposal forward, it needed the support of a powerful ally. The UFT could unilaterally veto the proposal. Alternatively, it could place some of its substantial political and economic capital at the disposal of CC9 to advance the lead teacher campaign. At significant points during the organizing campaign, the UFT proved to be a vital, trustworthy partner.

Collaboration with the DOE presented a number of difficult obstacles for CC9. To begin with, when CC9 was established in 2001, the bureaucracy was suspicious and resistant to any reform proposal that emerged from outside its decision-making process. This was especially the case if change initiatives emerged from parents or community groups. The new leadership of DOE was more receptive to working with grassroots organizations. Cahill was the most notable example of a leader who had a demonstrated commitment to involving parents in decision making. As the campaign progressed, however, there were a number of moments in which CC9 felt that certain officials advanced an approach that diminished the ambition of the parents' lead teacher initiative.

This lack of commitment from key DOE officials, combined with what CC9 parents perceived as a general lack of urgency regarding the implementation of the lead teacher proposal, tested parents' patience. As well, it raised questions about both the potential and limits of collaborating with DOE. Clearly, some conversation and a measure of collaboration were necessary if parents hoped to produce needed change in the public schools. What CC9 had to consistently balance was confronting DOE about its less than collaborative approach, on the one hand, and working with public education professionals to reach a meaningful settlement on the lead teacher proposal, on the other. This was a delicate dance of pushing key decision makers to accept

CC9's plan but not to the point of alienation, causing them to abandon the negotiation. Equally important, as the school year was quickly drawing to a close, the pressure was mounting for leadership to strike a deal.

Because the DOE is an arm of the state, it can never be an ally of a parent-led campaign for public education reform in the same way as a union. Individual administrators might offer such support, but the institution cannot. Collaboration with the DOE is generally limited to its assurance of access, willingness to entertain parent proposals, and provision of authentic forms of negotiation with community groups. Significantly, the collaboration cannot result in a political alliance that pits the DOE against other parts of the state to advance a community agenda for change. This is particularly the case if the proposal demands a substantial infusion of new resources or dramatic restructuring of the lines of accountability and authority. That is a boundary that DOE administrators will not cross. For example, an initiative supported by particular administrators but opposed by the mayor or governor will be resisted and, in the end, opposed by the DOE. This was, of course, not the case with the lead teacher proposal, an initiative of mutual interest that offered a basis for collaborative negotiation. But this may pose an issue in the future when parents contest another issue, such as class size.

As we review the collaborative institutional relationships developed by CC9, it is important to draw a few basic distinctions. IESP's constant attention to CC9's development through the extension of technical assistance, staff support, and fund-raising promoted an alliance of membership relationship. This form of collaboration is not unlike the relationships that were developed between the six member agencies that constituted CC9. Both parents and participating agencies perceived IESP as a key member of the collaborative because of both the quality and consistency of its contributions. Parents did not view the UFT as a member organization, but they did see it as an ally. It provided episodic but critical support to the lead teacher campaign. As well, the UFT sponsored a number of events to cement and deepen its relationship with parents. The UFT asked CC9 to support its budget agenda with the state assembly and the city council. This reciprocal exchange was an essential ingredient in building the alliance between CC9 and the UFT. Finally, as was noted earlier, the DOE collaborated with CC9 by assuring parents' access to its decision makers. Nevertheless, the DOE was the target of the lead teacher campaign because of its budgetary and policy-making roles in New York City public education.

CC9 was a community group prepared to push back against the persistent failures of public education policy and disinvestment. It asserted a need to reinvest in public education through the recruitment of a seasoned cohort of professional mentors in the poorest communities. Such an agenda could not be achieved at a district or regional level. To the contrary, it required the support of the city and the UFT precisely because it had broader contractual and policy implications.

Building a Movement

CC9 organizers and leaders always understood that the lead teacher proposal potentially had a broad trajectory beyond the single district. CC9's hope was that the experiment in District 9 would prove successful and be replicated in other poor communities throughout the city. The intention was, as Oakes and Lipton note in "Struggling for Educational Equity in Diverse Communities," "for educators to join with parents in collective activist projects, public projects to improve the quality of teaching."

CC9's power, both independently and in alliance, was considered a countervailing force to the continued decay of public education in very poor communities. As such, its ambition extended beyond lead teachers and District 9 to a broader movement for educational justice. Leaders and members anticipated that over time a broader alliance would be built with teachers struggling to make a difference as instructors in the midst of the gradual starvation of public schools. More generally, this alliance was expected to join community groups and teachers' unions in the common struggle to improve the performance of public schools through increased investment.

Over the longer term, CC9 hoped to build a social movement for educational justice. It was clear to CC9 organizers and parents that only a political and social movement of community-based organizations and labor interests has the potential to build a countervailing power to the neoliberal policies that led to a disinvestment and degradation of public education.

Dilemma as a Source of Struggle and Innovation in CC9's Campaign for Educational Justice

Organizing campaigns spawn practice dilemmas. Any project intended to create collective identity, challenge centers of political authority, reconfigure public space, and amass an independent community power has set a most ambitious agenda. The aspirations of CC9, however, were consistently confronted with interpersonal, communal, and institutional obstacles. The struggle was, at its essence, a push-pull between constraint and the collective will of parents.

Practice dilemmas, or the tension between the goals of an organizing campaign and the various constraints that contest its imagined reform arc, are not always resolvable, but in the course of a successful campaign like CC9's, they must be addressed. Effective change organizations recognize that the push-pull between reform aspiration and social reality is the grist for developing a robust organizing practice. Equally important, effective practitioners must develop the capacity to work with the uncertainty of how specific kinds of dilemmas will be resolved within the motion of a change campaign. Critically, such uncertainty has the significant potential value of forcing a campaign leadership to rethink direction, tactic, and strategy.

The Fragility of Collaboration

The founding of CC9 produced a series of internal challenges. Despite reaching agreement on internal standards of accountability, the authority of CC9 in relationship to its member organizations remained uncertain. The resources CC9 allocated to individual organizations were a source of leverage. As well, shared norms regarding increased public investment and the need to build parent power to reverse the failure of the school system were a basis of agreement on an ambitious platform for change.

For Zachary, the work of holding the collaborative together was often about recognizing both the uniform and distinctive contributions member agencies were capable of making to the joint project. The task was in holding individual agencies accountable for minimal standards of performance while understanding that the quality and quantity of their contributions would vary, at times substantially. This was very difficult terrain to navigate, particularly as the higher-performing agencies grew weary or resentful. The underperforming agencies were seen by some as "free riders" in the CC9 project. What CC9 leaders and organizers understood, however, was that an agency could exit the project without difficulty. It could simply determine that the benefits, such as organizing money or prestige associated with participation in CC9, failed to offset its expenditure of agency resources. If CC9 pushed too hard, it risked having agencies exit. If this occurred, the collaborative's experiment would unravel.

Parent Attentiveness to Change Work over the Long Haul

For poor parents, the commitment to fight for an issue such as improved public education is often both heartfelt and drawn from a deep well of frustration. Yet the commitment to remain in such struggle can be washed away by other pressing demands. The predominantly poor women who made up CC9's core leadership were often fighting to sustain housing, earn a living, and/or fend off violent partners. Time and energy were scarce commodities for many of these women. Additionally, many of CC9's leaders were attempting to build careers and migrate to other communities. As Alejandro Portes notes in "Embeddedness and Immigration," part of the push-pull in any social change organization "is a fear that a solidarity born out of common adversity would be undermined by the departure of more successful members" (1342).

These pulls away from the orbit of CC9 were compelling. A number of parent leaders had to scale back the time they allocated to CC9 as they transitioned back into school, took new jobs, or simply determined that their families required greater attention. Always, those who pulled back were replaced by new parents. But the lack of continuity among the leadership was costly to CC9. The accumulated expertise of parents constantly had to be replenished. Additionally, the historic memory of CC9's accomplishments and commitments was dimmed. At the very beginning of the lead teacher campaign, the importance of the platform had to be relearned by CC9 leaders. In part, this was a consequence of the natural growth of CC9's parent base after the development of the platform. However, it was also a consequence of seasoned leaders having less and less time to informally introduce neophytes to the CC9 change agenda.

In general, parents did not cut their ties to CC9. Instead, they reduced the time they invested in meeting and organizing. The access CC9 afforded parents through child care, meals, car service, and translation explains, in part, parents' continued engagement with the work despite other compelling demands. Parent leaders often complained, however, about the mushrooming number of meetings, particularly as the campaign intensified. Some suggested that it was simply untenable and they were burning out. Others thrived as the demands intensified, and stepped up to do more of the work. These parents had the strongest identification with both CC9 and the politics of educational justice. Many of the most committed parents likened their work with CC9 to the political fights during the civil rights movement or the liberation struggles in South America. The load that this relatively small cohort of parents carried was not tenable, however, over the long haul.

Scarce time was not the only factor causing parents to rethink and reconfigure their levels of commitment to CC9. For many leaders, patience was also in short supply. Their children carried the burden of failed schools, and parents felt deeply a sense of urgency to improve local school performance. As CC9 gradually developed both external alliances and an independent parent base, there emerged an implicit demand for a disciplined patience in building the power necessary to change the schools. Appadurai suggests that patience as a long-term political strategy for the very poor is most difficult. More to the point, a strategy of long-term asset building runs up against the crises and emergencies that characterize the daily life of the urban poor. Many parents questioned both the pace and ambition of CC9's agenda given the dire situations of their children. Others were loath to compromise the goals of the campaign, because even a total victory was not enough. Many conversations within CC9 at biannual community meetings and retreats focused on these questions. For some parents, the discussions enlarged both their time frame regarding meaningful reform and the politics of educational justice. They came to understand that, as in the civil rights or other movements, present organizing, while capable of achieving immediate successes, might also plant the seeds for more transformational change in a near or distant future. In general, parents were prepared to defer some part of their dream. However, they were also clear that the organizing work had to produce concrete, immediate successes in order to enlist new parents and sustain the commitment of seasoned leaders. They accomplished this, in part, through the success of the lead teacher campaign.

The more enduring tension of continued patience in the midst of their children's academic frustration and failure persisted, however. Impatience caused some parents to vent their frustration by advocating for more confrontational approaches. These heated discussions inevitably transitioned to political and strategic assessments of CC9's power and the most effective tactics to achieve its objectives. Ultimately, the demands of time and patience caused many parents to recalibrate their commitment to CC9's work. In turn, CC9 staff and leaders worked to sustain the engagement of members. This tension required both a vigilant attention to retaining present membership and investment in developing a next generation of leaders.

Organizer Turnover and the Strains of Collaboration

CC9 had great difficulty retaining its organizing staff. New Settlement Apartments was the one exception to a general pattern of relatively rapid organizer turnover. Staff rarely remained more than one year. At a number of CBOs, the position turned over more than once during the course of a year. Some agencies did not fill vacant organizing positions for months and addressed this gap on an ad hoc basis with substitutes. Critically, the turnover and delays in filling staff positions undermined the continuity of organizing work. Repeatedly, parents complained that they were simply unable to build relationships with organizers or fully develop their school-based or district campaign work as a result of the turnover.

This turnover of organizing staff occurred for many reasons. First, CBOs historically have had great difficulty retaining underpaid and overworked entry-level organizers. Additionally, a number of the organizers were based in agencies that were structured primarily to deliver direct services. Consequently, they often felt isolated and marginalized in agency cultures that emphasized individual client relationships and ignored collective liberatory forms of practice. Finally, agency investment in training, supervision, and other supports for organizers was modest at best. In the end, the steady drip of strain and estrangement produced an out-migration of organizers.

Clearly, strain is embedded in the very structure of a collaborative such as CC9. For example, supervisory support, outcome measures, and agency accountability were negotiated and renegotiated between member agencies and CC9 coordinators from the IESP. CC9 tried to mediate these strains by challenging agencies to provide specific forms of support for organizers, create more concrete outcome standards, and reconfigure the work to create better fit between agency strengths and CC9 needs. Over time, this challenge yielded specific structural changes. For example, the IESP developed a more ambitious training and support program for organizing staff to increase morale and capacity. These initiatives were part of a learning loop that began with the frustration of staff turnover. Through these trainings, frustrations were transformed into reflective conversations about the difficulties of collaboration. Slowly, the discussions yielded concrete proposals, many of which were tested. Initiatives directed at supporting staff, such as technical assistance and training, proved relatively effective in slowing turnover. These interorganizational experiments in structure did little, however, to reduce the consistent strain and fallout of collaboration. This experimentation continues as this book is being written. Despite the discontinuities of staff turnover and uneven contributions of member agencies, the lead teacher campaign proceeded and proved effective. Equally important, in the heat of the campaign, CC9 leadership paused to consider these vexing questions. The dynamic interplay between staff turnover and collaborative strain remains an important question not only for CC9 but for any organizing project that aims to work with community agencies to build a change campaign.

The Implementation and Value of the Lead Teacher Victory

Although the lead teacher campaign was a landmark victory, its importance will ultimately be determined on the basis of the contribution it makes to the improved academic performance of students from the poorest neighborhoods in the city. The value of parent organizing as a public education change strategy will be measured not on the basis of the victories it amasses, but on the positive and long-term change produced in the learning and instruction culture of public schools. The dilemma for parents and organizers is to assure that what they have achieved through an organizing campaign is implemented to maximize students' chances for success. This is a very complex undertaking. It demands new forms of partnership between professional staff and parents. CC9 parents, for example, had to transition from the "outsider" role of community change agent to the demands of working inside the system and helping to develop and implement an effective lead teacher program.

For parents, the choice to invest in implementation did not come without cost. The focus on program hiring and planning pulled parents away from the important work of developing the next organizing campaign. Much of the leadership was clear, however, that a trade-off in favor of implementation needed to be made in the short term. Parents and organizers understood that the program's chances for success increased to the extent that they were part of the decision making during early implementation. However, they also understood that CC9 could not be a part of an open-ended process of program development. The focus of their work needed to shift back to organizing as soon as the lead teacher program was launched in District 9. In the past many organizing groups had experienced the quicksand-like demands of housing creation, shelter management, or service delivery to victims of domestic violence, for example. Critically, many of these groups abandoned organizing in favor of service delivery. CC9 leadership was determined not to make that choice. Therefore, CC9 leaders struck a balance between the immediate and critical demands of implementation prior to and at the beginning of the new school year and the development of a next-stage organizing campaign in the spring.

As CC9 shifted its attention back to organizing, the day-to-day work of implementing and monitoring the lead teacher program would be increasingly influenced by public education administrators. The value of the lead teacher program to the academic achievement of students would largely be determined by professional staff, often distanced from the day-to-day difficulties of teaching and learning in the poorest districts of New York City. CC9 decided, however, that it simply could not satisfactorily address both the ongoing questions of lead teacher implementation and the need to launch a new campaign.

This tension also reveals the limitations of external organizing as a singular strategy for transforming public education. Although parents and organizers may win victories that are essential to changing learning and instruction conditions, these reforms will not reach their full potential unless they are a part of the ongoing conversation regarding program development and impact. The relationships among public schools, the communities they serve, and democratic decision making are essential to any sustained change in the learning culture and performance of public education. The reconfiguration of power between professional decision makers and parents through external organizing campaigns is essential to correcting public sector decision making that excludes the very communities they intend to affect. It is only on this basis that meaningful involvement of parents and community groups in the internal conversation and decision making to improve local public schools can be assured. Yet the dilemma of sustaining this "outsider" and "insider" change work, when constrained by various forms of resource scarcity, remains an ongoing, unresolved tension.

Reproducing and Expanding Grassroots Leadership

CC9 developed a hardy and capable group of parent leaders prior to the lead teacher campaign. Although organizers continued to test new approaches, recruitment of new parents remained relatively flat. The base expanded just enough, and seasoned leadership ratcheted up its investment sufficiently to meet the escalating demands of the campaign. A critical question remained, however: How could CC9 both stabilize and expand its base of parent leaders?

Some of the difficulty, as was noted earlier, can be traced to the internal challenges agencies faced in locating the resources, issues, and practices necessary to draw parents to a community change project. However, part of the difficulty is external and historic. Many parents have simply given up. They do not believe they can make a difference in improving public institutions such as schools and, more generally, their community. This encrusted sense of hopelessness is, at least in part, a product of failed schools, dead-end jobs, unsafe streets, and the absence of any countervailing vision or movement to change those conditions. It is especially difficult to persuade parents that school improvement from the bottom up is possible, and that CC9 can help achieve such change. In some sense, CC9 is asking parents to resist the powerful cultural pull to deride all things public and to locate some part of their hope in a struggle, without guarantee, to improve public schools. This is a very tall order. CC9's struggle to develop an expansive cohort of increasingly capable and effective parent leaders has produced some palpable results. However, the task of growing its parent base remains a vexing issue with no easy solution. The stakes are very high for the larger project of public education. Only an expansive number of parent activists in a cross section of poor communities can leverage the investment and structural change necessary to revive public education. Most recently, CC9 has added school safety to its platform. It is perceived by leadership as a concrete and compelling issue that may attract a large, new cohort of parents to CC9.

What Is at Stake?

This book has attempted to convey both the hope and challenge of reviving public education through the democratic participation of parents in decision making that shapes their children's schools. The challenges of entrenched bureaucratic power, increasing support for a neoliberal agenda, and the immediate survival pressures on poor communities are daunting obstacles to fully realizing such possibility. That said, another truth is that the hope of public education is highly intertwined with its role as an incubator of democratic experience.

An empowered, participatory citizenship evolves at least in part from a public education system that consciously provides lessons of participatory democracy inside and outside of the classroom. Those lessons are part of an academic experience that challenges students to think more deeply about democratic culture and prepares them to more fully participate in a rapidly changing economy. Public schools have failed students in the poorest neighborhoods on both counts. Increasingly, the testing culture of schools eliminates critical thinking from the day-to-day work of instructional staff. Public education pedagogy in the aftermath of No Child Left Behind singularly focuses on lifting test scores. Clearly, concrete academic achievement test scores have an independent value. However, despite some recent modest success regarding testing outcomes, the fact remains that the academic achievement of poor students of color is a scandal. They continue to drop out of the system in record numbers, and their test scores lag well behind those of students in neighboring, more affluent communities. The present failure of public education in these largely urban communities is most fundamentally a failure of democratic will—the will of the body politic to make an investment of resources, imagination, and persistence necessary to reinvigorate the democratic project of public education.

The experience of CC9 is instructive because it demonstrates how the struggle to revive public schools is ultimately a fight for democratic citizenship waged at many levels. Despite the various dilemmas associated with its organizing work, CC9 created a public space that promoted new forms of participation and enfranchisement for parents. That foundation was used to build a democratic alliance with the UFT. This conscious, internal process of building democratic experience led to relationships of solidarity between parents as they focused on their common problem of failing public schools. Let us make no mistake: parent voices were heard because of their independent base of power and sophisticated strategies to push a common agenda of lead teachers. For CC9 parents, this was a chance to improve local schools and perhaps more largely revive hope in public institutions, but it is important not to overstate their victory. The campaign did not produce a huge infusion of new resources or an overhaul of public education. How could this possibly have occurred, given the size of CC9 and the scope of public education failure? Conversely, the importance of the CC9 experiment must be understood as a major step in a democratic reclaiming of public schools by parents. Against very steep odds, parents in District 9 waged a campaign that led to both a redistribution of resources and a change in the learning and instruction environments of classrooms in local public schools. This is a signal victory because a community group, drawing on its own experience, shifted the focus to the learning and instruction culture within public schools, created alliance with other powerful stakeholders, developed a reform agenda with citywide implications, and imposed its will on the education establishment.

Despite many difficulties, CC9 was able to point the way to the next stage of parent organizing for public education change in New York City. As well, CC9 offers a practice framework for thinking about a new form of public space that joins democratic culture and process with organizing campaigns to contest public policies.

Most generally, CC9 is resisting a neoliberal policy regimen, which, on the one hand, promotes disinvestment or the privatization of public institutions, and, on the other hand, imposes business practices that destabilize the collective purposes of public institutions. This phenomenon is not restricted to either public schools or New York City. Neoliberal attacks on public institutions are an international trend. CC9's political and policy intentions challenge neoliberal ideological assumptions that have foreclosed the possibility of parents being full partners in the remaking of public education. As Morris and Mueller note, grassroots organizing such as CC9's lead teacher campaign also challenges the increasingly hegemonic presumption that public schools cannot work, especially in very poor communities. District 9 and communities like it continue to generate the persistent challengers seeking political change to shape a different future for the most deprived citizens. It is that democratic challenge, combined with organized parent power, that represents the best hope for reviving a public education that consistently fails the poorest children of color in New York City and the nation.

The Ongoing Work for Educational Justice

The lead teacher program quickly evolved into a featured element of the DOE's reform agenda. In part this was a consequence of the dramatic turnaround of key indicators of student performance in District 9. In spring 2005, data on the reading and math tests of fourth-grade students documented dramatic improvement. The *New York Times* reported that for years "the district's reading scores were the worst in the city." Six years earlier only 17.1 percent of the district's fourth-grade students read at grade level. The most recent data indicated that the percentage of fourth-grade students reading at grade level had jumped to 47.6, "still low but hardly last." David Herszenhorn of the *New York Times* reported that one official remarked that achieving this increase in performance in a brief period of time was like "climbing Mount Everest."

Much of the change in student achievement levels was attributed to new forms of collaboration between key stakeholders and the introduction of the lead teacher program. In May 2005 the *New York Times* reported that senior administrators attributed the student success "to cooperation between parents, the school system, community groups and the teachers union." In addition, the CC9-led lead teacher reform was described as having made a significant contribution to this turnaround in student achievement. An evaluation of the lead teacher program developed by an independent consulting firm in fall 2006 concluded that a number of positive outcomes in local district elementary schools could be attributed to this reform. More specifically, the instructor turnover rates of seven of the ten schools involved in the lead teacher experiment fell substantially. As well, test scores for students directly exposed to the program from 2004 to 2006 exceeded gains made by students in all New York City schools and all District 9 schools. Clearly, preliminary evidence indicated that the program had produced impressive results. This conclusion must be tempered, however, by the limitations of the data that were collected. The factors that led to the substantial changes in teacher turnover and student achievement are likely multiple and complex. The degree to which these changes can be attributed to the lead teacher program remains unclear. What is clear, however, is that in the aftermath of the introduction of lead teachers, school performance improved in ways that were consistent with the promise of the reform. That association in the very arid desert of public education success was enough for the City of New York to expand the lead teacher experiment. In the fall the lead teacher program was expanded to over a hundred elementary schools across the city.

In the midst of the reported successes of the lead teacher program, CC9 enlarged its organizing locus to include all of the Bronx and renamed itself the Community Collaborative to Improve Bronx Schools (CCB). It pushed forward on other elements of its reform program that were linked to school safety. After much struggle, both internally between parent leaders impatient with the slow progress being made with city agencies and externally with the Department of Transportation, an agreement was reached. The settlement, although important, achieved far less than initially proposed or imagined by CCB. The very labor-intensive campaign waged over the better part of a year produced speed bumps for the busy streets in front of PS 218, 53, and 64. Increasingly, however, parents and the CBOs were feeling the tension between the scope of their agenda, organizational capacity, and the magnitude of the systemic failures of the New York City public schools. Norm Fruchter, the director of the Community Involvement Program at the Annenberg Institute, remarked, "If we could build these associations with enough depth—and if we could raise expectations and hope in enough places—we could create the real public will needed to change priorities." In general, it was presumed that such associations should be embedded in local communities, perhaps over time cohering into structures with greater reach. The limitations of local organizing campaigns in altering either the education priorities of DOE or the systemic failure of public schools led to the conclusion that a city-wide parent organization needed to be founded to create the power necessary to influence systemwide policy and failure.

This realization was joined to the recent establishment of parent-led collaboratives in three of the five boroughs of New York City. They included the CCB, the Brooklyn Education Collaborative (BEC), and the Brooklyn Queens 4 Education group. These associations' structural commitment to democratic decision making, foundational institutional partnership between parents and CBOs, education change agendas, and interest in building alliances with a cross section of stakeholders were significantly influenced by the experience of CC9. The time was therefore ripe for founding a citywide parent-led coalition for public education reform.

In 2006, a citywide collaborative was founded. The three boroughwide groups formed the New York City Coalition for Education Justice (CEJ). Importantly the design and matrix were created by an intermediary organization, the Community Involvement Program (CIP), which was established through CC9's "old friend" NYU's IESP. The staff person from IESP most central to both founding and later helping to guide CEJ was Eric Zachary. The effort to "scale up" parent-led organizing from the neighborhood to the borough to the entire city at every step provided both opportunity and dilemma for parent leaders and organizers. Clearly, the most striking benefit was an increased capacity to address public education issues that had festered for years, produced dismal outcomes, and demanded new approaches. A particularly powerful example of such persistent, often invisible failure was, as Diane Ravitch remarked in April 2006 to the *New York Times,* "that the city's four year high school graduation rate of 53 percent had barely budged during Mr. Bloomberg's tenure." The greater reach of a citywide parent-led coalition to address systemic failure was a clear benefit. However, what would likely be traded off was a capacity to reach more deeply into the learning and instruction culture of local schools to transform the conditions that produced school-based failure. This choice for breadth over depth certainly had a powerful logic given the finite resource of parent activism and the profound failures of public schools citywide. That said, the cost of failing to introduce and monitor reform in local schools should not be underestimated. Targeted programmatic investment can be won at the city level and produce little discernable change in local schools. In fact, too often that has been the process and consequence of public education reform initiatives. What distinguished the CEJ initiative from earlier reform efforts was that the agenda would originate from a grassroots group and not the education bureaucracy, DOE. Although the point of origin and source of pressure for a particular reform are important factors that influence its impact, the locus of struggle is also critical. Importantly, the choice was made to invest parent energy in citywide campaigns.

CEJ was committed to organizing a citywide parent movement to assure a sound education to all of the city's schoolchildren. Importantly, as the three borough collaboratives scaled up their work to build on recent successes, it was met with an increasingly resistant and centralized school system. With the consolidation of mayoral control through legislation, as LynNell Hancock

reported in the July 9, 2007, issue of *The Nation,* "no matter how competent and committed the players at the top, public sector reforms . . . may be
doomed if the people most affected are left outside." This was bought into
vivid relief by the *New York Times* in March 2006 when it reported that the
DOE refused to consult with CCB about its plan to expand the lead teacher
program citywide. A CEJ organizing campaign would offer another pathway for change to often frustrated parents. In its first year, CEJ focused on
developing the participatory culture necessary to building a high parent
investment and ownership of collective change projects. As well, CEJ created
guidelines to help structure and govern its internal expectations and accountability. This early emphasis on creating a democratic culture and documents
on internal expectations was significantly informed by the experience of CC9.
After both reaching agreement and developing partnership relationships, CEJ
began to develop its first organizing campaign.

In fall 2006, CEJ developed a citywide middle school campaign. This initial organizing effort was focused on New York City's middle school failure
because of its significant contribution to the high school dropout rates. Much
evidence accumulated by CEJ indicated that middle school was a critical
transitional period for poor students that significantly influenced their later
academic performance and retention. Two reports developed by CEJ, *New
York City's Middle-Grade Schools: Platforms for Success or Pathways to Failure?*
published in January 2007, and *Our Children Can't Wait: A Proposal to Close
the Middle-Grades Achievement Gap* issued a year later, were important tools
in this organizing campaign. They both established the content of the problem and articulated a change platform for solving it. During the process of
developing and distributing these documents, CEJ built key strategic alliances with union officials, political leaders, and a cross section of community advocates. The CEJ platform and its emerging alliance were a large part
of the underpinning for its citywide organizing campaign. It organized parents, community residents, and key stakeholders for a number of rallies,
press conferences, and actions at DOE. The structure of the campaign—parents developing an independent platform and base while building strategic
alliances and pressure tactics—was borrowed from the organizing text developed by CC9 during the lead teacher campaign.

Of particular importance in this middle school campaign was a successful collaboration with the Speaker of the New York City Council Christine
Quinn. This collaboration resulted in the development of a city council task
force and comprehensive report with specific recommendations for the

middle-grade schools. This stage of the organizing yielded an agreement between the mayor, the city council speaker, the chancellor, and CEJ in August 2007. The *New York Times* reported that the agreement created a new DOE Middle School Initiative that included an investment of $5 million to implement the recommendations of the city council in fifty-one low-performing schools. Critically, the CEJ campaign helped to change the discourse regarding both the middle school crisis and its relationship to low high school graduation rates. The DOE and the mayor's office were not initially receptive to CEJ's platform for change. Only by broadening its alliance and applying a range of private and public pressure tactics was CEJ able to prevail in advancing its agenda. That said, CEJ organizers understood that an investment of $5 million in its ambitious program was only a first step in addressing the middle schools' deep crisis of performance. The campaign would need to both scale up its demands and bolster its alliance to heighten the visibility of the middle schools' failure and create a serious public investment to solve the problem.

CEJ's continuing effort to direct resources to low-performing middle schools met stiff resistance. This was in part a consequence of the $700 million in proposed cuts to the New York City and New York State education budgets in fall 2008. Earlier in the year, however, CEJ had joined with a number of other organizations including the UFT to create the Keep the Promises Coalition (KTP). The coalition was successful in persuading the New York State legislature and governor to restore all of the funding to New York City that it had committed the prior year. The coalition then turned its attention to both Mayor Bloomberg and the city council and pressured them to restore its proposed cuts to the education budget. Importantly, CEJ provided this larger coalition with its most effective parent leadership and mobilized the largest number of people to attend rallies. The work of CEJ and KTP resulted in the restoration of the education budget and an agreement that the city would invest in a comprehensive reform of low-performing middle schools. Again, it is important to note that both the impetus and pressure for this important reform did not come from the education establishment, but rather from effective grassroots citywide organizing. If not for this campaign, the failure of the middle schools would likely have festered at least in the short run on the back burner of DOE reform focused on testing, corporatization of school culture, and consolidation of mayoral control. Instead, middle school reform, like lead teacher innovation, became a featured part of education officials' reform program because of the pivotal role played by parent agenda and organizing campaigns. The new initiative committed

$30 million to the "DOE Blueprint for Middle School Success," which was informed by earlier reports of both the city council and CEJ. Equally important, a committee was established that included CEJ members to both guide and monitor implementation, in a role much like that played by CC9 during the introduction of the lead teacher program in district elementary schools.

In August 2008, The Office of the Mayor issued a press release that acknowledged the role played by CEJ in developing the "Blueprint for Middle School Success" when he noted, "the menu of options for principals to improve their options is based on the recommendations of the DOE, City council and CEJ reports." Mayor Bloomberg also noted, as CEJ had years earlier, that the city would continue to focus its attention on the middle schools because "that is where the rubber hits the road for many of our students. . . . this public–private partnership will help ensure that more students enter their freshman year with the tools they need to succeed in the classroom."

CEJ has carried on the work citywide that CC9 developed in a small corner of the Bronx. As noted earlier, its participatory culture, development of a proactive agenda, and attention to building both its parent base and a larger alliance replicate the earlier work of CC9. As well, its commitment to employing pressure tactics publicly while privately continuing to negotiate and to sustaining relationships with public officials mimics what CC9 practiced earlier in the decade. Importantly, CEJ also represents a next step in parent organizing. It marks the transition to a citywide power to hold public officials accountable not simply for local school failure but also for systemic breakdown. In addition, the clearer, more focused roles of organizers to create systemic change campaigns and not attend to local school-based organizing have contributed to a dramatically reduced turnover rate. The importance of organizer stability in helping to shape an effective campaign and build the base of CEJ over time cannot be underestimated. The middle school campaigns have established CEJ as an important player in New York City public education politics and decision making.

CEJ's task in the coming years, however, remains daunting. While CEJ has achieved substantial success and legitimacy, the crisis of public education has continued to deepen. The kind of redistributive investment and targeted programming necessary to produce systemwide results is far more substantial than what has been achieved to date. CEJ will need to increase its parent base, extend and deepen its alliances, and push state decision makers in ways that may challenge historic relationships if it is to make significant differences for the million-plus children attending New York City's schools. To have such success, CEJ may have to test its funders to finance more powerful challenges to New York City public education decision makers. Some part of its future work may also require CEJ to develop a political action committee that allows it to more effectively and directly lobby politicians. Finally, the dilemma of drawing more parents to the struggle over improved public schools system-wide continues to persist. CEJ, although it has involved hundreds of parent leaders citywide, is reaching but a small fraction of the low-income parents whose children attend New York City public schools. This part of its work must also be "scaled up." That challenge, which collides with parent inertia, daily struggles to survive, and the limited visibility of CEJ in public schools, is perhaps the most difficult and important work faced by any grassroots project intending to change the course of public education policy citywide. Yet within a neoliberal conservative context that continues to corporatize, privatize, and underfund public education, CC9's and CEJ's successes in re-directing and increasing public investment in strategically important pro-gramming has been remarkable. That has not been an accident but rather a consequence of paying careful attention to building the parent and col-laborative power necessary to hold public education officials accountable. The lessons of CC9 and its descendant collaborative CEJ can be generalized to campaigns in other parts of the country. However, the struggle to build democratic cultures of participation, create platforms for change that are collectively owned, evolve more robust alliances over time, and apply pres-sure tactics that challenge but do not permanently estrange decision makers requires the delicate mix of practice and leadership skill described earlier in this volume. That skill and disposition must be systematically incorporated into the training and leadership development of the organizing work even in the most frenetic and demanding periods of a campaign.

As CEJ contemplates next steps in its organizing work, part of the politi-cal landscape is changing locally and nationally. These changes will signifi-cantly influence public education discourse and policy making. To begin with, the financial meltdown of the private sector has resulted in proposals to reduce the budget of public education that are of far greater magnitude than in the recent past. Simultaneously, in fall 2008, the political landscape shifted with the election of Barack Obama, who campaigned on a platform of change. During the election he promised a new urban agenda that in large part would focus on school reform. Many progressive activists and advocates are therefore hopeful that the new president will make the kinds of targeted program investments in urban public schools that will help to transform the learning and instruction conditions for poor children of color. Shortly after the election and after much deliberation, President-elect Obama signaled some part of his agenda for public schools when he appointed Arne Duncan as the secretary of education. Duncan was described by the *New York Times* in December 2008 "as a compromise candidate on the debate that divides Democrats on the proper course for public school policy after the Bush years." The *New York Times* reported in the same article that the debate within the Democratic Party immediately before the appointment resulted in competing manifestos being circulated, "with one group espousing a get tough policy based on pushing teachers and administrators harder to raise achievement; and another arguing that schools alone could not close the achievement gap thus urging new investments in school-based health clinics and other social programs to help poor students learn." Duncan was the only big-city superintendent who signed both statements. The *New York Times* noted that he offered as his reasoning that the "nation's schools needed to be held accountable for student progress, but also needed major new investments, new talent and new teacher training efforts." "In straddling the two camps," the *New York Times* reported, "Mr. Duncan seemed to reflect Mr. Obama's impatience with what he has called 'tired educational debates.'" More recently, this rhetoric has been accompanied by new streams of Department of Education funding. The initiative titled Race to the Top, like No Child Left Behind, will only sustain investment in schools that are "productive" or "accountable" as measured by rising test scores. Finally, the administration has indicated that the primary force for innovation in education is charter schools. It is consequently advancing a political agenda to substantially increase the number of charter schools nationally.

Some labor, business, and political leaders greeted Duncan's appointment with much enthusiasm. Randi Weingarten, the president of the American Federation of Teachers, praised Duncan noting his record of working effectively with teachers. As well, Susan Traiman, director of educational policy at Business Roundtable, was cited in the *New York Times* as indicating "Obama found the sweet spot with Arne Duncan. . . . both camps will be OK with the pick." Especially noteworthy is Duncan's record in developing the talent of both teachers and principals. Advocates have noted that he understands the importance of the relationship between student achievement and teachers as well as principal capacity development. Importantly, his record indicates a commitment to invest in such programming. Some part of his public education reform agenda is, therefore, consistent with the kinds of targeted investment sought by CC9. A number of labor leaders have been quick to add that the Chicago schools, which were plagued by nine teacher strikes in the 1970s and 1980s, have experienced labor peace and relative stability since Duncan was appointed superintendent. The *New York Times* joined this chorus of strong endorsement when it noted in January 2009 that "he is an administrator who has a reputation for confronting pressing issues in public education, like how to raise teacher quality, how to transform weak schools, and when to shutter those that are irredeemably failing." This drumbeat of strong endorsement included George Miller, the chairman of the House Education and Labor Committee, who said in a December 2008 *New York Times* article that Duncan is "a good choice for school reform and our school children."

Some part of the question that still remains, however, is what kind of policy change will follow Duncan's appointment. Despite the broad support for his candidacy, the answer to that question is less clear. As noted, Duncan's record suggests a commitment to invest in recruiting and developing school-based professionals. Such policy initiative would represent a departure from the Bush administration record of creating unfunded mandates such as No Child Left Behind and subsequently blaming teachers as well as principals for failing to meet achievement and testing standards established by the legislation. Equally important, his record suggests a willingness to work with labor unions and community groups to improve student achievement. Such collaboration is an important departure from the Bush administration practice of governing by fiat. It recognizes the importance of partnership between critical stakeholders if the most distressed public schools are to be improved. It is on the basis of this inclination to collaborate that Duncan has been seen as a compromise candidate, more acceptable than, for example, Joel Klein, who has an embattled history with both the teachers' union and a number of community groups. On the matter of education policy, however, a number of advocates have suggested that Duncan's basic reform agenda is little different than either Klein's or the Bush administration's. In an article by Alfie Kohn in the December 29, 2008, issue of *The Nation*, Michael Klonsky, an education activist from Chicago, describes his agenda as a blend of more standardized testing, closing neighborhood schools, militarization, and the privatization of school management. Critically, groups that supported the Duncan candidacy, like Democrats for Education Reform, are disconcertingly allied with conservatives. Kohn reports that to be a school reformer in either political party is to support "(1) a heavy reliance on fill-in-the-bubble standardized tests to evaluate students and schools, generally in place of more authentic forms of assessment; (2) the imposition of prescriptive, top-down teaching standards and curriculum mandates; (3) disproportionate emphasis on rote learning—memorizing facts and practicing skills—particularly for poor kids; (4) a behaviorist model of motivation in which rewards (notably money) and punishments are used on students and teachers to compel compliance or raise test scores; (5) a corporate sensibility and an economic rationale for schooling, the point being to prepare children to 'compete' as future employees; and (6) charter schools, many of which are run by for-profit companies."

What, then, does this portend for public education advocates during an anticipated sea change from conservative to progressive politics? Clearly, the Obama administration will be less hostile to labor and committed to developing both teacher and principal capacity. However, the larger questions regarding federal public education policy remain unanswered. Questions having to do with the role of charter schools, the centrality of standardized testing in measuring the success of both students and teachers, targeted investments in programming, and curricula being driven by a culture of testing will define a large part of this administration's agenda and success. At least of equal importance is the degree to which the promise of the Obama administration to involve grassroots constituencies will be realized by something more than electronic polls. Will this new administration invest some part of its political capital to develop programs and opportunities for grassroots parent groups to have an enlarged role in improving the performance of inner-city public schools? Some part of the answer to these questions will be provided by both the early policy direction charted by policy makers and politicians and the pressure applied by grassroots leadership for the enactment of a new national agenda for public education. As in the past, this push-pull will determine the course of political decision making.

The new administration has opened some space for both discourse and alternate policy regarding public education. What remains to be seen, however, is whether grassroots and national leadership will produce a new policy direction that does more than simply tweak or paper over failed policies of the recent past, encoded in No Child Left Behind. The present moment calls for a bold new policy architecture that promotes partnership between stakeholders, and targeted investment extending beyond testing and the privatized option of charter schools as the solutions to public education failure. The focus must be on the restoration of public education as the venue for a first-class education. The early signals offered by the Obama administration about such focus are mixed. The past and present record of Duncan raises a number of serious concerns about the degree to which the Obama administration is prepared to depart from policies of testing and privatization as the cosmetic answer to public education failure. The contested terrain of public education will remain a hotbed of both debate and policy experimentation.

As in the past, the outcome of this next stage of struggle to improve public schools will be determined by the degree to which parent-led grassroots groups like CEJ accumulate the regional and national power necessary to rewrite both the assumptions and direction of present policy making. This will not be easy, but such proximity to both the failure and transformative possibility of public education is one of the best hopes for producing the public will necessary to change schools' learning and instruction culture. Let us hope that the next decade promotes the kinds of struggle necessary to invent and enact the long overdue just public education reform that inner-city youngsters and all children so richly deserve.

Bibliography

Academy for Educational Development. *Lead Teacher Project Second Year Report.* New York: Academy for Educational Development, 2006.

Albro, Robert. "The Water Is Ours Carajo! Deep Citizenship in Bolivia's Water Wars." In *Social Movements,* ed. June Nash. Malden, Mass.: Blackwell Publishing, 2005.

Anyon, Jean. *Radical Possibilities: Public Policy, Urban Education, and a New Social Movement.* New York and London: Routledge, 2005.

Appadurai, Arjun. "Deep Democracy: Urban Governmentality and the Horizon of Politics." *Environment and Urbanization* 13, 2 (October 2001): 23–43.

Apple, Michael. *The State and the Politics of Knowledge.* New York and London: RoutledgeFalmer, 2003.

"Arne Duncan." *New York Times,* Web site, January 5, 2008.

Astin, Alexander W. "Educational 'Choice': Its Appeal May Be Illusory." *Sociology of Education* 65, 4 (1992): 255–60.

Barber, Benjamin. *Strong Democracy: Participatory Politics for a New Age.* Berkeley: University of California Press, 1984.

Bascia, Nina, and Andy Hargreaves, eds. *The Sharp Edge of Educational Change: Teaching, Leading and the Realities of Reform.* London and New York: RoutledgeFalmer, 2000.

Bastian, Ann. *Making a Difference: Collaborative Organizing for School Improvement in New York City.* New York: Rockefeller Brothers Fund, 2006.

Biddle, Bruce, ed. *Social Class, Poverty, and Education: Policy and Practice.* New York and London: RoutledgeFalmer, 2001.

Bohte, John. "Examining the Impact of Charter Schools on Performance in Traditional Public Schools." *Policy Studies Journal* 32 (2004): 501–20.

Bourdieu, Pierre. "Structures, Habitus, Power: Basis for a Theory of Symbolic Power." In *Outline for a Theory of Practice.* Cambridge: Cambridge University Press, 1977.

Bryk, Anthony S., Penny Bender Sebring, David Kerbow, Sharon Rollow, and John Q. Easton. *Charting Chicago School Reform: Democratic Localism as a Lever for Change.* Boulder, Colo.: Westview Press, 1998.

Buchen, Irving H. "Education in America: The Next 25 Years." *The Futurist* 37 (2003): 44–50.

Burghardt, Steve. *The Other Side of Organizing*. Cambridge, Mass.: Schenkman Publishers, 1981.

Coleman, James. "Social Capital in the Creation of Human Capital." *American Journal of Sociology* 94 (1988) (Supplement): S95–S120.

Comer, James. *School Power: Implications of an Intervention Project*. New York: The Free Press, 1980.

Connell, N. "The Midnight Hour: A Progressive Strategy for School Reform." *New Labor Forum* 2, 1 (1998): 17–24.

di Leonardo, Micaela. "Introduction: New Global and American Landscapes of Inequality." In *New Landscapes of Inequality*, ed. Jane Collins, Micaela di Leonardo, and Brett Williams, 3–21. Santa Fe, N.Mex.: School for Advanced Research Press, 2008.

Dillon, Sam. "School Slow in Closing Gaps between Races." *New York Times*, July 28, 2004.

———. "Schools Chief from Chicago Is Cabinet Pick." *New York Times*, December 16, 2008.

Emirbayer, Mustafa, and Ann Mische. "What Is Agency?" *American Journal of Sociology* 4 (1998): 962–1023.

Evans, Peter. "Government Action, Social Capital, and Development: Reviewing the Energy on Synergy." *World Development* 24, 6 (1997): 1119–32.

Fabricant, Michael, and Steve Burghardt. *The Welfare State Crisis and the Transformation of Social Service Work*. Armonk, N.Y.: M. E. Sharpe, 1992.

Freire, Paulo. *The Pedagogy of the Oppressed*. Trans. Myra Bergman Ramos. New York: Continuum, 2000.

Gecan, Michael. "The Discovery of Power." In *Hope Dies Last: Keeping the Faith in Difficult Times*, ed. Studs Terkel. London: Granata Press, 2005.

Gilderbloom, John Ingram, and Robert Lee Mullins. *Promise and Betrayal: Universities and the Battle for Sustainable Urban Neighborhoods*. New York: State University of New York Press, 2005.

Gittell, Marilyn. "School Reform in New York and Chicago: Revisiting the Ecology of Local Games." *Urban Affairs Quarterly* 30, 1 (1994): 136–51.

Gold, Eva, Elaine Simon, Leah Mundell, and Chris Brown. "Bringing Community Organizing into the School Reform Picture." *Nonprofit and Voluntary Sector Quarterly* 33, 3 (2004): 54–76.

Goode, Judith, and Jeff Maskovsky. *The New Poverty Studies: The Ethnography of Power Politics and Impoverished People in the United States*. New York: NYU Press, 2002.

Grissmer, David, Ann Flanagan, and Stephanie Williamson. "Does Money Matter for Minority and Disadvantaged Students." In *Assessing New Empirical Evidence*, ed.

William Fowler, 13–30. Developments in School Finance. Washington, D.C.: U.S. Department of Education, 1998.

Hancock, LynNell. "Schools Out: For New York City Schools Chancellor Joel Klein Corporate Reforms Trump Democracy." *The Nation*, July 9, 2007, 16–21.

Harvey, David. *A Brief History of Neoliberalism*. Oxford: Oxford University Press, 2005.

Herszenhorn, David. "How a District in the Bronx Got Results from Pushing." *New York Times*, May 20, 2005.

———. "City May Gain 200 Teachers Designated as Masters." *New York Times*, March 10, 2006.

———. "Three Years Later, New York Revisits School Reformation." *New York Times*, April 9, 2006.

———. "City Weighs Bigger Private Role in Managing the Public Schools." *New York Times*, October 5, 2006.

Hess, G. Alfred. "Understanding Achievement (and Other) Changes under Chicago School Reform." *Educational Evaluation and Policy Analysis* 21, 1 (Spring 1999): 67–83.

Hill, Paul Thomas, Christine Campbell, and James Harvey. *It Takes a City: Getting Serious about Urban School Reform*. Washington, D.C.: Brookings Institute Press, 2000.

Hirshman, Albert. *Exit, Voice, and Loyalty: Responses to Decline in Firms, Organizations, and States*. Cambridge, Mass.: Harvard University Press, 1970.

Horton, Myles, with Judith Kohl and Herbert Kohl. *The Long Haul: An Autobiography*. New York: Doubleday, 1990.

Jasper, James. "The Emotions of Protest: Affective and Reactive Emotions in and around Social Movements." *Sociological Forum* 13, 3 (1998): 397–424.

———. *The Art of Moral Protest: Culture, Biography and Creativity in Social Movements*. Chicago: University of Chicago Press, 2000.

Jonnes, Jill. *We're Still Here: The Rise, Fall, and Resurrection of the South Bronx*. Boston and New York: Atlantic Monthly Press, 1986.

Kamens, David. "Education and Democracy: A Comparative Institutional Analysis." *Sociology of Education* 61, 2 (1998): 114–27.

Kohn, Alfie. "Beware Social Reformers." *The Nation*, December 29, 2008, 7–8.

Kozol, Jonathan. *Death at an Early Age: The Destruction of the Hearts and Minds of Negro Children in the Boston Public Schools*. New York: Penguin Group, 1985.

———. *The Shame of the Nation: The Restoration of Apartheid School in America*. New York: Crown Publishers, 2005.

Lareau, Annette. *Home Advantage: Social Class and Parental Intervention in Elementary Education*. London: Falmer Press, 1989.

Lieberman, Myron. *Privatization and Educational Choice*. New York: St. Martin's Press, 1989.

Lubienski, Chris. "Redefining 'Public' Education: Charter Schools, Common Schools, and the Rhetoric of Reform." *Teachers College Record* 103, 4 (2001): 634–66.

Mansbridge, Jane J. *Beyond Adversary Democracy.* New York: Basic Books, 1980.

Margonis, Frank, and Laurence Parker. "Choice: The Route to Community Control?" *Theory Into Practice* 38, 4 (1999): 203–8.

McAdam, Doug, and Ronnelle Paulsen. "Specifying the Relationship between Social Ties and Activism." *American Journal of Sociology* 99, 3 (1993): 640–67.

McNeil, Linda. *Contradictions of Control: School Structure and School Knowledge.* New York: Routledge Kegan and Paul, 1986.

———. *Contradictions of School Reform: Educational Costs of Standardized Testing.* New York: RoutledgeFalmer, 2000.

Medina, Jennifer. "Citing Learning Slumps, Mayor Presents Plan for Low-Performing Middle Schools." *New York Times*, August 14, 2007.

Mediratta, Kavitha. *Constituents of Change: Community Organizations and Public Education Reform.* Institute for Education and Social Policy, Steinhardt School of Education, New York University, 2004.

Mediratta, Kavitha, Norm Fruchter, and A. C. Lewis. *Organizing for School Reform: How Communities Are Finding Their Voices and Reclaiming Their Public Schools.* Institute for Education and Social Policy, Steinhardt School of Education, New York University, 2002.

Mediratta, Kavitha, Seema Shah, and Sara McAlister. *Organized Communities, Stronger Schools: A Preview of Research Findings.* Annenberg Institute for School Reform at Brown University, 2008.

Meier, Deborah. *The Power of Their Ideas: Lessons for America from a Small School in Harlem.* Boston: Beacon Press, 2002.

Mollenkopf, John, and Ken Emerson, eds. *Rethinking the Urban Agenda: Reinvigorating the Liberal Tradition in New York City and Urban America.* New York: Century Foundation Press, 2001.

Morris, Aldon D., and Carol McClurg Mueller, eds. *Frontiers in Social Movement Theory.* New Haven, Conn.: Yale University Press, 1992.

Murray, Charles. *Losing Ground: American Social Policy, 1950–1980.* New York: Basic Books, 1984.

NYC Coalition for Educational Justice. *New York City's Middle-Grade Schools: Platforms for Success or Pathways to Failure?* Annenberg Institute for School Reform, January 2007.

NYC Coalition for Educational Justice. *Our Children Can't Wait: A Proposal to Close the Middle-Grades Achievement Gap.* Annenberg Institute for School Reform, January 2008.

Oakes, Jeannie, and Martin Lipton. "Struggling for Educational Equity in Diverse Communities: School Reform as Social Movement." *Journal of Educational Change* 3 (2002): 383–406.

Oakes, Jeannie, John Rogers, and Martin Lipton. *Learning Power: Organizing for Education and Justice*. New York: Teachers College Press, 2006.

Payne, C., and M. Kaya. "So Much Reform, So Little Change: Building-level Obstacles to Urban School Reform." *Social Policy* 37 (2007): 30–37.

Payne, Charles. *I've Got the Light of Freedom: The Organizing Tradition and the Mississippi Freedom Struggle*. Berkeley: University of California Press, 1993.

Podair, Jerald. *The Strike That Changed New York: Blacks, Whites, and the Ocean Hill–Brownsville Crisis*. New Haven, Conn.: Yale University Press, 2002.

Portes, Alejandro. "Embeddedness and Immigration: Notes on the Social Determinants of Economic Action." *American Journal of Sociology* 98, 6 (1993): 1320–50.

———. "Social Capital: Its Origins and Applications in Modern Sociology." *Annual Review of Sociology* 24 (1998): 1–24.

Portes, Alejandro, and Patricia Landolt. "Social Capital: Promise and Pitfalls of Its Role in Development." *Journal of Latin American Studies* 32, 2 (2000): 529–47.

Reed, Adolph. "The 2004 Election in Perspective: The Myth of 'Cultural Divide' and the Triumph of Neoliberal Ideology." *American Quarterly* 57, 1 (2005): 1–15.

Rooney, Jim. *Organizing the South Bronx*. New York: State University of New York Press, 1995.

Ruben, Matthew. "Suburbanization and Urban Poverty under Neoliberalism." In *The New Poverty Studies: The Ethnography of Power, Politics, and Impoverished People*, ed. Judith Goode and Jeff Maskovsky, 435–70. New York: New York University Press, 2002.

Sarason, Seymour. *The Predictable Failure of Educational Reform: Can We Change Course Before It's Too Late?* San Francisco: Jossey-Bass, 1990.

Schein, Edgar. "Culture: The Missing Concept in Organization Studies." *Administrative Science Quarterly* 41 (1996): 229–40.

Schorr, Lizbeth. *Within Our Reach: Breaking the Cycle of Disadvantage*. New York: Anchor Books, Doubleday, 1979.

Serrgeldin, Ismail. "The Wars of the Twenty-first Century Will Be about Water." World Bank, unpublished paper, date unknown.

Shirley, Dennis. *Community Organizing for Urban School Reform*. Austin: University of Texas Press, 1997.

Sullivan, Elizabeth. *Civil Society and School Accountability: A Human Rights Approach to Parent and Community Participation in NYC Schools Center for Economic and Social Rights*. New York University, Institute for Education and Social Policy, 2003.

Tough, Paul. "Can Teaching Poor Children to Act More Like Middle-Class Children Help Close the Education Gap? What It Takes to Make a Student." *New York Times Magazine*, November 26, 2006.

Walsh, Joan. *Stories of Renewal: Community Building and the Future of Urban America*. A Report from the Rockefeller Foundation, 1996.

Warren, Mark. *Dry Bones Rattling: Community Building to Revitalize American Democracy.* Princeton, N.J.: Princeton University Press, 2001.

———. "Communities and Schools: A New View of Urban Education Reform." *Harvard Educational Review* 75, 2 (2005): 133–73.

Williams, Michael. *Neighborhood Organizing for Urban School Reform.* New York: Teachers College Press, 1989.

Williams, Timothy. "Now Booming, Not Burning, the Bronx Fears a Downside." *New York Times,* March 19, 2006.

Wilson, William Julius. *The Truly Disadvantaged: The Inner City, the Underclass, and Public Policy.* Chicago: University of Chicago Press, 1987.

Zachary, Eric, and Shola Olatoye. *Community Organizing for School Reform in the South Bronx.* New York University, Institute for Education and Social Policy, 2001.

Index

MICHAEL B. FABRICANT is professor in the School of Social Work and executive officer of the Ph.D. program in social welfare at Hunter College and the Graduate Center of the City University of New York.